Praise for *Zinky*

"[Svetlana] Alexievich has become one of my heroes."
—Atul Gawande

"Alexievich is like a doctor probing the scar tissue of a traumatised nation."
—Guy Chazan, *Financial Times*

"Alexievich put in thousands of hours with her tape recorder across the lands of the former Soviet Union, collecting and collating stories from ordinary people. She wove those tales into elegant books of . . . power and insight."
—Shaun Walker, *Guardian*

"Shattering and addictive . . . this is a polyphonic tour de force that shines a light on war, the plight of heroes, and why post-Soviet Russia is as it is."
—Kapka Kassabova, *Herald Scotland*

"Alexievich's 'documentary novels' are crafted and edited with a reporter's cool eye for detail and a poet's ear for the intricate rhythms of human speech. Reading them is like eavesdropping on a confessional. This is history at its rawest and most uncomfortably intimate."
—Andrew Dickson, *Evening Standard*

"An affecting, often haunting, compilation of first-person testimony on the Soviet experience in Afghanistan."
—*Kirkus Reviews*

SVETLANA ALEXIEVICH

Zinky Boys

Soviet Voices from the Afghanistan War

Translated by Andrew Bromfield

W. W. NORTON & COMPANY
Celebrating a Century of Independent Publishing

First published in Russian in 1989 as *Цинковые мальчики*
This translation first published in 2017 by Penguin Classics
Text copyright © 1989, 2013, 2023 by Svetlana Alexievich
Translation copyright © 2017 by Andrew Bromfield
First American Edition

This translation first published as a Norton paperback in 2023

For information about permission to reproduce selections from this book,
write to Permissions, W. W. Norton & Company, Inc., 500 Fifth Avenue,
New York, NY 10110

For information about special discounts for bulk purchases, please contact
W. W. Norton Special Sales at specialsales@wwnorton.com or 800-233-4830

Set in 10.5/13 pt Dante MT Std
Typeset by Jouve (UK), Milton Keynes
Printed in the United States of America by LSC Communications, Harrisonburg

A CIP catalogue record for this book is available from the British Library

ISBN 978-1-324-05112-1 pbk.

W. W. Norton & Company, Inc., 500 Fifth Avenue, New York, N.Y. 10110
www.wwnorton.com

W. W. Norton & Company Ltd., 15 Carlisle Street, London W1D 3BS

1 2 3 4 5 6 7 8 9 0

Contents

On 20 January 1801 the Cossacks of the Don Hetman Vasily Orlov were ordered to march to India. A month was set for the stage as far as Orenburg, and three months to march from there 'via Bukharia and Khiva to the Indus River'. Soon thirty thousand Cossacks would cross the Volga and advance deep into the Kazakh Steppe . . .

V bor'be za vlast':
Stranitsy politicheskoi istorii Rossii XVIII veka
(In the Struggle for Power:
Pages from the Political History of Russia in the Eighteenth Century) *(Moscow: Mysl, 1988), p. 475*

In December 1979 the Soviet leadership took the decision to send its troops into Afghanistan. The war continued from 1979 to 1989, lasting nine years, one month and nineteen days. More than half a million soldiers of the 'limited contingent' of Soviet forces passed through Afghanistan. The total number of lives lost by the Soviet Armed Forces was 15,051. Four hundred and seventeen military servicemen went missing in action or were taken prisoner. As of the year 2000, the number of men who had not returned from captivity and remained unaccounted for was 287 . . .

Polit.ru, 19 November 2003

Prologue

I walk alone . . . I'll be walking alone for a long time now.

He killed someone . . . My son . . . With a kitchen axe – I used to trim and beat meat with it. He came back from the war and killed someone here. He brought the axe back in the morning and put it away in the little cupboard where I keep the kitchenware. I think it was the same day I cooked pork cutlets for him. After a while they announced it on the television and they wrote in the evening newspaper that some fishermen had pulled a dead body out of the town lake. In pieces . . . A friend of mine called me:

'Did you read it? A professional murder . . . With the Afghan signature . . .'

My son was at home, lying on the sofa, reading a book. I didn't know anything yet, I didn't suspect a thing, but for some reason when she said that I looked at him. A mother's heart . . .

Can you hear the dogs barking? No? But I can, as soon as I start telling anyone about it, I hear dogs barking. And dogs running . . . In the prison where he's serving his time now, there are big black Alsatians. And the people are all dressed in black, nothing but black. I get back to Minsk and I walk along the street, past the bread shop and the kindergarten, carrying a long loaf and some milk, and I hear that barking. That deafening barking. It blinds me. Once I almost got run over by a car.

I'd be willing to visit my son's grave mound. I'd be willing to lie there beside him. But I don't know . . . I don't know how to live with this. Sometimes I feel afraid to go into the kitchen and see that cupboard where the axe used to lie. Can't you hear it? Don't you hear anything?

Now I don't even know what he's like, my son. What will he be like when I get him back in fifteen years? They gave him fifteen years in maximum security. How did I bring him up? He was interested in ballroom dancing. The two of us used to go to the Hermitage in Leningrad. We read books together . . . (*She cries.*) It was Afghanistan that took my son away from me . . .

We got a telegram from Tashkent: 'Meet such-and-such a plane' . . . I dashed out on to the balcony, I wanted to shout out with all my might: 'He's alive! My son has come back alive from Afghanistan! That terrible war is over for me!' And I passed out. We got to the airport late, of course, our flight had arrived ages ago, and we found our son in the public garden. He was lying on the ground and clutching the grass, amazed that it was so green. He couldn't believe that he was back. But there was no joy in his face . . .

In the evening the neighbours came round. They have a little girl and they tied a bright blue ribbon in her hair. He sat her on his knees, held her tight and cried: the tears just kept flowing on and on. Because they killed out there. And so did he . . . I realized that later.

On the border the customs men had 'trimmed off' his foreign shorts. American. Not permitted. So he arrived without any underwear. He was bringing a dressing gown for me; I turned forty that year. They took the dressing gown away from him. He was bringing his granny a shawl and they took that too. The only thing he had when he arrived was flowers. Gladioli. But there was no joy in his face.

When he got up in the morning he was still normal: 'Mama! Mama!' By evening his face had turned dark, his eyes were heavy with pain. I can't describe it to you . . . He didn't drink at first, not a drop, just sat there looking at the wall. He would spring up off the sofa and grab his jacket.

I used to stand in the doorway.

'Where are you going, Valyushka?'

He just looked straight through me. And went out.

I used to come back home late from work – the factory's a long way away – and ring the doorbell, but he didn't open up. He didn't recognize my voice. It's so strange – after all, he might not recognize his friends' voices, but mine! And especially 'Valyushka' – I'm the only one who ever called him that. It was like he was expecting someone all the time; he was afraid. I bought him a new shirt and started trying it on him for size, and I saw cuts all over his arms.

'What's this?'

'It's nothing, mama.'

I found out about it later. After the trial. In the training camp he slit his wrists . . . At an exercise he was a radio operator and he didn't manage to heave the radio up into a tree in time, he took longer than was allowed, and the sergeant made him rake out fifty bucketsful from the toilet and carry it all across in front of the assembled ranks. He started carrying it and passed out. In the hospital they diagnosed mild nervous shock. That same night he tried to slit his wrists . . . And a second time in Afghanistan. Just before they went out on a raid they checked, and the radio wasn't working. Some parts that were in short supply had disappeared: one of their own men had stolen them. The commander accused him of cowardice, as if he'd hidden the parts in order to avoid going with all the others. But they all stole from each other out there. They took trucks to pieces for the spare parts and took them to the *dukans* – those shops they had out there – to sell. They bought drugs. Drugs and cigarettes. Food. They were hungry absolutely all the time.

There was a programme about Edith Piaf on the television, we watched it together.

'Mama,' he asked me, 'do you know what narcotics are?'

'No,' I lied. But I was already keeping an eye on him, wondering if he was smoking something.

There were no signs. But they used drugs out there – I know that.

'How is it there, in Afghanistan?' I asked him one day.

'Shut up, mama!'

When he went out I reread his letters from Afghanistan. I wanted to get to the bottom of things, understand what was wrong with him. I didn't find anything special in them. He wrote that he missed the green grass; he asked his granny to get her photo taken in the snow and send it to him. But I couldn't see, I couldn't feel that there was anything happening to him. They sent me back a different man. He wasn't my son. And I was the one who sent him into the army – he had a deferment. I wanted him to become a real man. I persuaded him and myself that the army would make him better and stronger. I sent him off to Afghanistan with his guitar; I arranged a sweet buffet to see him off and he invited his friends, and girls. I remember I bought ten cakes.

There was only one time he spoke about Afghanistan. It was early evening. He came into the kitchen. I was preparing a rabbit. The bowl was bloody. He soaked his fingers in that blood and looked at it, examined it. And he said to himself:

'They brought my friend back with his stomach completely shattered . . . He asked me to shoot him . . . And I shot him . . .'

His fingers were covered in blood . . . From the rabbit meat. It was fresh. He grabbed a cigarette with those fingers and went out on to the balcony. And he didn't say another word to me all that evening.

I went to the doctors: 'Give me back my son! Save him!' I told them everything. They checked him, they looked, but apart from radiculitis they didn't find anything wrong with him.

Once I came home and there were four young men I didn't know sitting at the table.

'Mama, they're from Afghanistan. I found them at the railway station. They've got nowhere to spend the night.'

'I'll bake you a fruit pie right now. This very moment. In a jiffy.' I was absolutely delighted.

They lived with us for a week. I didn't count, but I think they drank about three crates of vodka. Every evening I met five strangers at home. The fifth one was my son . . . I didn't want to listen to their conversations, I was frightened. But I couldn't help overhearing. They said that when they had to wait in an ambush for two weeks at a time, they were given stimulants to boost their courage. But that's all kept secret. What weapons were best for killing . . . From what distance . . . I remembered that later, when it all happened . . . I started thinking later, frantically trying to remember. But before that there was only fear. 'My God,' I used to tell myself, 'they're all mad. They're not right in the head.'

That night . . . Before that day when he killed . . . I had a dream that I was waiting for my son. I kept waiting and waiting, but he didn't come. And then they brought him to me. Those four 'Afghanis' brought him to me. And they threw him on the dirty concrete floor. You know, the floor at home is concrete. Our kitchen floor's like in a prison.

By that time he had already got into the foundation studies department at the radio engineering college. He wrote a good essay. He was happy that everything was going really well. I even started to think that he was calming down. That he would go to college. Get married. But when the evening came . . . I was afraid of the evening. He used to sit there and stare blankly at the wall. Fall asleep in the armchair . . . I wanted to dash to him, throw myself over him and not let him go. And now I dream about my son: he's little and he's asking for something to eat. He's always hungry. He reaches out his hands . . . In my dreams I always see him as little and humiliated. And in real life? A meeting every two months. Four hours of talking to him through a pane of glass . . .

Two meetings a year when I can at least feed him. And those dogs barking. I dream about that barking. It won't ever let me be.

This man started courting me. He brought flowers. When he brought me the flowers I started shouting: 'Get away from me, I'm the mother of a murderer.' At first I was afraid of meeting someone I knew. I shut myself in the bathroom and waited for the walls to fall in on me. I felt like everyone in the street recognized me and pointed me out to each other and whispered: 'Remember that gruesome business? It was her son who killed him. He quartered the man. The Afghan signature . . .' I only went out into the street at night. I learned all the night birds. I could recognize them from their calls.

The investigation went on and on. It lasted months. He didn't say anything. I went to the Burdenko Military Hospital in Moscow and found some boys there who served in the special operations forces, like he did. I confided in them.

'Boys, what would my son kill someone for?'

'If he did, there must have been a reason.'

I had to convince myself that he could have done it . . . Killed someone. I questioned them about it for a long time and realized that he could have! I asked about death. No, not about death, but about killing. But talking about that didn't make them feel anything special, the kind of feelings that any killing usually arouses in a normal person who has never seen blood. They talked about war as a job, where you had to kill. Then I met some boys who had been in Afghanistan too, and when the earthquake happened in Armenia they went there with the rescue teams. What interested me, I was already obsessed with it, was: were they afraid? What did they feel at the sight of death? No, they weren't afraid of anything, even their sense of pity was blunted. Blown to pieces . . . squashed flat . . . skulls, bones . . . entire schools buried under the ground. Classes of children. Sitting there, doing their lessons. They all disappeared under the ground, just like that. But there was something else the boys remembered and told me about: the rich wine cellars they dug up, the fine cognac and wine they drank. They joked: 'It would be good if somewhere else got zapped too.' Only it had to be a warm place, where grapes grow and they make good wine. Are they sane, then? Are they really right in the head?

'He's dead but I still hate him.' That's what he wrote to me recently. After five years. What happened out there? He doesn't say anything. All I know is that boy – his name was Yura – boasted that in Afghanistan he'd earned lots of checks for the Beriozka hard currency shops. But afterwards it turned out that he'd served in Ethiopia, a warrant officer. He lied about Afghanistan.

At the trial it was only the lawyer who said we were trying a sick man. He said the accused wasn't a criminal, he was unwell. He needed treatment. But back then, that's seven years ago, there wasn't any truth about Afghanistan yet. They called them all 'heroes'. 'Internationalist soldiers'. But my son was a murderer . . . Because he did here what they did out there. What did they give them all medals and decorations for out there? Why did they only judge him and not the ones who sent him there? Who taught him to kill? I didn't teach him that . . . (*She loses control and shouts.*)

He killed a man with my kitchen axe . . . And in the morning he brought it back and put it in the cupboard. Like an ordinary spoon or fork.

I envy a mother whose son came back with no legs. What if he does hate her when he gets drunk? If he hates the whole world? What if he does go for her like a wild beast? She buys him prosti-tutes, so that he won't go insane . . . She was his lover herself once, because he was clambering on to the balcony and wanted to throw himself off the tenth floor. I'd do anything. I envy all the mothers, even those whose sons are lying in their graves. I'd sit by the little mound and feel happy. I'd bring flowers.

Can you hear the dogs barking? They're running after me. I can hear them . . .

A mother

From the Notebooks
At War

June 1986

I don't want to write about war any more . . . To live enveloped in a 'philosophy of extinction' instead of a 'philosophy of life'. To compile the interminable experience of non-existence. When I finished *The Unwomanly Face of War* I couldn't bear to see a child bleeding from an ordinary bang to the nose. On holiday I fled from fishermen merrily tossing on to the sandy shore the fish they had snatched out of the distant depths; those frozen, goggling eyes made me feel sick. Everyone has only so much strength to defend themselves against pain – both physical and psychological – and my reserves were totally exhausted. The howling of a cat struck by a car drove me demented. I turned my face away from a squelched earthworm. A dried-out frog on the road. Again and again I had the thought that animals, birds and fish also have a right to their own history of suffering. It will be written some day.

And then suddenly, if you can really call it 'suddenly', the war is in its seventh year. But we know nothing about it, apart from the heroic reporting on television. From time to time zinc coffins brought from faraway places, which don't fit into the pencil-box dimensions of five-storey Khrushchev-era apartment blocks, bring us up short with a shudder. Then the mournful peal of the farewell rifle volley fades away – and once again there is silence. Our mythological mindset is unshakeable – we are righteous and great. And always just. The final vestiges of the ideas of world revolution smoulder on, still not burned-out yet. No one notices that now the

9

conflagration has come home. Our own house is ablaze. Gorbachev's perestroika has begun. We are straining eagerly towards a new life. What awaits *us* up ahead? What will we prove capable of after so many years of artificially induced, lethargic sleep? Our boys are being killed somewhere far away and we don't understand what for.

What are the people around me saying? What are they writing about? About international duty and geopolitics, about our sovereign interests and our southern borders. And people believe it. They believe it. Mothers, who only recently were sobbing and shuddering in despair over the metal coffins in which their sons had been returned to them, give talks in schools and war museums, appealing to other boys 'to fulfil their duty to the Homeland'. The censor watches carefully to make sure that articles on the war don't mention our soldiers being killed: they assure us that a 'limited contingent' of Soviet forces is assisting a fraternal nation to build bridges, roads and schools, to send fertilizer and flour to the villages, and Soviet doctors are delivering the children of Afghan women. Returned soldiers bring guitars into schools in order to sing about things that ought to make people scream.

I had a long talk with one of them. I wanted to hear about what an agonizing choice it was – to shoot or not to shoot? But for him there didn't seem to be any drama to it. What is good? What is bad? Is it good to kill 'in the name of socialism'? For these boys the boundaries of morality are delineated by military orders. Although they talk about death more cautiously than we do. On this point the distance between us and them becomes obvious immediately.

How can you simultaneously experience history and write about it? You can't just grab any chunk of life, take the entire existential mire by the scruff of the neck and drag it into a book. Into history. You have to 'crack open' the times and 'capture their spirit'.

'Each substance of a grief hath twenty shadows' (William Shakespeare, *Richard II*).

At the bus station an officer with a travelling bag was sitting in a half-empty waiting room. Beside him was a boy with his hair shorn in an army buzz cut, digging about in a box of dried-up figs with a fork. Some countrywomen sat down ingenuously beside them and started asking questions: where to, what for, who? The officer was escorting home a soldier who had gone insane: 'He's been digging since Kabul. Whatever he can lay his hands on, he digs with it: a spade, a fork, a stick, a pen.' The boy raised his head: 'I've got to hide . . . I'll dig out a slit trench. I work quickly. We used to call them "communal graves". I'll dig out a big trench for all of you.'

It was the first time I'd ever seen pupils that covered the entire eye.

I stand in a municipal graveyard, surrounded by hundreds of people. At the centre there are four coffins, sheathed in red calico. Military men give speeches. A general has taken the floor . . . Women in black weep. The people don't say anything. Only a little girl with plaits sobs over a coffin: 'Papa! Pa-a-pa! Where are you? You promised to bring me a doll. A beautiful doll! I drew a whole sketchbook of little houses and flowers for you. I'm waiting for you . . .' A young officer picks up the little girl and carries her to a black Volga limousine. But for a long time we can still hear her crying: 'Papa! Pa-a-pa . . . Darling pa-a-pa . . .'

The general gives his speech. The women in black weep. We don't say anything. Why don't we say anything?

I don't want to remain silent. And yet I can't write about war any more.

September 1988

5 September

Tashkent. The airport is sweltering and smells of melons; not an airport, but a melon field. Two o'clock in the morning. Fat, semi-feral cats – they tell me they're from Afghanistan – dive fearlessly under the taxis. Among the tanned resort crowd, among the crates and the baskets of fruit, young soldiers (boys) hop about on crutches. No one takes any notice of them, everyone's used to them already. They sleep and eat right here on the floor, on old newspapers and magazines, vainly trying for weeks to buy a ticket to Saratov, Kazan, Novosibirsk, Kiev. Where were they crippled? What were they defending there? No one's interested. Only a little boy gapes incessantly at them, wide-eyed, and a drunken beggar woman walks up to one young soldier.

'Come over here. I'll comfort you . . .'

He waved her aside with his crutch. But she didn't take offence and added something else in a sad, soft, womanly tone of voice.

There are officers standing beside me, talking about how bad our Soviet prosthetic limbs are. About typhoid fever, cholera, malaria and hepatitis. About how during the first years of the war there were no wells or kitchens or bathhouses, not even enough water to wash the kitchen dishes with. And also about who had brought back what: some had 'videos', some had cassette players – Sharp or Sony. I remember their eyes as they looked at the beautiful, well-rested women in their low-cut dresses.

We wait a long time for the military plane to Kabul. They tell us that they'll load the equipment first, and then the people. About a hundred people are waiting. All military personnel. A surprisingly large number of women.

Snatches of conversations:

'I'm going deaf. Birds that sing on high notes were the first thing I stopped hearing. It's because of a concussion . . . A meadow warbler, for instance, I simply can't hear it for the life of me. I recorded one on my cassette player and I play it at full volume.'

'You fire first, and then you check to see if it's a woman or a child. Everyone has his own nightmare.'

'During the shelling a donkey lies down, and when the shelling's over, it jumps back up.'

'Who are we in the Soviet Union? Prostitutes? We know that. If I could get a job in a new cooperative company at least. And the men? What about the men? They all drink.'

'The general talked about our international duty, about defending our southern borders. He got quite maudlin: "Get them some boiled sweets. They're just children. Sweets are the best present." '

'The officer was young. When he found out they'd cut his leg off, he started crying. His face was like a girl's, white with rosy cheeks. I was afraid of dead men at first, especially if they had arms or legs missing. But then I got used to it . . .'

'They take them prisoner. Cut off their arms and legs and bind them round with tourniquets, so they won't bleed to death. And they leave them in that state. Our men pick up the stumps. They want to die, but the doctors treat them forcibly anyway. And after the hospital they don't want to go back home.'

'At the customs they saw my empty travelling bag: "What are you carrying?" "Nothing." "Nothing?" They didn't believe me. They made me strip to my underpants. Everybody brings in two or three suitcases.'

In the plane I got a seat beside an armoured personnel carrier that was chained in place. Fortunately the major beside me turned out to be sober, everyone else nearby was drunk. Not far from me someone was sleeping on a bust of Karl Marx. Portraits and busts of the socialist leaders were dumped on board without any packaging. We weren't carrying just arms, but also a full set of all the prerequisites for Soviet rituals. There were red flags and red ribbons lying there.

A siren howling . . .

'Get up. Or else you'll sleep through the kingdom of heaven.' That was above Kabul.

We come in to land.

The rumble of big guns. Patrols carrying automatic rifles and wearing bulletproof vests demand to see our passes.

I didn't want to write about war any more. But here I am in a genuine war. War people on all sides. War things. War time.

12 September

There's something immoral about scrutinizing someone else's courage and risks. Yesterday we went to breakfast in the mess and exchanged greetings with the sentry. Half an hour later he was killed by a stray piece of shrapnel that came flying into the garrison. All day long I tried to recall that boy's face . . .

Here they call the journalists 'storytellers'. And the writers too. Our writers' group consists entirely of men. They're champing at the bit to reach the furthest outposts; they want to get into the action. I ask one of them:

'What for?'

'I'm interested. I'll say: "I was in Salang." And I'll do a bit of shooting.'

I can't rid myself of the feeling that war is a creation of the male nature and incomprehensible to me in many ways. But the prosy mundaneness of war is colossal. Apollinaire: *'Que la guerre est jolie!'* 'Oh what a lovely war!'

At war everything's different: you, and nature, and your thoughts. Here I have realized that human thoughts can be very cruel.

I ask and I listen everywhere: in the soldiers' barracks, in the mess, on the football pitch, at the dances in the evening. There are elements of peacetime life that are surprising here.

'I shot point-blank and saw a human skull fly to pieces. I thought: "The first one." After the battle, the wounded and the dead. No one says anything . . . I dream about trams here. About riding home in a tram . . . My favourite memory: my mother cooking pies. The place smells of sweet pastry . . .'

'You're friends with a nice guy . . . And then you see his guts hanging on the rocks. You start taking revenge.'

'We're waiting for a caravan. In the ambush for two or three days. Lying in the hot sand, relieving ourselves right where we are. By the end of the third day you start freaking out. And you let loose that first burst of fire with such a feeling of hatred. After the firing, when it was all over, we discovered the caravan was carrying bananas and jam. We gorged ourselves on enough sweet stuff to last the rest of our lives.'

'We took some "spirits" prisoner. (That's what we used to call the mujahedeen.) We question them: "Where are the arms depots?"

They don't talk. We took two up in helicopters: "Where? Show us!"
They don't talk. We dropped one of them out on to the rocks . . .'

'Making love at war and after war aren't the same thing . . . At
war it's always like the first time.'

'The Grad rocket launcher is firing. The missiles are flying. And
there's just one impulse hovering over it all: live! live! live! But you
don't know anything, you don't want to know anything about the
sufferings of the other side. Just live – and that's all. Live!'

To write (to tell) the whole truth about yourself is, as Pushkin
remarked, a physical impossibility.

At war a man is saved by the way his mind becomes distracted
and abstracted. But the death around him is ludicrous and gratuit-
ous. Without any higher meanings.

Written on a tank in red paint: 'We'll pay them back for Malkin'.

A young Afghan woman knelt in the middle of the street in front
of her killed child and screamed. Probably only wounded animals
can scream that way.

We drove past devastated *kishlaks* – Afghan villages – that
looked like ploughed-up fields. The dead clay that only recently
was a human dwelling was more terrifying than the darkness that
they could shoot out of.

In the hospital I put a teddy bear on the bed of a little Afghan
boy. He took hold of the toy with his teeth and played with it, smiling; both his arms were missing. 'Your Russians shot him' – his
mother's words were translated for me. 'Do you have children? A
boy or a girl?' I couldn't make out whether her words contained
more horror or forgiveness.

They talk about the cruelty with which the mujahedeen treat
Russian prisoners. It's like the Middle Ages. It really is a different
time here: the calendars show the fourteenth century.

In Lermontov's novel *A Hero of Our Time* Maximych comments
on the actions of the mountain tribesman who killed Bela's father:
'Of course, according to their ways, he was absolutely right' –
although from a Russian point of view it's a bestial atrocity. The

writer captured an amazing Russian trait – the ability to assume the viewpoint of a different people and see things 'according to their ways'.

But now . . .

17 September

Day after day I see man slipping lower. And only rarely rising higher.

Dostoyevsky's Ivan Karamazov remarks: 'An animal can never be as cruel as a human being, as artfully, artistically cruel.'

Yes, I suspect that we don't want to hear about this, we don't want to know about this. But in any war, no matter who leads it and in the name of what – whether it's Julius Caesar or Joseph Stalin – people kill each other. This is murder; but it's not the done thing to reflect on that here. For some reason, even in our schools we don't talk about 'patriotic' education, but 'military and patriotic' education. But then why I am surprised? It's all quite clear – military socialism, a military country, military thinking.

A human being should not be subjected to trials like this. A human being cannot endure trials like this. The medical term for this is 'vivisection'. Experimenting on living creatures.

In the evening they put on a cassette player in the soldiers' hostel opposite the hotel. I listened to the 'Afghani' songs too. Childish voices, not yet fully formed, growled, Vysotsky-style: 'The sun fell into the *kishlak* like a massive bomb' – 'I don't want glory. Life is the only award for us' – 'Why are we killing? Why are they killing us?' – 'Now I've even started forgetting faces' – 'Afghanistan, you're bigger than our duty. You're our universe' – 'Big seabirds with one leg hopping along the seashore' – 'He's dead, he's no one's any more. There's no more hatred in his face.'

That night I have a dream: our soldiers are leaving, going back to the Soviet Union, and I'm one of the people seeing them off. I walk up to one boy. He has no tongue; he's mute after being in captivity. His hospital pyjamas protrude from under his army tunic. I ask him about something, but all he does is write his name: 'Vanechka . . . Vanechka . . .' I can make out his name so clearly – Vanechka. His face resembles the face of a boy I spoke to during the afternoon; he kept repeating: 'Mama's waiting for me at home.'

We drove through the lifeless streets of Kabul, past the familiar posters in the centre of the city: 'The bright future is communism' – 'Kabul – city of peace' – 'The people and the Party are united'. Our posters, printed in our printshops. Our Lenin, standing here with his arm raised . . .

I met some cameramen from Moscow.

They were filming the loading of a 'black tulip' – an An-12 plane that takes coffins back home. Without raising their eyes they tell me that the dead are dressed in old army uniforms from the 1940s, still with breeches instead of trousers; sometimes even these uniforms are in short supply, and they're put in the coffin without being dressed. Old wooden boards, rusty nails . . . 'They've brought more dead for the freezer. The smell's a bit like rank wild sheep.'

Who will believe me if I write about this?

20 September

I saw military action . . .

Three soldiers were killed. In the evening everyone ate supper. They didn't recall the dead, although they were lying somewhere nearby.

It is a human right not to kill. Not to learn to kill. A right that is not recorded in a single constitution.

War is a world, and not an event. Everything here is different: the landscape, a human being, words. What is remembered is the theatrical part of war: a tank swivelling round, the bark of commands, the glittering tracer lines in the darkness.

Thinking about death is like thinking about the future. Something happens to time when you think about death and see it. Close to the fear of death – the attraction of death . . .

No need to invent anything. There are passages everywhere in the great books. In every one.

★

In the stories (rather often!) the aggressive naivety of our boys, of yesterday's final-year Soviet schoolboys, is astounding. But what I want from them is a dialogue of one human being with another human being.

Well, after all, in what language do we talk with ourselves and others? I like the language of conversational speech: it's unencumbered, it lacks any external, imposed burdens. Everything rambles in discursive, exuberant style: syntax, intonation, accents – and feeling is reconstructed precisely. What I track is the feeling, not the event. The way our feelings have developed, not the events. Perhaps what I do is similar to the work of a historian, but I am a historian of the untraceable. What happens to great events? They migrate into history, while the little ones, the ones that are most important for the little person, disappear without a trace. Today one boy (so frail and sickly that he didn't look much like a soldier) told me how strange and at the same time exhilarating it feels to kill together. And how terrifying it is to shoot someone.

Is that really going to go down in history? I strive desperately (from book to book) to do one and the same thing – reduce history to the human being.

I thought about how impossible it is to write a book about war while at war. You are hampered by pity, hate, physical pain, friendship . . . And the letter from home, after which you want so much to live. They tell me that when they kill they try not to look into the eyes, even if it's a camel. There are no atheists here. And everyone is superstitious.

They reproach me (especially the officers; the soldiers not so often), telling me that I've never fired a gun and never been caught in anyone else's sights. So how can I write about war? But perhaps it's a good thing that I have never fired a gun.

Where is the man for whom the very thought of war causes suffering? I can't find him. But yesterday there was a dead bird lying beside the staff headquarters. And strangely enough the officers walked up to it and tried to guess what kind of bird it was. They pitied it.

There's a kind of inspiration in dead faces . . . And another thing I simply can't get accustomed to is the insanity of the ordinary at war – water, cigarettes, bread. Especially when we leave the garrison and go up into the mountains. Up there the human being is face-to-face with nature and chance. Will a bullet fly past or won't it? Who'll shoot first – you or him? Up there you start seeing the human being of nature, not of society.

And on the television in the Soviet Union they show trees being planted to line avenues of friendship, which none of us here have ever seen or planted . . .

In *Demons*, Dostoyevsky says: 'Certainty and the human being seem to be two separate things in many ways . . . Everyone is guilty . . . If only everyone was certain of that!' And he adds that humankind knows more, a lot more, about itself than it has so far managed to document in literature and science. He said that this was not his thought, but Vladimir Solovyov's.

If I hadn't read Dostoyevsky, I would be in even greater despair . . .

21 September

Somewhere far away a Grad truck-mounted rocket launcher is at work. It's spine-chilling even at this distance.

After the great wars of the twentieth century and the mass deaths, writing about modern (small) wars, like the war in Afghanistan, requires different ethical and metaphysical stances. What must be reclaimed is the small, the personal and the specific. The single human being. The only human being for someone. Not as the state regards him, but who he is for his mother, for his wife, for his child. How can we recover a normal vision of life?

I am also interested in the body, the human body, as the link between nature and history, between the animal and speech. All the physical details are important: the way blood changes in the sun, the human being just before he passes away. Life is incredibly artistic in itself and – cruel as this may sound – human suffering is especially artistic. The dark side of art. Just yesterday I saw them assembling the pieces of boys who had been blown up by an anti-tank mine. I didn't have to go and watch, but I did, so that I could write about it. Now I'm writing . . .

But after all, should I have gone? I heard the officers laughing behind my back, saying how scared the fine lady would be. I went and there was nothing heroic about it, because I fainted there. Perhaps it was from the heat, perhaps from the shock. I want to be honest.

23 September

We went up in a helicopter. From up there I saw hundreds of zinc coffins readied in advance, glittering in the sun with an appalling beauty . . .

You come across something like that and immediately think: literature is stifled within its own boundaries. With copying and facts you can only express what is visible to the eye, and who needs a simple, comprehensive account of what is taking place? What is needed is something else. Captured moments, snatched out of life . . .

25 September

I shall return from here a free human being. I wasn't one until I saw what we are doing here. It was terrifying and lonely. I shall return and never go into a single war museum again.

* * *

I don't name real names in the book. Some people requested the secrecy of the confessional, others want to forget everything. To forget what Tolstoy wrote – that man is fluid. That he has everything in him.

But in this diary section I have kept the names. Perhaps some day my characters will want to be known:

Vladimir Agapov, senior lieutenant, artillery crew commander; Sergei Amirkhanian, captain; Dmitry Babkin, private, artillery- man; Saya Emelyanovna Babuk, mother of the killed nurse Svetlana Babuk; Victoria Vladimirovna Bartashevich, mother of the killed private Yury Bartashevich; Olimpiada Romanovna Baukova, mother of the killed private Alexander Baukov; Maria Terentievna Bobkova, mother of the killed private Leonid Bobkov; Taisia Nikolaevna Bogush, mother of the killed private Victor Bogush; Anatoly Devetyarov, major, artillery regiment propa- ganda officer; Tamara Dovnar, wife of the killed senior lieutenant Pyotr Dovnar; Tamara Fadeeva, medical bacteriologist; Nina Ser- geevna Galovneva, mother of the killed senior lieutenant Yury Galovnev; Vadim Glushkov, senior lieutenant, interpreter; Gen- nady Gubanov, captain, pilot; Galina Fyodorovna Ilchenko, mother of the killed private Alexander Ilchenko; Vadim Ivanov, senior lieutenant, commander of a mine-clearing platoon; Taras Ketsmur, private; Anna Khakas, civilian employee; Ludmila Kharitonchik, wife of the killed senior lieutenant Yury Kharitonchik; Valery Khudyakov, major; Marina Kiselyova, civilian employee; Alexander Kostakov, private, radio operator; Yevgveny Kotelnikov, sergeant, reconnaissance company combat medic; Nadezhda Sergeevna Kozlova, mother of the killed private Andrei Kozlov; Vasily Kubik, warrant officer; Pyotr Kurbanov, major, commander of a mountain warfare company; Alexander Kuvshinnikov, senior lieutenant, commander of a mortar platoon; Denis L., private, grenadier; Oleg L., helicopter pilot; Alexander Lavrov, private; Alexander Leletko, private; Oleg Lelyushenko, private, grenadier; Valery Lisichenok, sergeant, radio operator; Sergei Loskutov, army surgeon; Vera Lysenko, civilian employee; Tomas M., sergeant, commander of an infantry platoon; Lidia Yefimovna Mankevich, mother of the killed sergeant Dmitry Mankevich; Maxim Medvedev, private, aviation gunlayer; Artur Metlitsky, private, scout; Vladimir Mikh- olap, private, mortar operator; Galina Mlyavaya, wife of the killed captain Stepan Mlyavy; Yevgeny Stepanovich Mukhortov, major, battalion commander, and his son Andrei Mukhortov, junior lieutenant; Alexander Nikolaenko, captain, commander of a helicopter squadron; Natalya Orlova, civilian employee; Vladimir Pankratov, private, scout; Galina Pavlova, nurse; Yekaterina Nikitichna Platitsyna, mother of the killed major Alexander Platitsyn; Sergei Rusak, private, tank crewman; Vitaly Ruzhentsev, private, logistics driver; Valentina Kirillovna Sanko, mother of the killed private Valentin Sanko; Nina Ivanovna Sidelnikova, mother; Vladimir Simanin, lieutenant-colonel; Mikhail Sirotin, senior lieutenant, pilot; Timofei Smirnov, sergeant, artillery warrant officer; Alexander Sukhorukov, senior lieutenant, commander of a mountain warfare platoon; Leonid Ivanovich Tatarchenko, father of the killed private Igor Tatarchenko; Vadim Trubin, sergeant, special forces; Vladimir Ulanov, captain; Victoria Semyonovna Valovich, mother of the killed senior lieutenant Valery Valovich; Valentina Yakovleva, warrant officer, security service head of department; Vladimir Yerokhovets, private, grenadier; Natalya Zhestovskaya, nurse; Sofya Grigorievna Zhuravlyova, mother of the killed private Alexander Zhuravlyov; Maria Onufrievna Zilfigarova, mother of the killed private Oleg Zilfigarov.

Day One

'For many shall come in my name . . .'

In the morning a long trill on the phone, like a burst of automatic fire: 'Listen,' he began, without introducing himself, 'I read your grubby libel. If you print even one more line . . .'

'Who are you?'

'One of the ones you write about. We'll get the call again, they'll put guns in our hands again, for us to sort out the mess. All of you will have to answer for everything. Only print more of your names and don't hide behind pseudonyms. I hate pacifists! Have you ever climbed a mountain in full combat gear, ridden in an armoured personnel carrier when it's fifty degrees Celsius? Do you smell the acrid stench of camelthorn at night. No, you don't . . . So keep your hands off! This is ours! What do you need this for? You're a woman: have children!'

'Why won't you say who you are?'

'Keep your hands off! My best friend, he was my brother, I brought him back from a raid in a plastic sack . . . The head separate, the arms and legs all separate . . . The skin ripped off him, like a wild boar . . . A butchered carcass . . . And he used to play the violin and write poetry. He could have written about it, but not you . . . Two days after the funeral his mother was taken off to the loony bin. She was sleeping in the graveyard, on his grave. Sleeping in the snow, in winter. You! You . . . Keep your hands off this! We were soldiers. We were sent there. We were following orders. I swore an oath of loyalty. I kissed the banner, down on my knees.'

' "Take heed that no man deceive you. For many shall come in my name." The New Testament. The Gospel according to Matthew.'

'Smart asses! After ten years they've all turned into smart asses! You want to stay clean, is that it? And we're all filthy black, then. You don't even know how a bullet flies. You've never held an automatic rifle in your

hands . . . I don't give a rotten damn for your New Testaments! I carried my own truth in a plastic sack. The head separate, the arms separate. There isn't any other truth . . .' And then a vague rumbling in the phone, like the sound of a distant explosion.

Even so, I regret that we didn't finish our conversation. Perhaps he was my main character . . .

The author

Only the voices got through to me . . . No matter how hard I strained, the voices had no faces. They kept going away and coming back again. It seems to me like I just managed to think, 'I'm dying.' And then I opened my eyes . . .

I came round in Tashkent, on the sixteenth day after being blown up. When you recover consciousness you feel really lousy, you think things will never get better . . . Not coming back any more would have been more comfortable. Mist and nausea. It's not even nausea, but choking, as if there's a load of water in your lungs. It takes a long time to get out of that state. Mist and nausea . . . Your own whispering makes your head hurt; I couldn't speak louder than a whisper. I'd already been in the Kabul hospital. In Kabul they opened up my skull and it was full of mush. They took out small pieces of bone and screwed my left arm together without any joints. The first thing I felt was regret that nothing would ever come back. I wouldn't see my friends again, and worst of all – I wouldn't be able to get on to the pull-up bar.

I spent just two weeks short of two years lying about in hospitals. Eighteen operations – four under general anaesthetic. Students wrote dissertations about me: what I still had and what was missing. I couldn't shave myself; the boys shaved me. The first time, they poured a bottle of eau de cologne over me and I shouted: 'Let's try a different bottle!' Because there wasn't any smell. I couldn't smell it. They dragged everything out of the bedside locker: sausage, cucumbers, honey, sweets – nothing had any smell! There was colour, there was taste, but no smell. I almost lost my mind! Spring arrived, the trees blossomed, I could see it all, but I couldn't smell it. They took out one and a half cubic centimetres of my brain and apparently some kind of centre was removed, the one responsible for smells. Even now, after five years have gone by, I can't tell how flowers, tobacco smoke and women's perfumes smell. I can smell eau de cologne if it's a crude, powerful smell, but the bottle has to be shoved right under my nose. Apparently the remaining part of the brain has taken over the lost function. I think that's it.

In the hospital I got a letter from a friend. I learned from him that our personnel carrier was blown up by an Italian blast mine. He saw a man come flying out together with the engine . . . That was me . . .

They discharged me and gave me welfare compensation – three hundred roubles. For a minor injury you're supposed to get a hundred and fifty; for a serious injury it's three hundred. After that, how you live is up to you. The pension is peanuts. Move in with your parents and be dependent on them. My father's fighting a war of his own anyway. He's turned grey and developed high blood pressure.

I didn't wise up about things at the war, I started wising up afterwards. And everything started spinning in the opposite direction . . .

I was drafted in '81. The war had already been going on for two years, but in ordinary life they didn't know or talk about it much. My family thought that if the government had sent the troops in it needed to be done. That was the way my father and the neighbours reasoned. I don't remember anyone having any other opinion. Not even the women cried. It was all still a long way away and not very frightening. A war and not a war; if it was war, then it was a strange kind of war, without anyone being killed or taken prisoner. No one had seen any zinc coffins yet. It was later that we found out they'd already brought coffins into the city, but they were burying them in secret, at night, and on the headstones they wrote 'died', not 'killed'. But nobody bothered to ask themselves: how come nineteen-year-old boys have suddenly started dying in the army? Is it from vodka or the flu? Or maybe they gorged themselves on too many oranges? Their relatives wept, and everyone else carried on living the same way as ever, if they weren't affected. They wrote in the newspapers that our soldiers were building bridges and planting avenues of friendship and our doctors were treating Afghan women and children.

At the Vitebsk training camp it was no secret that we were being trained for Afghanistan. Lots of guys tried to dodge the army at any cost. One confessed he was afraid that we would all get shot out there. I started despising him. Just before we left, another one refused to go: at first he tried to trick them, said he'd lost his Komsomol membership card. Then the card was found and he made up a story about his girl having a baby. I thought he was a headcase. We were going to make a revolution! That was what they told us. And we believed it. We imagined something romantic in store for us.

When a bullet hits someone you hear it; there's no way to forget it or confuse it with anything else – that distinctive wet splat. A young guy you know falls face down in dust as bitter as ashes. You turn him over on to his back; the cigarette that you just gave him is still clutched in his teeth. It's still smoking . . . I wasn't prepared to shoot at anyone, I was still from ordinary life. From the normal world . . . The first time you act as if it's a dream: you run, drag, shoot, but you don't remember anything. Afterwards you can't tell anyone about it. It's like it's all behind a sheet of glass . . . Behind a wall of rain . . . As if you're having a terrible dream. You wake up in fright and you can't remember a thing. It turns out that to feel the horror you have to remember it, get used to it. After two or three weeks there'll be nothing of the old you left, just your name. You aren't you any longer, but someone else. I think that's how it is . . . Clearly that's it. And that someone else . . . That person isn't frightened any longer by the sight of someone who's been killed. He thinks calmly or with a feeling of annoyance about how he'll have to drag him down a cliff or lug him for kilometres through the heat. He doesn't picture it. But he already knows how spilled-out guts smell in the heat and how the smell of human excrement and blood doesn't wash out. Imagination? The imagination goes silent. You see a dirty puddle of molten metal with charred skulls grinning in it – as if a few hours ago they weren't screaming here, but laughing as they died. But suddenly it's all normal . . . simple . . . You get this acute thrill of excitement at the sight of a dead man: they didn't get me! It happens so quickly, that kind of transformation . . . It's very quick. It happens to everyone.

For men at war there's nothing secret about death. Killing is simply pulling the trigger. We were taught that the one who stays alive is the one who fires first. That's the law of war. 'You have to know how to do two things here: walk quickly and shoot accurately. I'll do the thinking,' the commander said. We shot at whatever we were told to shoot at. I was taught to shoot at whatever I was told to shoot at. I shot without feeling any pity for anyone. I could have killed a child. After all, everyone there was fighting against us: young men, women, old men, children. A column's driving through a *kishlak*. The engine of the lead vehicle stalls. The driver climbs out and lifts the hood. A kid about ten years old knifes him in the back. Right where the heart is. The driver collapsed across the engine. They riddled the kid with bullets . . . If they'd given us the order we'd have reduced that *kishlak* to dust. Erased it.

Everyone tried to survive. There was no time to think. We were eighteen to twenty years old. I got used to other people's deaths, but I was afraid of my own. I saw how it took just one second, and there was nothing left of a man, as if he had never existed. And they sent a dress uniform back to the Homeland in an empty coffin. They used to pour in some foreign soil to make up the weight . . . I wanted to live. I've never wanted to live as much as I did there. When we got back from action we laughed. I've never laughed as much as I did there. Old jokes passed as first-rate with us. Take this one for instance . . .

A black marketeer ended up at the war. The first thing he did was find out how many hard currency checks a captured 'spirit' cost. One 'spirit' was valued at eight checks. Two days later there's a cloud of dust beside the garrison: it's him leading along two hundred prisoners. A friend of his says: 'Sell me one. I'll give you seven checks.' 'Ah, come on, old buddy. I bought them for nine.'

Someone could tell that a hundred times – and we'd laugh a hundred times. We laughed until our bellies hurt at any little piece of nonsense.

A 'spirit' is lying there with a dictionary. A sniper. He sees three little stars – a senior lieutenant . . . he leafs through the dictionary: three little stars is fifty thousand afghanis. Bang! One big star, a major – that's two hundred thousand afghanis. Bang! Two little stars – a warrant officer. Bang! That night the leader pays out: for the senior lieutenant – pay him the afghanis; for the major – pay him the afghanis; for . . . 'What's this? A warrant officer! You've killed the man who feeds us. Who's going to sell us condensed milk and tinned food, who's going to sell us blankets? Hang him!'

We talked a lot about money. More than about death. I didn't bring anything back. Just the piece of shrapnel they took out of me – that's all. Some brought back things . . . China, precious stones, jewellery, carpets. That was from combat missions, when we went into the *kishlaks*. Some bought and swapped. A magazine of cartridges for a make-up set: mascara, face powder and eye shadow for the girl you love. They sold boiled cartridges . . . A bullet from a boiled cartridge won't fly out of the barrel, it just gets spat out. You can't kill with it. They heated up buckets or basins, threw the cartridges in, boiled them for two hours and they were done! In the evening they took them off to sell. This trade was carried on by commanders and common soldiers, heroes and cowards. Knives, bowls, spoons and forks disappeared from the messes. Mugs, stools and hammers went missing from the barracks. The bayonets of automatic rifles disappeared, and car mirrors and spare parts. Even medals as well . . . In the *dukans* they took everything, even the rubbish that was carted out of the garrison: tin cans, old newspapers, rusty nails, pieces of plywood, plastic bags. Rubbish was sold by the truckload. The dollar and water will always find a way. Everywhere. A soldier dreamed . . . There were three soldier's dreams: to buy a shawl for his mother, a make-up set for his girlfriend and swimming trunks for himself. There weren't any swimming trunks in the Soviet Union then.

They call us 'Afghanis'. A foreign name. Like a badge. A mark. We're not the same as everyone else. We're different. What are we like? I don't know who I am: a hero, or a fool who people should point their fingers at? Or maybe a criminal? They're already saying that it was a political blunder. They say it quietly today, tomorrow it will be louder. And I left blood behind there. My own. And others' . . . They gave us medals that we don't wear. We'll return them some day. Decorations won honourably in a dishonourable war. They invite us to speak in schools. But what can we talk about? The military action? The first man we killed? . . . About how, even now, I'm still afraid of the dark; if something falls, I shudder . . . About taking prisoners, but not getting them all the way back to the regiment? Not always . . . (*He pauses.*) In a year and a half of war, I never saw a single live *dushman*, or mujahedeen, only dead ones. About the collections of dried human ears? Trophies of war. Men boasted about them. About the *kishlaks* after a pounding by artillery, looking more like a ploughed-up field than a place where people live? Is that what they want to hear about in our schools, then? No, what they want there are heroes. But I remember the way we used to kill and destroy, then immediately build and hand out presents. It all existed so close together that even now I can't separate things. I'm afraid of these memories. I hide from them. I push them aside. I don't know a single man who came back from there and didn't drink and smoke. Weak cigarettes are no good to me. I look for Hunter's, which are what we used to smoke out there. But the doctors forbid me to smoke. Half my head's made of metal. And I can't drink . . .

Only don't write about our 'Afghani' brotherhood. It doesn't exist. I don't believe in it. At the war we were all united: we were deceived in exactly the same way, we wanted to live in exactly the same way and we wanted to go home in exactly the same way. Here we're united by the fact that we've got nothing, and in our country benefits are handed out to those who have pull and privileges. But they owe us for our blood. We all have the same problems: pensions, apartments, decent medicine, artificial limbs, furniture . . . If we solve those our clubs will fall apart. Let me just get myself an apartment, force it through, grab it with my teeth if I have to – with furniture and a fridge and a washing machine and a Japanese video – and that's it! It'll be clear immediately that I don't need that club for anything any more.

The young people haven't reached out their hands to us. They can't understand us. Supposedly we're equated with the men who fought in the Great Patriotic War. Only they were defending their Homeland; but what were we doing? We played the part of the Germans – that's what one young guy told me. I think that's . . . that's . . . that's the way they look at us . . . And we resent that. They were listening to music here, dancing with girls and reading books, while we were eating half-cooked grain and getting blown up with mines. Anyone who wasn't there with me, who didn't see it, experience it, suffer it – to me he's no one. In ten years' time, when our hepatitis, blast injuries and malaria start showing through they'll try to get rid of us. At work and at home . . . They'll stop planting us on the committees of various organizations. We'll be a burden to everyone.

What's your book for? Who's it for? None of us who came back from there will like it anyway. How can you possibly tell people how it was? The dead camels and dead men lying in a single pool of blood, with their blood mingled together. Who wants that? We're strangers to everyone back here. All I have left is my home, my wife and the child she's going to have soon. A few friends from there. I don't trust anyone else.

And I never will now.

A private, grenadier

I kept quiet for ten years . . . I kept quiet about everything.

They wrote in the newspapers that the regiment had completed a training manoeuvre. And held a live-firing exercise. We read it and we felt insulted. Our platoon was escorted by trucks. You could stick a screwdriver through a truck – it was just a target for a bullet. Every day they fired at us and killed us. They killed a young guy I knew right beside me. The first one, right in front of my eyes. We didn't know each other very well yet. The shot came from a mortar. He took a long time to die, there was lot of shrapnel stuck in him. He could recognize us. But he called for people we didn't know.

Just before I was sent off to Kabul I almost got into a fight with one guy, but his friend dragged him off me.

'What are you quarrelling with him for? He's flying to Afghanistan tomorrow.'

Out there we never had one mess tin each or one spoon each. If there was a mess tin we all used to fling ourselves on it, about eight men. But Afghanistan isn't a thriller or an adventure story. A dead peasant farmer lying there – a scrawny body with big hands . . . During a bombardment you beg (who you're begging I don't know; you beg God): 'Let the ground open up and hide me. Let the stone part . . .' Dogs whining. The mine detection dogs whining pitifully. They were killed and wounded too. Dead Alsatians and men. Bandaged dogs and men. Men with legs missing; dogs with legs missing. You can't tell where it's dog's blood on the snow and where it's human. They toss the captured weapons into a single heap: Chinese, American, Pakistani, Soviet, English – I was amazed to see that they were beautiful, but it was all for killing us. Fear! I'm not ashamed of that fear. Fear is more human than courage. I realized that. When you're afraid you have pity, at least for yourself. You look round and start noticing life . . . Everything will stay alive, but you'll disappear. You don't want to think that you'll be lying here, so small and gruesome, a thousand kilometres from home. People are already flying into space, but they're still killing each other the way they did thousands of years ago. With a bullet, a knife, a rock . . . in the *kishlaks* they stabbed our soldiers to death with wooden pitchforks.

I came back in '81. It was all cheers and applause. We fulfilled our international duty! Our sacred duty! Heroes! I reached Moscow in the morning, early. I arrived on a train. There wasn't a bus until the evening. I couldn't wait, so I hitched rides. I arrived in Mozhaisk on a commuter train, reached Gagarin on a local bus and got to Smolensk on all sorts of things. And then from Smolensk to Vitebsk on a truck. Six hundred kilometres altogether. No one took any money when they realized I was from Afghanistan. I haven't forgotten that. And I covered the last two kilometres on foot. At a run. I ran all the way home.

At home there was the scent of the poplars, the clanking of the trams, a little girl eating ice cream. And that smell of the poplars, the poplars – that's a green zone, 'the bush' as it was called; they fire out of there. I wanted so badly to see a birch tree and our Russian blue tit. I was afraid of corners, of going round the corner of a building. When there's a corner ahead everything inside me clenches up tight: who's round that corner? For a whole year I was afraid to go out in the street: no bulletproof vest, no helmet, no automatic rifle – like being naked. And at night the dreams: someone aiming a gun at my forehead, and the calibre's big enough to blow half my head off. I fling myself against the wall . . . The phone starts jangling and sweat springs out on my forehead. They're firing! Where from? My eyes start darting around. They run into the bookshelf . . . A-a-ah! I'm at home . . .

In the newspapers they were still writing the same things: 'Helicopter X has completed a training flight . . .' 'Awarded the Order of the Red Star . . .' 'A concert to celebrate May Day was held in Kabul with Soviet soldiers participating . . .' Afghanistan set me free. It cured me of the belief that everything here is right, that they write the truth in the newspapers and show the truth on the television. 'What should I do? What should I do?' I used to ask myself. I wanted to make my mind up and do something, go somewhere. But where? My mother discouraged me from doing it and none of my friends supported me. 'Everyone's keeping quiet,' they said. 'It's the right thing to do.'

So now I've told you . . . For the first time I've tried to say what I think. It feels strange.

A private, motorized infantry

I'm afraid to start telling you about it. Those shadows will pounce on me again . . .

Every day . . . Every day out there I used to tell myself: 'I'm a fool, a fool. Why did I do it?' Especially at night I used to get thoughts like that, when I wasn't working. But during the day they were different: how can I help everyone? The wounds are terrible . . . I was staggered: what were bullets like this for? Who invented them? Could a human being really have invented them? The entry hole is small, but inside . . . the intestines, the liver, the spleen – it's all chopped up and ripped apart. It's not enough to kill and injure, they have to make a man suffer all that torment. They always called out 'Mama!' when it hurt. That was the only word I heard . . .

I wanted to get away from Leningrad, maybe just for a year or two, but get away. My child died, then my husband died. There was nothing to keep me in that city. On the contrary, everything reminded me, it was driving me away. This is the place where I met him for the first time . . . This is the place where we kissed for the first time . . . I had my baby in this maternity home . . .

The chief physician summoned me. 'Will you go to Afghanistan?'

'Yes, I'll go.' I needed to see that others were worse off than me. And I saw it.

The war, we were told, was a just one. We were helping the Afghan people put an end to feudalism and build a bright socialist society. The fact that our boys were being killed was glossed over somehow. What we understood was that there were a lot of infectious diseases: malaria, typhoid fever, hepatitis. 1980 . . . The beginning . . . We flew to Kabul. The old English stables had been allocated for the hospital. There was nothing. One syringe for everyone . . . The officers drank the medical spirit and we had to treat the wounds with petrol. The wounds healed poorly. But the sun helped. Bright sunlight kills microbes. I saw my first wounded men in underwear and boots. Without pyjamas. It was quite a while before pyjamas appeared. Or slippers. Or blankets. One boy . . . I remember that boy: his body bent in all directions, as if there were no bones. His legs were floppy, like string. They took about twenty pieces of shrapnel out of him.

All through March we dumped the amputated arms and legs right there, beside the wards. The dead bodies . . . they lay in a separate ward. Half-naked with their eyes gouged out; one with a star carved into the stomach. I'd seen things like that before in films about the Civil War. There weren't any zinc coffins yet; they still hadn't laid in any stocks of them.

Soon we started thinking a little bit, wondering who we were. The command wasn't pleased by our doubts. There still weren't any slippers or pyjamas, but they were already hanging up the slogans, calls to action and posters that had been brought in. And against the background of those slogans – the thin, sad faces of our boys. They stuck in my mind forever. Twice a week there was political instruction. All the time they taught us: 'It's a sacred duty, the border must be locked down.' The most unpleasant thing in the army is informing on people, the order to inform about every tiny little thing. To rat on every wounded man, every patient. It was called 'knowing the mood'. The army had to be healthy. It was required to rat on everybody: you mustn't pity them. But we did pity them. Pity was what held everything together . . .

We went there to save, to help, to love. That's what we went for . . . After some time went by, I caught myself thinking that I hated everything. I hated this soft, light sand that burned like fire. I hated these mountains. I hated these stunted *kishlaks*, from which they can shoot at any moment. I hated the occasional Afghan, carrying a basket of melons or standing beside his house. Who could tell where he had been last night and what he was doing? They killed an officer I knew, who had been treated in the hospital recently. They slaughtered two wards of soldiers. In another place the water was poisoned. Someone picked up a beautiful cigarette lighter and it exploded in his hand. These were our boys who were being killed. Our own boys. You have to understand that . . . Have you ever seen a roasted man? You haven't. No face, no eyes, no body. Something shrivelled up, covered in a yellow crust. No screaming, just a growling from under the crust.

Hate helped people to live out there. They survived by hating. And a sense of guilt? That didn't appear there, but here, after I looked at things from the outside. There it had all seemed like justice. Here I was horrified to remember a little girl lying in the dust with no arms and no legs. Like a broken doll. After our bombardment . . . And we were astonished that they didn't like us. They were treated in our hospital: when I gave a woman medicine she didn't look up at me, she never smiled. It was actually insulting. I felt insulted there, but not here. Here I'm a normal human being and all my feelings have come back to me.

I have a good profession – saving people – and it saved me too. I can try to make excuses: we were needed there. We didn't save everyone we could have saved – that's the most terrible thing. I could have saved someone, but we didn't have the right medicine. I could have saved someone, but he was brought in too late. (Who were in the combat medical squads? Poorly trained soldiers, who had only learned how to apply bandages.) I could have saved someone, but I couldn't wake up the drunken surgeon. I could have saved someone . . . We couldn't even write the truth in the death notifications. They were blown up by mines. Often all that was left of a man was half a bucket of flesh . . . And we wrote: 'Killed in a road accident', 'Fell over a cliff', 'Food poisoning'. When there were already thousands of them, then we were allowed to tell the relatives the truth. I got used to dead bodies. But the fact that they were so young, so endearing, like little children – it was impossible to come to terms with that.

They brought in a wounded man. I happened to be on duty. He opened his eyes and looked at me.

'That's it then,' he said. And he died.

They searched for a man for three days in the mountains. They found him. They brought him in. He was raving: 'Doctor! Doctor!' He saw a white coat and thought: 'I'm saved!' But his injury was fatal. It was only there that I learned what it means to be wounded in the cranium . . . I have my own graveyard in my head, my own portrait gallery. With black frames.

Even in death they weren't equal. For some reason the ones who were killed in action were pitied more. The ones who died later in hospital were pitied less. Sometime they screamed out as they died . . . They screamed so terribly! I remember a major who died in intensive care. His wife had come to see him. He died in front of her eyes. And she started screaming. Like an animal. I wanted to close all the doors, so that no one would hear. Because soldiers were dying nearby. Boys. And there was no one to weep for them. They were dying alone. She was out of place among us . . .

'Mama! Mama!'

'I'm here, son,' I used to say, deceiving them.

We became their mothers and sisters. And we always wanted to justify that trust.

The soldiers would bring in a wounded man, hand him over and not leave. 'Girls, we don't want anything. Can we just sit with you for a while?'

But here, at home . . . They have their own mothers, sisters and wives. They don't need us here. Out there they trusted us with things about themselves that they wouldn't tell anyone in this life. Those conditions put a man under a spotlight. If he was a coward it soon became clear that he was a coward. If he was an informer then it was immediately obvious that he was an informer. If he was a womanizer then everyone knew he was a womanizer. I'm not sure anyone would admit it here, but there I heard more than one man say that you could get to like killing, that killing was a pleasure. It's a powerful feeling. A warrant officer I knew who was going back to the Soviet Union didn't even try to conceal it: 'How am I going to live now, when I've got the urge to kill?' It's probably another kind of passion: they used to talk about it quite openly. The boys used to tell us with real enthusiasm about how they burned a *kishlak* and flattened everything. They must be insane, surely? How many of them have come back like that . . . Killing a man means nothing to them . . . Once we were visited by a major; he had come from somewhere near Kandahar. In the evening we had to say goodbye to him, and he locked himself in an empty room and shot himself. They say that he was drunk, I don't know. It's hard. It was hard to live through a single day there. A boy on sentry duty shot himself after three hours in the sun. A home-loving boy, he couldn't bear it. There were a lot who were insane. At first they used to lie in the general wards, then they were accommodated separately. They started trying to escape: they were frightened by the barred windows. They felt better together with all the others. I remember one especially.

'Sit down. I'll sing you a discharge song.' He sang and sang until he fell asleep.

'When he woke up, he used to call out: 'Home! Home! To mama. It's too hot for me here . . .' He was always asking to go home.

Lots of them smoked. Hashish, marijuana, whatever they could get hold of. They explained to me that it makes you strong, free from everything. In the first place, from your body. As if you're walking on tiptoe. You feel a lightness in every cell. You can feel every muscle. You want to fly! It's as if you are flying! An irrepressible joy. Everything pleases you: you laugh at the merest trifle. You hear better. You see better. You can distinguish more smells, more sounds. In that state it's easier to kill – you're anaesthetized. There's no pity. It's easy to die – the fear goes away. You feel as if you're wearing a bulletproof vest, you're armoured. I could understand what they said. Twice I . . . I smoked it myself twice. In both cases when I couldn't take any more, psychologically or physically. I was work-ing in the infectious diseases ward. There were supposed to be thirty beds, but there were three hundred men lying there. Typhoid fever, malaria. They were issued sheets and a blanket, and they lay on their own greatcoats, on the bare ground. In their underpants, with their heads shaved. And the lice poured down off them . . . Body lice . . . Head lice . . . I'd never even imagined so many lice . . . And in the *kishlak* nearby the Afghans strolled about in our hospital pyjamas, with our sheets on their heads instead of turbans. I don't blame them for it. No . . . Most of the time I don't blame them. Our boys died for three roubles a month – our soldiers received eight hard currency checks a month. Three roubles . . . They were fed maggoty meat and fish that had turned rusty-looking. All of us had scurvy and all my front teeth fell out. They used to sell blankets and buy hash. Or something sweet. Trinkets . . . There were such bright little shops there, and so many attractive things in those shops. Back home in the Union there wasn't any of that, they'd never seen it before. And they used to sell guns and cartridges, only to be killed by those same automatic rifles and cartridges. They bought chocolate with them . . . Pies . . .

After everything out there I saw my country with different eyes. My pupils even changed: they got wider. It was frightening to come back here. Strange, somehow. As if all my skin had been ripped off. I kept crying all the time. I couldn't bear to see anyone except people who had been there. I could have spent all day and all night with them. Other people's conversations seemed like some kind of idle nonsense, silly nonsense. It went on like that for six months. But now I swear myself when I'm standing in the queue for meat. I try to live a normal life, the way I did 'before'. But I can't do it. I've become indifferent to myself and my own life. Life's over, there's not going to be any more. And for men the experience is even more agonizing. A woman can cling on to her children, but men have nothing to cling on to. They come back, fall in love and have children, but even so Afghanistan comes before everything else. I myself would like to figure out why it's like that. What was it all for? Why does it affect me so much? Back there everything was driven inside, and now it has come creeping out here.

They should be pitied. All of them who were there should be pitied. I'm a grown adult – I was thirty then – and look how it shattered me. But they were little children; they didn't understand anything. They were taken out of their homes and guns were put in their hands. They were told: 'You're going on a sacred mission. The Homeland won't forget you.' Now people turn their eyes away from them and try to forget the war. It's over! And the first ones to do that are the ones who sent us there. Even we talk about the war less and less often when we meet. Nobody loves that war. Although to this day I still cry when they play the Afghan national anthem. I learned to love all Afghan music. It's like a narcotic.

Not long ago I met a soldier in a bus. He was one of our patients. He'd lost his right arm. I remembered him well, another Leningrader.

'Perhaps I could help you in some way, Seryozha?'

But he just replied angrily: 'You go to hell!'

I know he'll find me and ask me to forgive him. But who will ask him to forgive them? And ask everyone who was there, everyone who was broken and mutilated, to forgive them? I'm not talking just about the cripples. What kind of loathing for your own people does it take to send them to something like that! It's not just every war that I hate now, I even hate little boys' fights. And don't tell me that the war is over. A hot, dusty breath of summer wind, a bright glint on a circle of stagnant water, the acrid odour of dry flowers . . . It's like a blow to the temple.

It will pursue us all our lives.

A nurse

I've had a rest after the war now, recovered a bit. How can I express everything that it was? That shuddering right through all your body, that fury . . . How?

Before the army I graduated from a road transport technical college and so I was given the job of driving the battalion commander. I had no complaints about the work. But they started going on and on at us about a limited contingent of Soviet forces in Afghanistan. Every single political awareness session fed us the same information: 'Our troops are securely protecting the borders of the Homeland, providing help to a friendly nation.' We started getting worried they might send us to the war. I realize now that they'd decided to trick us.

We were summoned to the commanding officer and asked: 'Well, boys, how would you like to work with some brand new vehicles?'

Naturally, we all chorused back: 'Yes! That's what we dream of.'

But what came next was this: 'Only first you have to go to the virgin lands and help harvest the grain.'

Everyone agreed.

In the plane I happened to overhear the flight crew saying we were flying to Tashkent. I couldn't help having doubts after that. Were we flying to the virgin lands or not? Then we really did land at Tashkent. They marched us away to an area fenced off with barbed wire, not far from the airfield, and we waited. The officers walked about, looking kind of nervous, whispering to each other. Lunchtime arrived and they lugged crates of vodka, one by one, over to our parking lot.

'Line up by two-o-os!' They lined us up and immediately announced that a plane would arrive in a few hours' time to collect us – we were being sent to the Republic of Afghanistan to perform our military duty. To fulfil our oath.

All hell broke loose! Fear and panic turned the men into animals – some into quiet ones, some into raging beasts. Some wept at the sheer effrontery of it, some were just dazed or fell into a trance at this squalid, unbelievable deception. So this was what they'd got the vodka ready for! To keep things simple, make it easier to handle us. After the vodka, when the alcohol went to their heads, some soldiers tried to run off or fling themselves at the officers and brawl with them. But the compound was cordoned off by soldiers with automatics, and they started forcing everyone towards the plane. They loaded us into the plane like crates, just flung us into its empty metal belly.

That's how we ended up in Afghanistan . . . Soon we saw the wounded and the dead, and we heard the words 'reconnaissance', 'action', 'operation'. It seems to me . . . The way I see things now, I was in a state of shock. It was months before I even started recovering, started getting a clear idea of my surroundings.

When my wife asked, 'How did my husband end up in Afghanistan?' they told her, 'He volunteered to go of his own free will.' They gave the same kind of answer to all our mothers and wives. If my life and my blood were needed for a great cause, I'd have told them myself: 'Put me down as a volunteer!' But they tricked me twice and sent me off to war without telling the truth about what kind of war it was. I only found out the truth eight years later. My friends are lying in their graves and they don't know how they were duped with this shabby war. Sometimes I even envy them. They'll never find out about that. And they'll never be tricked again.

A private, logistics driver

I was really homesick so far away from our Homeland. My husband had served in Germany for a long time, and then in Mongolia. Twenty years of my life had been spent outside my Homeland, which I loved with an immense, boundless love. I wrote to the General Staff to say I'd been abroad all my life, I couldn't bear it any more. Please help me get home . . .

We'd already got into the train, but I still couldn't believe it. I kept asking my husband over and over: 'Are we going to the Union? You're not tricking me, are you?' At the first station I picked up a lump of my native earth, looked at it and smiled – my very own. I ate it, believe me. I scrubbed my face with it.

My darling . . . My . . . Our . . . Yura was my eldest. It's not a good thing for a mother to admit, but I loved him more than anyone else in the world. More than my husband, more than my second son. I loved them all, but him in a special kind of way. When he was little I used to sleep holding him by his little foot. I couldn't imagine ever running off to the cinema and leaving my son with someone else. I used to take him when he was just three months old, and a few bottles of milk, and off we'd go to the cinema. I really can say I was with him all his life. I brought him up just with books, on ideal images: Pavel Korchagin, Oleg Koshevoi, Zoya Kosmodemyanskaya. In the first year at school he didn't know any fairy tales or children's poems off by heart, but he knew whole pages out of *How the Steel Was Tempered* by Nikolai Ostrovsky.

The teacher was thrilled.

'Who's your mother, Yura? You've already read so much.'

'My mama works in a library.'

He knew ideals, but he didn't know life. And, after living so far away from our Homeland for so many years, I imagined that life consisted of ideals as well. So this is what happened . . . We'd already returned to our part of the country and were living in Chernovtsy. Yura was studying in the military academy. One night, it was two o'clock in the morning, the doorbell rings and he's standing there on the step.

'You, son? Why so late? Why did you come in the rain? You're soaking wet.'

'Mama, I've come to tell you that life is hard for me. Those things you taught me . . . None of that exists. Where did you get all that from? And that's just the start. How am I going to carry on living now?'

The two of us sat in the kitchen right through the night. What could I tell him? Only the same things all over again: life is beautiful, people are good. It's all true. He listened to me quietly. In the morning he went back to the academy.

I tried to persuade him again and again: 'Yura, leave the academy. Go to a civilian college. That's the place for you. I can see how you're suffering.'

He wasn't happy with his choice, because he became a soldier by accident. He would have made a good historian. A scholar. He lived for books. 'What a wonderful country – ancient Greece.' And he read everything about Greece. And then about Italy: 'Mama, Leonardo da Vinci thought about space flight. Some day they'll solve the mystery of the Mona Lisa . . .' In the tenth year at school he went to Moscow for the winter holidays. I have a brother who lives there, a retired colonel. Yura confided in him: 'I want to join the philosophy faculty at the university.' His uncle didn't approve.

'You're an honest boy, Yura. It's hard being a philosopher in our times. You have to deceive yourself and others. If you tell the truth you'll end up behind bars or in the madhouse.'

But in the spring Yura made up his mind. 'Mama, don't ask me any questions. I'm going to be a soldier.'

I'd seen the zinc coffins in the garrison. But back then one of my sons was only in the seventh year at school and the other was even younger. I was hoping the war would be over before they grew up. Could a war really last that long? 'But it turned out that it lasted as long as school, ten years,' someone said at Yura's wake.

There was a graduation party at the academy: my son was an officer now. But I couldn't grasp the fact that Yura was going away. I simply couldn't imagine my life without him, even for an instant.

'Where can they send you?'

'I'll ask to go to Afghanistan.'

'Yura!'

'Mama, you brought me up that way. Now don't you dare try to re-educate me. You brought me up properly. All those degenerates I've met in my life, they're not my people and they're not my Homeland. I'll go to Afghanistan to prove to you that there is something exalted in life, that a fridge crammed with meat and a Zhiguli automobile aren't enough to make everyone happy. There's something more than that . . . That's what you taught me.'

He wasn't the only one who asked to go to Afghanistan. Lots of boys put in requests. All of them were from good families: one's father was the chairman of a collective farm, another's was a teacher in a rural school, and his mother was a nurse.

What could I tell my son? That his Homeland didn't need this? That the people he wanted to prove something to would still think what they had always thought – that no one went to Afghanistan except for the clothes and the hard currency checks? Or for medals, and their career? For them Zoya Kosmodemyanskaya was a fanatic, not an ideal, because no normal person was capable of doing that sort of thing.

I don't know what happened to me. I wept and I begged. I admitted to him what I was afraid to admit to myself, but people were already talking about. Already whispering about in their kitchens. I implored him:

'Yurochka, life isn't anything like what I taught you. And if I find out that you're in Afghanistan, I'll go out into the square . . . to the Place of Execution. I'll soak myself in petrol and set fire to it. You won't die for your Homeland there, you'll just get killed for no reason at all. Nobody knows why. How can the Homeland just send its finest sons to their deaths without any great idea?'

He tried to trick me. He said he would go to Mongolia. But I knew. He was my son: he would be in Afghanistan.

And at the same time my younger son, Gena, went into the army. I wasn't worried for him – he'd grown up different. He and Yura were always arguing.

'You don't read enough, Gena. I've never seen you with a book in your hands. It's always a guitar.'

'I don't want to be like you. I want to be like everyone else.'

Both boys left and I moved into the children's room to live. I lost interest in everything except their books, their things, their letters. Yura wrote about Mongolia, but he got his geography so confused that I had no doubts about where he was. Day and night I picked through my life, cutting myself into little pieces. No words can express that pain . . .

I was the one who sent him there. I did it!

. . . Some strangers walked in, but I could tell straightaway from their faces that they'd brought me sorrow and misery. I backed away into the room. There was just one terrible final hope left.

'Gena?'

They turned their eyes away. I asked again, willing to give them one son to save the other. 'Gena?'

One of them said it very, very quietly. 'No, Yura.'

I can't carry on like this . . . I can't carry on. I've been dying for two years. I'm not sick with anything, but I'm dying. I didn't burn myself in the square. My husband didn't take his Party card and fling it in their faces. We've probably died already. Only nobody knows.

We don't even realize it ourselves.

A mother

I immediately persuaded myself: 'I'm forgetting it all. I'm forgetting it all.'

The subject is taboo in our family. My wife has turned grey at forty. My daughter used to have long hair, now she wears it short. During the night-time bombardments of Kabul they couldn't get her to wake up and they used to pull her plaits.

But after four years suddenly I can't keep it in. I can't keep it in. I want to talk about it. Yesterday we had unexpected visitors, and I couldn't stop myself. I brought out the album. I showed the slides: copters hovering over a *kishlak*; a wounded man being laid on a stretcher, and his torn-off leg beside him with a trainer on the foot; prisoners condemned to be shot, looking naively into the lens – in ten minutes they won't exist any more . . . Allah Akbar! I looked round: the men were smoking on the balcony, the women had gone into the kitchen. Only their children were still sitting there. Teenagers. They find it interesting. I don't understand what's happening to me. I want to talk. Why all of a sudden? In order not to forget anything . . .

How it was then, what I felt then – I can't express that. I can talk about my feelings now. Four years later . . . After ten years it will all start to sound different. Perhaps it will all just get shattered to pieces.

It was a kind of rage. Frustration. Why do I have to go? Why has the choice fallen on me? But although I felt the weight of the burden I didn't break down – and that gave me some satisfaction. You start preparing with the smallest things: which kind of knife to take with you, which kind of razor . . . I was all organized. And then it got unbearable. I wanted to get on with it and meet the unknown quickly, so that the enthusiasm and the exalted feelings wouldn't pass off . . . It's this pattern. Anyone and everyone will tell you. And I'm breaking out in fits of the shakes or sweating . . . And then there's that moment, when the plane has landed, the relief of it – and at the same time the excitement: now it will all begin, we'll see it, touch it, start living it.

There are three Afghans standing there, talking about something and laughing. A dirty little kid runs along the market stalls and dives into some rags under a counter. He stares out at me with the green, unblinking eye of a parrot. I watch and I don't understand what's going on. They don't break off their conversation. The one with his back to me turns round . . . And now I'm looking into the muzzle of a pistol. The pistol moves higher . . . higher. There's the mouth. I can see it. At the same moment I hear a click – and I'm gone. I'm in this world and the next one at the same time. But I'm not lying down yet. I'm still standing. I want to talk to them, but I can't. A-a-ah . . .

The world appears slowly, like a photograph developing . . . A window . . . A tall window. Something white and something big and bulky in that whiteness. Someone. The spectacles get in my way and I can't make out the face. Sweat's dripping off it, and the drops hurt when they land on my own face. I lift my impossibly heavy eyelids and hear a sigh of relief.

'That's it, comrade lieutenant-colonel, you're back from your "assignment".'

But if I raise my head, if I even turn it, my brain collapses somehow. My consciousness flickers on and off . . . The kid dives into those rags under the counter again. He stares at me with the green, unblinking eyes of a parrot. The three Afghans are standing there. The one with his back to me turns round, and my eyes run smack into the muzzle of the pistol . . . There's the mouth. I can see it. This time I don't wait for the familiar click. I shout out: 'I've got to kill you! I've got to kill you!'

What colour is a scream? What does it taste like? And what colour is blood? In a hospital it's red; on dry sand it's grey; on a rock in the evening it's bright blue, not alive any longer. The blood flows rapidly out of a seriously injured body, like out of a broken glass jar . . . And the man rots away . . . he rots away. Only the eyes still gleam right to the end, and they look past you. They look past you stubbornly, at something else.

It's all been paid for! Everything! In full. (*He starts striding round the room nervously.*)

You look at the mountains from below – infinitely large, beyond reach. But go up in a plane and there are overturned sphinxes lying down there. Do you understand what I'm talking about? About time. About the distance between events. Back then, even those of us who were fighting that war didn't know what kind of war it was. Don't confuse today's me with yesterday's me, with the person I was in '79. Yes, I believed in it! In '83 I came back to Moscow. Here they were living and acting as if we didn't exist out there. As if there wasn't any war. In the metro people were laughing and kissing, the same as always. They were reading books. I walked along Arbat Street and stopped people.

'How long has the war in Afghanistan been going on?'

'I don't know . . .'

'How long has the war been going on?'

'I don't know. Why do you ask me that?'

'How many years?'

'Two years, I think.'

'How many years?'

'You mean there's a war going on? Really?'

Now they can laugh at us and mock us, say we were blind and stupid, like sheep. A docile herd! Gorbachev has permitted it . . . The reins have been dropped . . . Laugh away! But a wise old Chinese proverb says: 'Worthy of all contempt is the hunter who boasts over the body of a dead lion, and worthy of all respect is the hunter who boasts over the body of a lion he has conquered.' Some might talk about mistakes. True, I don't know who. But not me. When they ask me, 'Why didn't you say anything back then? You weren't a boy, were you? You were almost fifty years old', I have to understand . . .

Let me start by saying I used my gun there, but at the same time

I respect those people. I even like them. I like their songs, their prayers: calm and endless, like their mountains. But I myself – I'm only going to speak for myself – sincerely believed that a nomad's tent is worse than a five-storey house, that without a toilet bowl there is no culture. And we were going to swamp them with toilet bowls, and build them brick houses. Teach them to drive tractors. And we brought them desks for their offices, and carafes for water, and red tablecloths for official meetings, and thousands of portraits of Marx, Engels and Lenin. They hung in all the offices, above the head of every boss. We brought them black Volga limousines for the bosses. And our tractors and our pedigree bull calves. The peasants didn't want to take the land that we gave to them; because it belongs to Allah a man can neither take it nor give it. The smashed skulls of their mosques gazed at us as if they were looking from outer space.

We'll never know how an ant sees the world. Read about that in Engels. And the orientalist Spenserov says: 'Afghanistan cannot be bought.' One morning I light up a cigarette: sitting there on the ashtray is a lizard, as small as a May bug. I come back a few days later. The lizard is still sitting on the ashtray in the same pose; it hasn't even turned its head. Then I realize: that's it – the East. I can vanish and rise from the dead again ten times over and it still won't have turned its tiny little head. In their calendar it's the year 1361. Here I sit at home in an armchair in front of the television. Could I kill a man? Why, I wouldn't even kill a fly! For the first few days, even months, it feels unreal when the bullets slice branches off a mulberry tree. The psychology of war is different . . . You run along, trying to spot a target . . . up ahead, out of the corner of your eye. I didn't count how many I killed. But I ran. I tried to spot a target. Here, there . . . a living, moving target. And I was a target myself. A target . . . No, men don't come back from war as heroes. You can't come back from there as a hero.

And it's all been paid for! Everything! In full.

You picture him to yourself and you love that forty-five-year-old soldier who was adored by all of Europe. Naive-looking, with his simple face and his broad belt. He didn't want anything, he just wanted to win his victory – and go home. But *this* soldier, the one who has come back to our entrance hall, to our street, is different. *This* soldier wants his jeans and cassette player. He saw a different life and remembered it. He started wanting lots of things. The ancients used to say: 'Don't wake a sleeping dog.' Don't give a man temptations beyond human endurance. He won't withstand them.

I couldn't read my beloved Dostoyevsky there. Too gloomy. I carried Ray Bradbury around with me. Science fiction. Who wants to live forever? No one.

But it all really happened . . . It did! I remember. In the prison they showed me the 'chieftain', as we used to call them, of a gang. Lying on an iron bedstead and reading. The book's dust jacket was familiar – Lenin, *The State and Revolution*. 'It's a pity,' he said, 'that I won't finish it. Perhaps my children will read it.'

A school burned down, just one wall was left. Every morning the children came to their class and wrote on the wall with pieces of charcoal left after the fire. After classes they whitewashed it. And it looked like a clean sheet of paper again.

They brought a lieutenant back from 'the bush' without any arms or legs. Without any male parts. The first words he uttered after the shock were: 'How are my boys?'

It's all been paid for! And we paid more than anyone. More than you . . .

We don't want anything. We've been through everything. Just hear us out and understand us. But everybody's used to doing something – giving us medicine, giving us a pension, giving us an apartment. Giving us something and forgetting. This 'giving' has been paid for in expensive currency – blood. But we've come to you to unburden ourselves. We're making our confession.

And don't forget the secrecy of the confessional . . .

A military adviser

No, it's a good thing after all that it ended that way. In defeat. It will open our eyes.

It's impossible to tell you everything . . . What happened, happened. From that, what's left is what I saw and remembered. It's already only a part of the whole. And from that, there'll only be what I'm able to tell you about. There'll only be a tenth of it left in words. That's the very best case, if I try really hard. Strain myself. And for whose sake? For Alyoshka, who died in my arms – eight pieces of shrapnel in his stomach? It took us eighteen hours to carry him down from the mountains. He lived for seventeen hours and then died in the eighteenth. Remember for Alyoshka's sake? But it's only from the viewpoint of religion that you need to do that or a man, especially when he's up there, on high. I tend more to believe that he's not in pain, he's not afraid and he's not ashamed. So why stir things up? You want to find out something from us . . . Right. We're marked men, of course. But what can you find out from us? Maybe you've taken us for someone else? You have to understand, when you're in a foreign country, not knowing what you're fighting for, it's difficult to acquire any kind of ideals. To find a meaning. We were all the same there, but we didn't all think the same way. The same way as it is here, in the normal world. Chance could quite easily have swapped round those who were there and those who weren't. We're all different, but we're the same everywhere – there and here.

I remember, in the sixth or seventh year at school, the Russian literature teacher called me up to the board.

'Who's your favourite character, Chapaev or Pavel Korchagin?'

'Huckleberry Finn.'

'Why Huckleberry Finn?'

'When Huckleberry Finn was deciding whether to squeal on Jim the runaway black or burn in hell for him, he said to himself: "Well, damn him, I'll burn in hell" – but he didn't squeal on Jim.'

'And what if Jim was White and you were Red?' my friend Alyoshka asked after the lesson.

That's the way we live all our life – Whites and Reds. Whoever isn't with us is against us.

Near Bagram . . . We went into a *kishlak* and asked for something to eat. According to their laws, if a man's in your home and he's hungry you can't refuse to give him a hot, round bread cake. The women sat us down at the table and fed us. When we left, those women and their children were stoned and beaten to death with sticks by their own kind. They knew that they'd be killed, but even so they didn't turn us away. And we go to them with our laws . . . We used to walk into the mosque in our caps . . .

Why make me remember? It's all very intimate: the first man I killed, the first sight of my blood on the light sand, and the tall chimney of a camel's head swaying over me before I passed out. At that time I was like everyone else there. In my whole life I've only ever once refused to be like everyone else. Only once . . . In kindergarten they made us hold hands and walk in pairs, but I liked to walk on my own. The young teachers put up with my mischief for a while, but soon one of them got married and left, and to replace her they sent us Aunty Klava.

'Take hold of Seryozha's hand,' said Aunty Klava, leading another boy over to me.

'I don't want to.'

'Why don't you want to?'

'I like walking on my own.'

'Behave like all the good boys and girls do.'

'I won't.'

After the walk Aunty Klava undressed me – she even took off my underpants and little vest – then led me into a dark, empty room and left me there for three hours. And when you're a child, there's nothing more frightening than being left alone. In the dark. You think everyone's forgotten about you. That they'll never find you. The next day I walked hand-in-hand with Seryozha. I became like everyone else. In school it was the class that decided things; in college it was the course group that decided things; at the factory it was the collective that decided things. Everywhere things were decided for me. It was impressed on me that one man alone can't do anything. In some book or other I came across the phrase 'the murder of courage'. When I went out there, there was nothing left in me to kill. 'Volunteers, two paces forward.' Everyone took two paces – and I took two paces.

In Shindand I saw two of our soldiers who had gone crazy. They kept negotiating with the 'spirits' – the Afghans – all the time.

They explained to them what socialism was, according to the history textbook from the tenth year of school. Who Lenin was . . . Remember old Krylov's classic fable: the point was that the idol was hollow, and the priests used to get into it and sit there to answer the questions of the lay people . . . One day – I was about eleven at the time – an old aunty came to visit our school: a sniper who had killed seventy-eight 'Uncle Fritzes'. I went home and started stammering, and that night I developed a temperature. My parents decided it was flu. I stayed at home for a week, reading my favourite book, *The Gadfly*.

Why make me remember it all? When I got back from the war I couldn't wear any of my old jeans and shirts. Those clothes belonged to a stranger, someone I didn't know, even though they still had my smell on them, or so my mother told me. That person is gone, he doesn't exist any more. This other person, who I am now, only has the same name. Before the army I was dating a girl, I was in love. When I came back I didn't call her. She found out by chance that I was in town and she found me. She shouldn't have looked for me. We shouldn't have met . . . 'That man you loved, and who used to love you, is gone,' I told her. 'I'm a different person. Look, I'm not the same!' She cried. She came round lots of times. She called me. What for? I'm not the same! I'm different! (*He pauses for a while and calms down.*) I actually used to like that other person. I miss him. I miss him. 'Padre,' the Gadfly asked Montanelli, 'is your – God – satisfied?'

Who can I fling those words at? Like a grenade . . .

A private, artilleryman

How did I end up here? It's very simple. I believed everything they wrote in the newspapers. I told myself: 'People used to commit feats of heroism, they were capable of self-sacrifice, but our young people nowadays are no good for anything. And I'm just the same. There's a war on out there, and I'm making myself a dress, thinking up a new hairstyle.' My mother cried: 'I'll die before I ever forgive you. I didn't have you so that I could bury your arms and your legs separately.'

Some of my first impressions? The transfer camp in Kabul. Barbed wire, soldiers with automatic rifles. Dogs barking. Nothing but women. Hundreds of women. The officers come and choose the youngest and prettiest ones. Quite blatantly. I was called over by a major.

'Why don't I take you to my battalion, if you're not put off by my truck.'

'What kind of truck's that?'

'For "Load 200" . . .'

I already knew what 'Load 200' was. It was dead men, coffins.

'Are there any coffins?'

'They're just about to unload them.'

An ordinary KamAZ truck with a tarpaulin cover. They threw the coffins about like crates of cartridges. I was horrified. The soldiers realized I was a new girl. When we arrived at the unit it was sixty degrees Celsius. So many flies in the toilet they could've lifted you up on their wings. No shower. Water's worth its weight in gold and I was the only woman.

Two weeks later the battalion commander summoned me. 'You're going to live with me.' I fought him off for two months. Once I almost threw a grenade, and another time I grabbed a knife. I got sick of hearing 'You're just looking for someone with more stars . . . When you want butter with your tea, you'll come on your own . . .' I never used to swear before, but I did now. 'Get out, bugger off!' I turned the air blue – I became really crude.

They transferred me to Kabul, as a receptionist in a hotel. At first I used to attack everyone like a wild beast. They looked at me as if I was crazy. 'Why do you attack us like that? We're not going to bite you.' But I couldn't act any other way, I'd got used to defending myself. Someone might invite me in:

'Come and have a cup of tea.'

'Are you inviting me in for a cup of tea or to slip something else to me?'

That was until I found my . . . love? They don't use words like that here.

He would introduce me to his friends: 'My wife.'

And I'd whisper in his ear: 'For Afghanistan?'

We were travelling in a personnel carrier . . . I shielded him with my body, but fortunately the bullet hit the hatch. He was sitting with his back to it. When we got back he wrote to his wife about me. He hadn't had any letters from home for two months.

I like to go shooting. I let off a whole magazine in a single burst. And I feel better after that.

I killed one 'spirit' myself. We went up into the mountains to breathe the air and admire the view. There was this rustling behind a rock, a kind of electric tingle swung me round and I fired a burst. First. I went over to look: there was a strong, handsome man lying there.

'We could take you out on reconnaissance,' the boys said.

I got cocky then. But they liked the fact that I didn't rummage about in his bag for his things. I only took the pistol. They kept an eye on me all the way – in case I started feeling dizzy or sick. I was fine. My body suddenly felt very light. I got back, opened the fridge and ate a whole load of food, enough to last me a week at any other time. Nerves. They brought me a bottle of vodka. I drank, but didn't get drunk. I was filled with horror: if I'd missed, my mother would have got a 'Load 200'.

I wanted to be at war. Only not this war, but the Great Patriotic War.

Where did the hate come from? It's very simple. They killed your comrade, and you were there beside him. You used to eat out of the same mess tin. He used to tell you about his girlfriend, about his mother. And now he's lying there, scorched all over. Immediately everything's clear . . . You'll keep shooting until you go insane.

We're not used to thinking about the big questions. Who started this? Who's to blame? There's a joke about that. Armenian Radio is asked: 'What is politics?' Armenian Radio replies: 'Have you ever heard a mosquito piss? Well, politics is even subtler.' Let the government deal with that. But here people see blood and they turn into vicious brutes. They lose their minds. You only have to see the scorched skin scrolling up into a tube, like when a nylon stocking bursts, just once . . . And that's enough for you. It's horrifying when they kill the animals. They were shooting up a caravan – it was carrying weapons. They shot the men and the donkeys separately; and they all waited for death silently, in exactly the same way. But one wounded donkey screamed, and it was like a piece of iron being scraped across iron. This screeching sound . . .

I have a different face here, a different voice. You can imagine what we're like here from the girls sitting and talking like this: 'Well what a fool! He quarrelled with the sergeant and then went off to the "spirits". He should've just shot the sergeant. Full stop. He'd have been reported lost in action.' A frank conversation. After all, lots of officers have thought that they could hit a soldier and insult him here, just like in the Soviet Union. They've been found dead. They get shot in the back in action. Try and find out who did it. Just try and prove it.

At the outposts in the mountains the boys don't see anyone for years. A helicopter, three times a week. I arrived. The lieutenant walked over. 'Girl, take off your headscarf and let your hair down. I haven't seen anything but cropped soldiers' heads for two years.' I've got long hair. All the soldiers swarmed out of their trenches.

In one battle a soldier shielded me with his body. For as long as I live I'll remember him and light a candle for him in church. He didn't know me; he only did it because I'm a woman. You remember something like that. In ordinary life where can you tell if someone would protect you with his body? The best things here are even better and the bad things are even worse. They were bombarding us – this is a different incident – and a soldier shouted something vulgar at me. Something foul – something disgusting! 'Well, curse you!' I thought. And he was killed. Half his head was sliced off, and half his body. Right in front of my eyes. I started shuddering like I had malaria. Although I'd seen big plastic sacks with bodies in them before. Bodies wrapped up in foil, like . . . I can't even think of a comparison . . . I couldn't write it, I'd be searching for the words forever. Trying them out, seeing how they felt. You know . . . Like big toys. But for me to shudder like that, it had never happened before. And this time I just couldn't calm down.

I've never come across girls wearing military decorations, even if they have them. One put on her medal 'For Services in Battle' and everyone laughed 'For Sexual Services'. Because everyone knows you can get the medal for a night with the battalion commander . . . Why do they accept women here? They can't get by without them. Do you understand? Some of the gentlemen officers would go insane. And why are the women so keen to go to war? Money. Good money. You can buy a cassette player and things. When you go home you can sell them. You can't earn that much in the Union. You can't save it up. There isn't just one truth: there are different kinds. We're talking honestly. Some girls have got involved with *dukanshchiks* – the local shopkeepers – for clothes. You go into the *dukan* and the *bachata* – the children – shout 'Khanum! Lady! Dzhik-dzhik!' and show you the way to the storeroom. Our officers pay with checks, and the first Soviet security forces were called the Cheka, so they say: 'I'm going to see the security girl.'

Have you heard this joke? Gorynych the dragon, Koshchei the Deathless and the witch Baba Yaga meet up at the transit point in Kabul. They're all off to defend the revolution. Two years later they see each other again on the way home. Only one of Gorynych's three heads is left – the others have been chopped off. Koshchei the Deathless is barely alive, and only because he's immortal. But Baba Yaga is all dolled up in Montana jeans and stone-washed denim gear. Looking cheerful.

'I'm signing up for a third year.'

'You're out of your mind, Baba Yaga!'

'In the Union I'm Baba Yaga, but here I'm Vasilisa the Beautiful.'

Soldiers . . . Kids . . . They leave here broken, eighteen or nineteen years old. Children. They've seen a lot here. A lot . . . A woman selling herself for a case – no, never mind a case – for two tins of meat. Afterwards he'll see a woman through those eyes. All women. The way they see things has been ruined here. We shouldn't be surprised that afterwards they don't behave properly in the Union. One boy I knew is already doing time in jail. They have a different kind of experience. They're used to deciding every-thing with automatic rifles, with force . . . A *dukanshchik* was selling watermelons, one watermelon for a hundred afghanis. Our soldiers wanted them cheaper. He refused. Oh, right then! And they shot up all the watermelons, an entire heap of watermelons, with an automatic. You try standing on the foot of someone like that in the trolleybus or not letting him into a queue. Just try it!

I used to dream that I'd go home, take the camp bed out into the garden and fall asleep under the apple tree. Under the apples . . . But now I'm afraid. You can hear lots of people say it, especially now, just before our forces are withdrawn: 'I'm afraid to go back to the Soviet Union.' Why? It's very simple. We'll get there, and everything will have changed: different fashions after these two years, different music, different streets. A different attitude to this war . . . We'll stick out like sore thumbs.

Come and find me in a year's time. At home. I'll give you my address.

A civilian employee

I believed so strongly that now I can't let go of it. And now . . . No matter what they tell me, no matter what I read, every time I leave myself a little loophole. The instinct for self-preservation kicks in. Defence. Before the army I graduated from a physical education college. I spent my last period of practical work, for my diploma, at the Artek pioneer camp, I was a camp counsellor. I used to pronounce those exalted sentiments 'the word of a pioneer' and 'the pioneer cause' so often when I was there. It sounds stupid now. But back then I had tears in my eyes.

At the military commissariat I told them: 'Send me to Afghanistan.' The deputy commander for political affairs gave us a lecture about the international situation. He was the one who told us that we had only got there an hour before the American Green Berets – they were already airborne. It hurts that I was so gullible. They kept on and on, hammering it into us that this was an 'international duty', and they finally succeeded. I can never get to the end of it and put the final full stop at the end of my thoughts. 'Take off those rose-tinted glasses,' I tell myself. I didn't go there in 1980 or '81, only in '86. But nobody was saying anything yet. In '87 I was already in Khost. We took one little hill. Lost seven of our boys . . . The

Moscow journalists arrived and they were given some 'greens' (the Afghan National Army), who were supposed to have taken the hill. The Afghans posed while our boys were lying in the morgue.

At the training camp they chose the very best for Afghanistan. It was frightening to end up in Tula, Pskov or Kirovabad – it was filthy and stifling there, so men asked to go to Afghanistan; they worked hard to get there. Major Zlobin starting trying to persuade me and Sasha Krivtsov, a friend of mine, to withdraw our requests.

'Let Sinitsin get killed instead of one of you two. The state has spent so much on you.' Sinitsin was a simple country boy, a tractor driver. I already had a college diploma. Sasha had studied in the faculty of Romance and Germanic Philology at Kemerovo University. He was an outstanding singer. He played the piano, violin, flute and guitar. He wrote music. He drew well. The two of us lived like brothers. At the political awareness sessions they spoke to us about heroism. Afghanistan, they told us, is the same as Spain all over again. Then suddenly – 'Let Sinitsin get killed instead of one of you two.'

It was interesting from a psychological point to view to see the war. First and foremost, to study yourself. I was attracted by that. I asked the guys I knew who had been there. One of them, I realize now, told us a load of bullshit. He had this large, very obvious mark on his chest, like a burn in the shape of the letter *P* – he used to wear his shirt open especially to show it off. He made up this story about how they used to land on the mountains at night from copters – and I remember him saying that for three seconds a paratrooper is an angel, until the parachute opens, and for three minutes he's an eagle, while he's flying, and the rest of the time he's a carthorse. We took it all at face value. If I could just get my hands on that Homer now! Afterwards I saw straight through his kind quick as a flash: 'If he had any brains, he'd have got concussion.' Another young guy, on the contrary, tried to change our minds.

'You shouldn't go here. It's a foul business, not a romantic adventure.'

I didn't like that. 'You've tried it, right? I want to try it too.'

He taught me how to stay alive. Once you've fired, roll two metres away from the spot you fired from. Conceal the barrel of your automatic behind a clay wall or a rock, so they won't see the flame and get a bearing on where you are. When you go out don't drink; don't go out if you do. First a paratrooper runs as far as he can, after that only as far as he needs to.

My father's a scientist, my mother's an engineer. They raised me as an individual from when I was a kid. I wanted to be an individual . . . That's why (*he laughs*) . . . I was thrown out of the Little Octobrists and for a long time they wouldn't let me join the Young Pioneers. I used to fight for my honour. After they'd knotted on my kerchief I used to wear while I slept. In our literature lessons the teacher used to snap at me.

'Don't say what you think; say what's in the book.'

'Am I telling it wrong?'

'Not the way it says in the book . . .'

Like that fairy tale, the one where the king didn't like any colours except grey. And everything in that kingdom – that state – was mouse-coloured.

This is what I ask my pupils to do now (I work in a school): 'Learn to think, so they won't make fools of you like all the rest. Little tin soldiers.'

Before the army it was Tolstoy and Dostoyevsky who taught me how to live my life. In the army it was the sergeants. The power of the sergeants has no limits, three sergeants to a platoon.

'Listen to my orders! What should a paratrooper have? Repeat this!'

'A paratrooper should have a brassy, ugly mug, a fist of iron and not a single gramme of conscience.'

'A conscience is a luxury for a paratrooper. Repeat!'

'A conscience is a luxury for a paratrooper.'

'You are the medical and sanitary battalion – the Medsanbat. That means you are the aristocrats of the airborne assault forces. Repeat!'

From a soldier's letter: 'Mum, buy me a sheep and call it "Sergeant". When I get home I'll kill it.'

The system itself stifles your conscience, I'm sick and tired of it. They can do anything to you . . .

At six in the morning it's reveille. Three times – reveille and then lights out. Get up – go to bed.

Three seconds to fall in on the 'launch pad'– white linoleum: white, so it has to be washed and polished more often. A hundred and sixty men have to leap out of their beds and get in line in three seconds. Then there's forty-five seconds to get dressed in uniform number three – full uniform, only without the belt and the cap. One day someone didn't get his footcloths wound on in time.

'Fall out and repeat!' He was too slow again. 'Fall out and repeat!'

PT. With hand-to-hand combat: a combination of karate, boxing, sambo wrestling and combat moves against a knife, a stick, an entrenching tool, a pistol, an automatic rifle. He's got an automatic rifle and you've got just your bare hands. You've got an entrenching tool and he's got just his bare hands. Cover a hundred metres, hopping and skipping on one leg . . . Break ten bricks with your fist. They took us to a building site: 'You're not leaving here until you learn to do it.' The hardest thing is overcoming your own resistance, the fear of hitting hard.

Five minutes to get washed. Twelve little taps for a hundred and sixty men.

'Fall in! Fall out!' One minute later, the same thing again. 'Fall in! Fall out!'

Morning inspection. They check our belt buckles – they've got to be gleaming, clean as a cat's bollocks – and white collar liners and the needle and thread in your cap.

'Forward! Quick march! Back to your starting positions!'

Only half an hour of free time in the whole day. After lunch – for letters.

'Private Krivtsov, why are you sitting there and not writing?'

'I'm thinking, comrade sergeant.'

'Why are you answering so quietly?'

'I'm thinking, comrade sergeant.'

'Why aren't you shouting the way you've been taught to shout?

You'll have to be potty-trained.' 'Potty-training' is shouting into a toilet bowl, to develop a commanding voice. The sergeant stands behind you, making sure there's a good, booming echo.

From a soldier's dictionary of songs and films: Lights out – 'Life, I Love You'. Morning inspection – 'Believe Me, People'. Evening rollcall – 'They Only Knew Their Faces'. In the lockup – 'Far from the Homeland'. Demobilization – 'The Light of a Distant Star'. Combat drill field – 'The Field of Fools'. Dishwashing is 'the discotheque' (the plates spin like discs). The political officer is 'Cinderella' (in the navy he's 'the passenger').

'The Medsanbat are the aristocrats of the airborne assault forces. Repeat!'

That constant hungry feeling. The canteen's a sacred place: you can buy a cake, sweets or chocolate there. Get full marks on the shooting range and you're allowed to go to the shop. If we haven't got enough money we sell a few bricks. We take a brick and two of us – big, strong guys – go up to a new kid who has money.

'Buy a brick.'

'What do I want it for?'

We close in on him.

'Buy a brick . . .'

'How much?'

'Three roubles.'

He gives us three roubles, goes round the corner and dumps the brick. And we eat our fill for three roubles. One brick is equivalent to ten cakes.

'Conscience is a luxury for a paratrooper. The Medsanbat are the aristocrats of the airborne assault forces.'

I'm probably a pretty good actor, because I soon learned to play the part I was given. The worst thing of all is to get a reputation as a 'wimpino' – from 'bambino', something weak, not even male. After three months I ended up on leave. I'd forgotten everything! Just recently I'd been kissing a girl, sitting in a café, dancing – it was like three years had gone by, not three months, and I'd returned to civilization.

In the evening: 'Form up, you apes! What's the most important thing for a paratrooper? The most important thing for a para-trooper is not to drift right past the edge of the world.'

Just before I left we celebrated the New Year. I was Grandfather Frost, Sasha was the Snow Maiden. It reminded me of school.

We marched for twelve days. The only thing worse than mountains is more mountains . . . We were trying to get away from an armed gang of guerrillas. Keeping ourselves going with dope.

'Combat medic, give me some of your Berserker pills.'

'That was Mesocarb. You've guzzled all the pills.'

And we were still joking.

'What's your complaint?' the doctor asked Leopold the Cat. Everyone tried to come up with something first.

'Mice.'

'Then hunt them . . . You don't mouse . . . That's it then. You're way too kind-hearted. You need to get really good and angry. Take one tablet three times a day after food.'

'And then what?'

'You'll go totally berserk.'

On the fifth day one soldier went and shot himself. He let everyone go ahead and put his automatic to his throat. We had to lug his body, his backpack, his bulletproof vest, his helmet. No one felt any pity. He knew we didn't leave bodies behind – we took them with us. We only remembered him and felt pity for him when we were going home, when we were demobilized.

'Take one tablet three times a day . . .'

'And then what?'

'You'll go totally berserk.'

The wounds from explosions are the most horrible . . . A leg torn off at the knee. The bone sticking out. The heel torn off the other leg . . . A prick sliced off. An eye knocked out. An ear ripped off . . . The first time, I got the cold shakes. I had a dry tickle in my throat. I tried to persuade myself: 'Do it now, or else you'll never be a combat medic.' I crept up to him, and he'd got no legs. I put on tourniquets, stopped the bleeding, anaesthetized him, put him to sleep. I held him for four hours . . . He died.

We were short of medical supplies. There wasn't any basic liquid antiseptic. Either they hadn't shipped it in or we'd run through our allocation – our planned economy. We tried to get captured stuff, imported. I always had twenty-five Japanese disposable syringes in my bag. They're in soft polythene packaging: you just take off the wrapper and make the injection. The paper liners on our Record brand glass syringes used to fray and their sterility was compromised. Half the dose didn't get sucked in – defective goods. Our blood substitutes were in half-litre bottles. To help one severely wounded man takes two litres – four bottles. How can you hold the rubber tube out at arm's length for about an hour out on the battlefield? It's virtually impossible. And how many bottles can you take out with you? So what do the Italians suggest? A one-litre polythene bag – you can jump on it in your boots and it won't burst. To continue: ordinary bandages, Soviet sterile bandages. Really solid packaging – it weighs more than the bandage does. The imported bandages – from Thailand or Austria – they're thinner and whiter for some reason. There weren't any elastic bandages at all. I used to take captured bandages too . . . French and German . . . And what about our Soviet splints? They're skis, not medical devices. How many of them can you take out with you? I had English ones: different types for the forearm, the shin, the thigh. With zippers, inflatable. Just reach in and zip it up. The broken bone doesn't shift about and it's protected against any blows when the man's moved.

In ten years they haven't started producing anything new here. The bandages are the same; the splints are the same. The Soviet soldier is the cheapest soldier there is. The most long-suffering, the most uncomplaining. Unequipped and unprotected. Expendable. The same way it was in 1941 . . . It'll still be the same in fifty years' time. Why?

The frightening thing is when they're blazing away at you, not when you're firing. In order to survive you have to think about it all the time. I did. I never got into the vehicles at the front or the rear of the column. I never sat with my legs inside the hatch – better to stay outside and dangle them over the armour plating, so they wouldn't get sliced off in an explosion. I kept a supply of German tablets for suppressing feelings of fear. But no one took them any more. I had a bulletproof vest . . . The same thing again! You can't lift one of our bulletproof vests, and it's impossible to move in them. The American ones don't have a single metal part: they're made of some special kind of bulletproof material. It's just like wearing a tracksuit. A Makarov pistol can't penetrate it at point-blank range, and an automatic rifle bullet only pierces it from closer than a hundred metres. Our helmets are from the 1930s – idiotic helmets. Left over from the old war . . . (*He ponders briefly.*) Lots of things there made me feel ashamed. Why are we like this? American sleeping bags, the 1949 model, they're filled with swan's down, they're light. Japanese sleeping bags are excellent, but too short. But our cotton-wadding sacks weigh at least seven kilogrammes. We used to take gear off mercenaries who were killed: jackets, caps with long peaks, Chinese trousers that didn't chafe you in the crotch. Everyone took them. We took underpants, because underpants were in short supply, and socks, and trainers too. I picked up a little torch and a little knife like a dagger.

Apart from that, I was always hungry. Hunger! We used to shoot wild sheep. Any sheep that lagged five metres behind the flock was considered wild. Or we traded: two kilogrammes of tea for one sheep. The tea was captured goods. We brought money back from combat missions and the higher ranks took it from us. They divided it up right there in front of our eyes. Stick a couple of notes in a cartridge, sprinkle some gunpowder on top of it – and you can save them.

Some wanted to get drunk, some wanted to survive and some dreamed of medals. I wanted a medal too. But back here in the Union people asked me: 'Well then, what have you got? You were a sergeant, were you, in charge of supplies?'

The political officer's parting words before I came back home: what we could talk about and what we couldn't. We couldn't talk about fatalities, because we were a large and powerful army. We couldn't talk about harassment, because we were a large, powerful and morally sound army. Photographs should be torn up. Films should be destroyed. We didn't shoot, bomb, poison or blow up anyone. We were a large and powerful army, the best army in the world . . .

At the customs they nabbed the presents that we were taking home: perfume, headscarves, watches. 'Not allowed, guys.' They didn't draw up any inventories. It was just their business.

Ah, but that smell of the green spring leaves . . . The girls walking along in their light dresses . . . Svetka Afoshka flashes through my mind – an *afoshka* is the Afghan money, an afghani – and disappeared again. (I never did know her surname: she was always just Afoshka.) The first day she arrived in Kabul she slept with a soldier for a hundred *afoshkas*, before she'd got her bearings. A couple of weeks later she was taking three thousand a time. Way too much for an ordinary soldier.

And where's Pashka Korchagin now? His real name's Andrei, but they called him Pashka because of his surname, after Pavel Korchagin in *How the Steel Was Tempered*. 'Pashka, get an eyeful of those girls!' Pashka-Andrei used to have a girl, but she sent him photographs of her wedding. We stood watch over him at night – we were afraid. One morning he hung her photo on a rock and shot it up with his automatic. 'Pashka, get an eyeful of those girls!'

In the train I dreamed we were preparing to go out on a combat mission, and Sasha Krivtsov asked: 'Why have you got three hundred and fifty cartridges, and not four hundred?'

'Because I've got medical supplies.'

He paused for a moment and asked: 'Could you have shot that Afghan girl?'

'What Afghan girl?'

'The one who led us into the ambush. Remember, four guys killed?'

'I don't know . . . Probably not. In kindergarten they used to tease me and call me a "womanizer" for defending the girls. Could you?'

'I feel ashamed . . .'

He doesn't get a chance to say what he feels ashamed about – I wake up. At home there's a telegram for me from Sasha's mother: 'Please come. Sasha's been killed.'

I stood beside his grave. 'Sasha, I feel ashamed because I got an

"A" for the final exam in scientific communism; I criticized bour-
geois democracy. I made a comparative analysis. You understand
me . . . We went to Afghanistan blind . . . Now everyone says the
war is a disgrace, but not long ago they handed us brand new
"Internationalist Soldier" badges. I didn't speak up. I even said
"Thank you!" Sasha, now you're there and I'm here.'

I need to talk to him . . .

A sergeant, reconnaissance company combat medic

My boy was small. He was born small, like a girl – two kilogrammes,
thirty centimetres long. I was afraid to hold him in my arms.

I used to hug him close. 'My little sunshine . . .'

He wasn't afraid of anything except spiders. He came home
from school one day . . . It was after we'd bought him a new coat
for his fourth birthday . . . I hung that coat on a hanger and then
from the kitchen I heard this flop-flopping sound. I ran out and the
whole hallway was full of frogs, they were jumping out of the pockets of his coat. He collected them up.

'Mama, don't be afraid. They're friendly.' And he stuck them
back in his pocket.

'My little sunshine.'

He liked military toys. I gave him a tank, an automatic rifle, a
pistol. He used to hang the rifle over his shoulder and march round
the apartment.

'I'm a soldier, I'm a soldier.'

'My little sunshine. Why don't you play a peaceful game?'

'I'm a soldier . . .'

When he started school, we couldn't buy him a school uniform
anywhere. Everything we tried on just smothered him.

'My little sunshine . . .'

They took him into the army. I didn't pray that he wouldn't be
killed. I prayed they wouldn't beat him. I was afraid the stronger
boys would bully him, he was so small. He told me they could
make you clean the toilet with a toothbrush and wash other
people's underpants. That's what I was afraid of.

He wrote and asked: 'Send me your photos, mama, papa, little

sister. I'm going away . . .' He didn't write where he was going away
to. Two months later a letter arrived from Afghanistan: 'Don't you
cry, mama, our armour plating's good and strong.'

'My little sunshine . . . Our armour plating's good and strong . . .'

I was expecting him back home – he had one month left to serve.
I bought shirts, a little scarf, shoes. And now they're in the wardrobe. I'd have dressed him in them for his little grave . . . I'd have
dressed him myself, but they didn't allow us to open the coffin. If
I could only have looked at my son, touched him . . . Did they find
a uniform to fit him? What's he wearing in there?

The first to come was a captain from the military commissariat.

'Brace yourself, mother . . .'

'Where's my son?'

'Here, in Minsk. They'll bring him in a minute.'

I collapsed on the floor. 'My little sunshine!' I got up and started
flailing at the captain with my fists. 'Why are you alive and my
son's dead? You're so big and strong. And he's so small . . . You're a
man and he's a boy. Why are you alive?'

They brought the coffin and I knocked on it. 'My little sunshine!
My little sunshine!'

And now I go to his grave to visit him. And I always fall down
on the stones and hug him. My little sunshine . . .

A mother

I put a little lump of my own native earth in my pocket – this feeling came over me in the train . . .

Oo-ooh! War! I'm going to fight. Of course, we had some cowards among us too. One young guy failed the medical because of
his eyesight and came rushing out, overjoyed: 'I got lucky!' There
was another guy behind him in the queue who wasn't taken either.
He was almost crying: 'How can I go back to my unit? The boys
spent two weeks saying goodbye to me. If I had a stomach ulcer,
okay, but it's only my teeth that hurt.' He pushed his way through
to the general in just his underpants: 'If they won't take me because
two of my teeth are bad, they can pull them out!'

I got an 'A' in geography in school. I closed my eyes and pictured it: mountains and monkeys; we're sunbathing somewhere, eating bananas . . . But what happened was this. They put us on tanks, in our greatcoats, one machine gun on our right, another on our left, the last vehicle at the end of the column with a machine gun pointing backwards. All the gun ports are open, with automatic rifles sticking out of them. Like some kind of metal hedgehog. We meet two of our armoured personnel carriers – the guys are sitting on the armour plating, in their singlets, wearing sun hats, looking at us and splitting their sides with laughter. I saw a mercenary who'd been killed and I was staggered. He was in such good shape, a real athlete.

I ended up in the mountains and I didn't even know the right way to start climbing a cliff, that I ought to start with my left foot. Later I used to carry a phone ten metres down a sheer rock face. When there was an explosion I closed my mouth; but you're supposed to open it or your eardrums burst. They issued us with gasmasks. We threw them away the very first day – the 'spirits' don't have any chemical weapons. We sold our helmets in the *dukans*. Useless weight on your head; they heat up like frying pans. I had one problem: where could I steal another magazine of cartridges? They issued four to us; I bought a fifth one from a comrade out of my first pay; someone gave me a sixth. In battle you take out your last magazine and put the last cartridge between your teeth. That one's for you.

We came here to build socialism, but they fenced us in with barbed wire: 'You mustn't go out there, lads. No need to spread the word about socialism. There are special people to do that.' It hurt, of course, that they didn't trust us.

I talked to this shopkeeper: 'You weren't living right. We'll teach you now. We're going to build socialism.'

He smiled. 'I was buying and selling before the revolution and I'm still buying and selling now. Go home. These are our mountains. We'll work things out ourselves.'

We drove round Kabul and the women threw sticks and stones at our tanks. The little kids swore and cursed in Russian without any accent. They shouted: 'Russian, go home.'

What are we here for?

. . . They were firing at us with a grenade launcher. I managed to swing the machine gun round, and that saved me. The shell hit me on the chest, otherwise it would have smashed straight through one arm and all the shrapnel would have hit the other. I remember it was such a gentle, pleasant sensation, and no pain at all . . . And there was someone shouting somewhere above my head: 'Fire! Fire!' I pressed the trigger, but the machine gun didn't make a sound. Then I looked and my arm was dangling loose, scorched black all over. It felt like I was pressing my finger on the trigger, but there weren't any fingers . . .

I didn't pass out. Instead I crawled out of the vehicle with everyone else and they put on a tourniquet. We had to go, but I took two steps and fell over. I'd lost something like a litre and a half of blood. I heard voices. 'They're encircling us.' Someone said: 'We'll have to leave him, or we're all done for.'

I begged them: 'Shoot me . . .' One guy walked off straightaway. Another pulled back the bolt of his gun, but slowly. If you do it slowly, the cartridge can get jammed. And the cartridge did get jammed. He flung his automatic rifle down on the ground. 'I can't do it! Here, do it yourself.'

I pulled the gun over to me, but you can't do anything with only one hand. I was lucky. This was in a little gully and I was lying behind some rocks. I was sheltered by a big round boulder. The *dushmans* were walking around without seeing me. I thought: 'The moment they spot me, I have to kill myself with something.' I groped to find a small rock and pulled it over, got ready to swing it.

In the morning I was found by our boys. The two who ran off the night before carried me on a tunic. I realized they were afraid I might tell the truth. But I couldn't give a damn any longer. At the hospital they put me straight on the table. The surgeon came over: 'Amputation.' I woke up and I could feel my arm was missing . . . There were different kinds of patients lying there: with one arm missing, with both arms missing, with a leg missing. They cried on the quiet. And started knocking back the booze. I started learning to hold a pencil in my left hand.

I came back home to my granddad's place. I haven't got anyone else. My granny started weeping and wailing: her beloved grandson had lost his arm. My granddad shouted at her: 'Don't you understand the policy of the Party?'

People I know meet me and ask: 'Did you bring a sheepskin coat? Did you bring a Japanese cassette player? You didn't bring anything? Were you really in Afghanistan?' I should have brought my gun!

I started looking for our guys. If he was there and I was there we have a common language. Our language. We understand each other. The rector of the college called me in. 'We accepted you into the institute with "C" grades. We gave you a grant. Don't go to those people . . . Why do you meet at the cemetery? That's out of order.' At first they wouldn't allow us to meet together. They were afraid of us, said we were spreading morbid rumours. On the sly. Well, and what if we organized and fought for our rights? They'd have to give us apartments. We'd force them to help the mothers of the guys who were lying in their graves. We'd demand that they put headstones on these graves and fence them off. And who needs all that hassle, tell me? They tried to persuade us: 'Guys, don't go talking too much about what happened and what you saw. It's a state secret!' A hundred thousand soldiers in a foreign country is a secret. Even how hot it is in Kabul is a secret . . .

War doesn't make a man better. Only worse. That's for sure. I can never go back to the day I left for the war. I can never be who I was before the war. How can I become a better man when I've seen guys buy two glasses of a hepatitis patient's urine from a doctor for hard currency checks? Then drink it. And fall ill. And get invalided out. Men shooting their own fingers off. Mutilating themselves with the breech blocks of machine guns . . . And . . . And flying back home in the same plane as the zinc coffins and the suitcases full of sheepskin coats, jeans and women's panties . . . and Chinese tea . . .

The very word 'Homeland' used to set my lips trembling. I'm different now. Fighting for something . . . What is there to fight for? But we fought, didn't we? So okay. Maybe we actually fought for a cause. Every generation here gets its own war. If the newspapers say that it's just, then it will be just. Then again, the newspapers are starting to write that we're all murderers. Who should we believe? I don't know. I don't believe anyone any more. The newspapers? I don't even take any of them. We write one thing today and something else tomorrow – that's the way the times are. Perestroika. Lots of different truths. But *my* truth, where's that? Look, I've got friends. I trust one, two, three of them. I can always rely on them. But not on anyone else. I've been back here six years now. I can see all this.

They gave me an invalidity pension book – I'm entitled to benefits. So I walk up to the counter for war veterans. 'Where are you going, kiddo? You've got the wrong queue.'

I grit my teeth and say nothing. Behind my back I hear: 'I defended our Homeland, and this . . .'

A stranger asks me: 'Where's your arm?'

'I got drunk and fell under a train. It got sliced off.' Then they understand. And they feel sorry for me.

I read this not long ago in Valentin Pikul's novel *A Soldier's Honour* – it's the confessions of a Russian General Staff officer. He's talking about the shameful aftermath of the Russo-Japanese War of 1905: 'Many officers are resigning, since they are despised and mocked everywhere they appear. Things are so bad that an officer is ashamed to wear his uniform and tries to go out in public in civilian clothes. Not even the mutilated cripples arouse any sympathy. People give much more to one-legged beggars if they say the other one was sliced off by a tram on the corner of Nevsky and Liteiny Prospects, and they have nothing to do with Mukden and Liaoyang.' They'll start writing like that about us soon . . .

I think I could even change my Homeland now. Leave the country.

A private, signaller

I asked to be sent. I dreamed of getting into that war. I thought it was interesting . . .

I imagined how it was there. I wanted to know what it was like when you've got one apple and two friends, you're hungry and they're hungry, and you give them the apple. I thought they were all friends there, that they were all brothers.

I walked out of the plane and this guy who had been discharged and was flying back to the Soviet Union nudged me in the side.

'Give me the belt.'

'What?' It was my lucky belt, special.

'You fool, they'll take it anyway.'

They took it off me the very first day. And I used to think: 'Afghanistan, that's where everyone's friends.' What an idiot! A young soldier is just a thing. You can get him up at night and beat him, batter him with chairs and sticks, fists and feet. You can punch him, beat him up in the toilet during the day, take his backpack, his clothes, his tinned meat, his biscuits (that's if he has any, if he brought any). No television, no radio, no newspapers. Our amusements followed the law of the weak and the strong.

'Right now, little birdie, wash my socks . . .' That's more terrible than your first battle. The first battle is interesting! You watch it like a feature film. You've seen it a hundred times in the movies, the way they go into the attack, but it turns out that's all just stories. You don't walk, you run, and you don't jog along, you give it everything you've got, and in a battle you've got the strength of a madman, you dodge and weave like a mad March hare.

I used to love the parades on Red Square. All the military technology, I loved it . . . Now I know you shouldn't admire all that stuff. It'd be better if they just dumped all those tanks, personnel carriers and automatic weapons somewhere and put dust sheets over them. The sooner the better. Because they're all for killing men . . . For grinding them into the dust and the clay. Men like me . . . Even better would be if all the men from Afghanistan with artificial limbs marched through Red Square. I'd go . . . 'Look!'

Both my legs are amputated above the knee. If only it had been below the knee. I'd be a happy man. I envy the men with legs amputated below the knee. After they change the dressings you shudder for an hour or an hour and a half. And suddenly you're so short without your artificial legs. Lie down in your shorts and paratrooper's singlet, and the singlet's as long as you. In the beginning I wouldn't let anyone near me. I didn't talk. If only I had one leg left, but I don't. The hardest thing is to forget that you used to have two legs. Four walls, and the one you want is the one with the window.

I gave my mother an ultimatum: 'If you're going to cry, don't come.' Even out there what I was most afraid of was that I'd be killed. They'd take me home, and my mother would cry. After a battle people pity a wounded man, but not a dead man – they just pity his mother. In the hospital I tried to say thank you to the nurse, but I couldn't. I'd even forgotten the words.

'Would you go back to Afghanistan?' Yes.

'Why?' Out there a friend's a friend and an enemy's an enemy. But here there's always the question: 'What did my friends die for?' For the gorged black market dealers? For the bureaucrats? Or the young jerks who couldn't give a shit about anything, just as long as they have a can of beer in the morning? Everything's wrong here. I feel like an outsider. A stranger.

I was learning to walk and someone tripped me from behind. I fell. 'Easy now,' I told myself. 'Command number one – turn over and push yourself up on your hands. Command number two – get up and walk.' For the first few months it would be truer to say: 'Don't walk – crawl.' I crawled.

My most vivid memory from out there is a little dark-skinned kid with a Russian face . . . There are lots of them out there. We've been there since '79, after all. Seven years. I'd go there! If my legs weren't amputated above the knee . . . If only it was below the knee.

I'd go there.

A private, mortar operator

I used to ask myself: 'Why did I end up here?'

There are a hundred answers. But the most important one is in this poem, I just don't remember who wrote it . . . Maybe it was one of our boys?

> This world has two things sweet and fine:
> Women come first, and second comes wine.
> But the heart of a man is gladdened far more
> By the succulent sweetness of war.

I used to envy my colleagues who had been in Afghanistan: they had acquired immense experience. Where else in the world could you get that? I'm a surgeon – I'd already worked as a surgeon for ten years in the municipal hospital of a large town. But when the first transport of wounded men came in I almost went out of my mind. No arms, no legs; just a trunk lying there, breathing. Things you would never see even in a sadistic horror movie. I did operations there that I could only dream about back in the Union. The young nurses couldn't stand it. Some cried so hard they started hiccuping. Some laughed. One just stood there all the time, smiling. They sent them home.

The way a man dies isn't anything like in the movies. A man doesn't die like a Stalinist hero – a bullet hits him in the head, he throws his arms up and falls. In reality what happens is this: a bullet hits him in the head, his brains go flying out, and he runs after them – he can run half a kilometre, trying to catch them. It's crazy, way over the top. He runs until physiological death sets in. It would be easier to shoot him than to watch him lying there and listen to him sobbing or begging for death as a release. That's if he has any strength left. Another man can be lying there, and the fear creeps up on him. His heart falters. He shouts and calls for you. You check him and calm him down . . . But his brain is just waiting for the moment when the man relaxes . . . Before you can even leave the bed the boy's gone. And he was there just a moment ago.

You don't forget that in a hurry. When these boy-soldiers grow up they'll go through it all again. Their views will change and they'll forget some things, but other things will surface out of the vaults. In the Second World War my father was an airman, but he didn't tell me anything about it. He always kept quiet. I didn't understand him at the time, but I do now. I respect him for his silence. Remembering is like sticking your hand into a fire. A word or a hint is enough . . . In yesterday's newspaper I read this: 'He defended himself to the last cartridge and shot himself with it.' What does it mean to shoot yourself? Battle's a straightforward business: it's you or him. It's clear that you've got to stay. They've all gone, and you're covering them – it was an order or you've decided for yourself, knowing pretty much for certain that you've chosen death. I'm sure it's not hard psychologically at that moment. In that situation suicide seems perfectly normal. Lots of men are capable of it. Afterwards they call them heroes. It's here, in normal life, that people who kill themselves are abnormal. But out there? Everything's the other way round out there. Different rules. Just two lines in a newspaper, and you can't sleep a wink at night. It all surges up inside you. It all comes back.

The men who have been there won't ever want to fight again. You can't fool us by saying meat grows on trees. Whatever we might be like – whether we're naive or cruel, whether we love our wives and children or not – no matter what, we've killed. I realized what my place was out there in the foreign legion, but I don't regret anything. Everyone here has started talking about a sense of guilt. I don't have one. The guilty ones are the ones who sent us out there. I enjoy wearing my Afghan uniform: it makes me feel like a man. The women are crazy about it. One day I put it on and went to a restaurant. The manager fixed his eyes on me, but I was expecting that.

'What, is my uniform incorrect? Come on – make way for a blighted heart.'

Just let someone tell me that he doesn't like my battledress. Just let me hear a peep out of him. I don't know why, but I'm looking for that person . . .

A doctor

My first child was a girl. Before she was born, my husband said it didn't really matter if it was a boy or a girl, but a girl would be better. Afterwards she'd have a little brother and she could tie the laces on his little shoes. And that's the way it was.

My husband called the hospital and they said it was a girl. 'Good. So we'll have two girls.'

And then they told him the truth. 'You've got a son! A son!'

'Well, thank you! Thank you!' He started thanking them for his son.

One day went by, then another . . . The nurses brought

everyone their children, but not me. No one said anything. I started crying and my temperature went up. The doctor came and she said to me: 'What are you getting upset about, little mother? You've got a fine, big, strapping boy. He's still sleeping; he hasn't woken up. He isn't hungry yet. Don't worry.' They brought him and unwrapped him: he was asleep. Then I calmed down.

So what could we call our son? We chose from three names – Sasha, Alyosha and Misha. I liked them all. My husband and daughter came, and Tanya told me: 'I drew wots.' 'What's a wot?' It turned out they'd put some pieces of paper in a hat and drawn lots. 'Sasha' was pulled out twice. It was our Tanechka who decided things.

He was born heavy – four and a half kilogrammes; and big – sixty centimetres long. I remember he started walking at ten months. He could already speak well at a year and a half, but he couldn't get the hang of the letters *r* and *s* until he was three. He called his friend 'Tiglei' instead of 'Sergei'. His kindergarten teacher, Kira Nikolaevna, was 'Kila Kolavna'. When he saw the sea for the first time, he shouted: 'I wasn't born, a wave threw me out on to the shore!'

When he was five I gave him his first photo album. He's got four of them: from when he was little, his school years, the army (when he was in the military academy) – and for Afghanistan, with the photos that he sent. My daughter has her own albums. I gave them to both of them. I loved my home and the children. I used to write poems for them:

> A snowdrop thrust up through the snow
> On a clear bright springtime morn.
> When springtime came into its own
> My little son was born.

My pupils at the school used to love me. I was so full of joy.

For a long time he liked to play cops and robbers: 'I'm brave.' He was five and Tanechka was nine when we went to the Volga. We got off the boat and Sasha stopped dead. He wouldn't move.

'I won't walk. Carry me.'

'Such a big boy and you want to be carried?'

'I won't walk, and that's it.' And he didn't walk. We used to remind him about that all the time.

At kindergarten he liked to dance. He had a pair of baggy red trousers. He was photographed in them – I still have the picture. He used to collect stamps until the eighth year in school – I still have his stamp albums. He was keen on music – I have the cassettes with his favourite songs.

All through his childhood he dreamed of being a musician. But he must have absorbed the fact that his father was an army man. We lived all our life in a garrison town: he ate his buckwheat with the soldiers and washed cars with them. No one told him 'no' when he sent in his application to the military academy. On the contrary: 'Now you'll defend the Homeland, son.' He was a good student; he was always involved in activities at school. And he graduated from the academy with excellent marks too. The academy staff sent us a message of thanks.

1985 . . . Sasha was in Afghanistan. We were proud, we admired him – he was at war. I used to tell my pupils about Sasha and about his friends. We waited for him to come home on leave. Somehow you never think about anything bad happening . . .

Before Minsk we used to live in garrison towns and we were still in the habit of not locking the door when we were at home. He walked in without ringing the bell and asked: 'Did you call for someone to fix your television?' He and his friends had flown from Kabul to Tashkent, and from there they could only get tickets as far as Donetsk; there weren't any for anywhere closer. Minsk wasn't accepting flights, so they flew to Vilnius. In Vilnius they had to wait three hours for the train, and that was too long for them with home so near, only about two hundred kilometres away. So they took a taxi.

He was suntanned and thin, and his teeth gleamed so brightly.

'Son, you're so skinny!' I said and cried.

'Mama,' he said and lifted me up and carried me round the room. 'I'm alive! I'm alive, mama! Do you understand, I'm alive!'

Two days later it was the New Year. He hid presents for us under the New Year tree. A big shawl for me. A black one.

'Why did you choose black, son?'

'Mama, there were all kinds there. But by the time my turn came round there were only black ones left. Look, it suits you.'

I buried him wearing that shawl. I haven't taken it off for two years.

He always liked giving presents. He used to call them 'little surprises'. When he was still small, his father and I came home and the children weren't there. I went to the neighbours and out into the street. My children were nowhere and no one had seen them. Oh, how I wailed, how I cried! Then the box from our television opened (we'd bought a television and we hadn't thrown the box away yet) and out climbed my children. 'Why are you crying, mama?' They'd laid the table, brewed the tea and then waited for us, but we didn't come. Sasha thought up the 'little surprise' of hiding in the box. They hid in there and then fell asleep.

He was affectionate. Boys aren't often as affectionate as that. He always kissed me and hugged me: 'Mama . . . *mamochka*.' After Afghanistan he was even more loving. He loved everything about home. But there were moments when he sat there without saying anything, not seeing anybody. He used to jump up in the night and walk round the room. Once he woke me up by shouting: 'Flashes! Flashes! Mama, they're firing . . .' Another time I heard someone crying at night. Who could be crying in our home? We didn't have any little children. I opened the door of his room and he was holding his head in his hands and crying.

'Why are you crying, son?'

'I'm afraid, mama.' And he didn't say another word. Not to his father or to me.

He left the same way he usually did. I baked him a whole suitcase-full of 'nuts' – that was his favourite kind of biscuit . . . A whole suitcase-full, so there'd be enough for everyone. They were all missing home life. Their own lives.

The second time he came home it was for the New Year too. We were expecting him in summer at first. He wrote: 'Mama, make lots and lots of compote and jam. I'll come and drink and eat it all up.' He shifted his leave from August to September: he wanted to go into the forest and collect chanterelle mushrooms. But he didn't come. He wasn't here for the holidays in November either. I got a letter asking me what I thought – maybe he should come for the New Year again? There'd be a New Year tree, and papa's birthday was in December, and mama's was in January.

30 December. I stayed home the whole day, didn't go out anywhere. Just before that I got a letter: 'Mama, I'm putting in an advance order for blueberry dumplings, cherry dumplings and cottage cheese dumplings.' My husband came back from work and we decided he could wait in, and I'd go to the shop and buy a guitar. Just that morning we'd got a card to tell us they'd gone on sale. Sasha told us there was no need to get an expensive one; we should just get the ordinary 'backyard' kind.

When I got home from the shop, he was there. 'Oh, son, I was waiting but I missed you!'

He saw the guitar. 'What a beautiful guitar!' he said and danced round the room. 'I'm home. How good it is here. Even our entrance hall has a special smell.' He said we had the most beautiful city, the most beautiful street, the most beautiful building, the most beautiful acacias in our courtyard. He loved this building. Now it's hard for us living here – it reminds us of Sasha all the time. But it's hard to leave, because he loved everything here.

This time he came home different. We weren't the only ones who noticed, here at home, all his friends did too. He told them: 'How lucky you all are! You can't even imagine how lucky you are! Every day's a holiday for you.'

I came home from the hairdresser's with a new hairstyle. He liked it. 'Mama, always get your hair done that way. You're so beautiful.'

'It's expensive son, very expensive if I do it every day.'

'I brought money. Take it all. I don't need money.'

One of his friends had a son. I remember his face when he said, 'Let me hold him.' He took the baby and froze. When his leave was almost over his tooth started aching. He'd been afraid of the dentist ever since he was little, so I held his hand and dragged him to the clinic. We sat there, waiting for him to be called. When I looked at him his face was all sweaty – he was so afraid.

If there was a programme about Afghanistan on the television he used to go into the other room. A week before he left, this anxious look appeared in his eyes. They were brimming over with it. Perhaps it just seems that way to me now? But I was happy then: my son had come home as a major with an Order of the Red Star. In the airport I looked at him and I couldn't believe that this handsome young officer was really my son. I felt so proud of him.

A month later we got a letter. He wished his father a happy Soviet Army Day and he thanked me for the mushroom pies. After that letter something happened to me. I couldn't sleep. When I went to bed I just lay there until five o'clock with my eyes open. I couldn't sleep a wink.

On 4 March I had a dream. A big field, with white flashes all over it. Something exploded, and there were long white streamers of smoke. My Sasha was running, running like mad, tearing along . . . He had nowhere to hide. A flash on one side, then on the other. I was running after him, trying to catch up with him. I wanted to be in the front, with him behind me. Once, when he was little, we got caught in a thunderstorm out in the country. I covered him with my body and he scrabbled about underneath me, like a little mouse: 'Mama, save me!' But now I couldn't catch up with him. He was so tall and his strides were so very, very long. I was running as hard as I could. I thought my heart would burst. But I couldn't catch up with him . . .

The front door banged and my husband came in. My daughter and I were sitting on the sofa. He walked straight across the room to us in his shoes and coat and hat. He'd never done that before. He was always so particular, because he'd been in the army all his life. He had to have discipline in everything. He walked over and went down on his knees in front of us. 'Girls, something terrible has happened.'

Then I noticed there were other people in the hallway. A nurse came in, and a military commissar, teachers from my school, friends of my husband . . .

'Sashenka! My little boy!'

It was three years ago. And we still can't open the suitcase with Sasha's things in it. They brought it with the coffin. I think they smell of Sasha.

He was hit by fifteen pieces of shrapnel simultaneously. The only thing he had time to say was: 'Mama, it hurts.'

What for? Why him? So affectionate and kind. How can he be gone? These thoughts are slowly killing me. I know I'm dying – there's no point in living any longer. When I used to go out to see people, I had to drag myself there. I went with Sasha, in his name. I talked about him. I was giving a talk at the polytechnic college and a student came up to me and said: 'If they hadn't stuffed him so full of patriotism he'd still be alive.' I felt unwell after she said that and I collapsed.

I used to go for Sasha's sake. For the sake of his memory. I was proud of him . . . And now they say it was a fatal mistake, not good for anybody. Not for us, not for the Afghan people. I used to hate the men who killed Sasha. Now I hate the state that sent him there. Don't speak his name. He's only ours now. I won't let anyone have him. Not even his memory . . .

(*A few years later she called me.*) I wanted to go on with my story. It didn't have an ending. I didn't finish it that time . . . I wasn't ready yet, but . . . Of course, I'm not young any more. But six months ago we adopted a boy from an orphanage. He's called Sasha and he's a lot like our Sasha when he was little. Instead of 'I'll do it myself' he says 'myshelf'. And he hasn't got the hang of the letters *r* and *s* yet. We've got our son back. Do you understand me? But I swore, and I made my husband swear, that he would never be a soldier. Never!

A mother

I fired. I fired like everyone else. I don't know how it all works, how this world works . . . I just fired . . .

Our unit was based in Kabul . . . (*He suddenly laughs.*) We had a 'library and reading room' – it was an immense toilet, this incredible dump, twenty metres by five, and you had to go down six metres to get into it. There were forty holes with wooden-plank partitions and the newspapers *Pravda*, *Komsomolskaya Pravda* and *Izvestiya* hanging on a nail in every partition. Just drop your trousers, stick a cigarette in your mouth, light up and sit there, reading. Find the reports on Afghanistan. 'Afghan government forces have entered such-and-such a place' . . . 'They've taken such-and-such a place.' Not a word about us, fuck it . . . But only yesterday forty of our boys were torn to shreds. Two days earlier I was sitting here in the latrine with one of them and reading these papers, hooting with laughter. Holy shit! Enough to make you stick the barrel in your mouth and blow your brains out, it's so bloody depressing. Lies everywhere . . .

The barracks was repulsive. The food was so bad, it made you want to puke. The only joy in life was going out to fight the war. On a raid or some other mission you might get killed or you might not; but we were really keen to go on combat missions because life was just too tedious. We'd been sitting behind barbed wire for months. For four months we'd eaten nothing but boiled buckwheat: breakfast, lunch and supper – nothing but buckwheat. But on combat missions they gave you field rations with tinned meat, sometimes even Alyonka chocolate. And after the action you could frisk the dead 'spirits' and maybe get a good haul: a jar of jam, some good tinned stuff and filter cigarettes. My God! Marlboro! And all we've got is Hunter's. You've probably heard about them before? On the pack there's this man with a stick, walking through a swamp – we used to call them 'Death in the Swamp'. There were Pamir cigarettes too – they were 'Death in the Mountains'. I tried crab for the first time in Afghanistan, American tinned stuff. And I smoked an expensive cigar. You could drop into a *dukan* along the way and nick something. Not because we were great looters, but a man always like, to eat a bit sweeter and sleep a bit longer.

They took us away from our mamas and said: 'Forward, guys, it's your sacred duty – you're obliged to do it, you're eighteen.' Holy shit! They took us to Tashkent first. The political officer came out, with this big belly, and he said: 'All those who want to go to Afghanistan, write an application.' The guys scribbled it down: 'I request to be posted . . .' I didn't write it, but the next day they gave all of us our rations and money allowance, loaded us into trucks and drove us to the transit point. That evening at the transit point the old-timers came up to us and said: 'Right, you guys, give us your Soviet money. Where you're going it's afghanis.' What the shit? They transported us like sheep. Some were glad; they'd asked to be sent. Some didn't want to go: they got hysterical and started crying. Some got pissed on eau de cologne. Bloody hell . . . I was just devastated, I couldn't give a shit any longer. 'Why, fuck it,' I thought. 'Why didn't they give us any special training? Holy shit! They're taking us to a real war.' They didn't even teach us to shoot. How much shooting did I do on exercises? Three single shots and a burst of six . . . Bloody fantastic!

My first impressions of Kabul – sand, a mouthful of sand. And the day we arrived the 'demobbers' beat the shit out of me in the guardhouse. And in the morning it started: 'Over here, at the double! Have you washed your mess kit? At the double! Halt! Name?' They didn't hit us on the face, so the officers wouldn't notice. They hit us on the chest, on our uniform buttons. They made a neat dent in the skin, like a little mushroom. I was happy when I was put on sentry duty: the 'granddads' and the 'demobbers' left me alone for two hours. Four days before we arrived a 'youngster' walked up to a tent of 'demobbers' and flung a grenade into it. Seven 'demobbers' wiped out at a single stroke. Afterwards he put his gun barrel in his mouth and blew his brains out. They wrote them all off as lost in action. Dear old Mother War, she can write off anything at all . . . Holy shit!

After supper the 'granddads' called us over: 'Right then, Moscow' – I'm from the Moscow region – 'some spuds. Note the time – you've got forty minutes. Off you go!' And a kick up the backside. Question: 'But where will I get them?' Answer: 'Do you want to live?' The potatoes had to come with onions, pepper and sunflower oil – it was called a 'civilian'. And it had to have a bay leaf on the top. I took twenty minutes too long and they gave me a real walloping . . . Holy shit! I found the spuds at the helicopter crews' place. The 'youngsters' were sitting there, peeling potatoes for the officers. I just asked: 'Guys, give me some, or they'll fucking kill me.' They gave me half a bucket. 'Go to our cook for the oil,' they told me. 'He's an Uzbek. Sing him a song about the friendship of the peoples – he likes that.' The Uzbek gave me some oil and onions from the bosses' table. I fried it all up on a campfire in a gully and I then ran – so I wouldn't bring them a cold frying pan.

Now when I read about brotherhood in Afghanistan I just want to laugh. Some day they'll make a movie about that brotherhood and everyone will believe it. But if I go to watch it, it will only be to see the Afghan landscapes. Just raise your head and there are the mountains. Purple mountains. And the sky! But it's like you're in prison. If the Afghan 'spirits' don't kill you, your own side will. Afterwards I told an ex-convict about it, back in the Union, and he didn't believe guys could give someone on the same side such a hard time: 'That's not possible!' And he'd done ten years inside. He'd seen a thing or two. Fuck it . . .

To stop yourself going right round the bend you couldn't let them beat you! Some drank, others smoked grass. They made moonshine out of whatever they could find: raisins, sugar, mulberries, yeast, bread – they flung it all in. When there weren't enough cigarettes, instead of tobacco they smoked tea rolled up in newspaper. It tasted like shit, but there was smoke. And 'chars' of course. 'Chars' is hemp pollen. When some of the guys tried it they used to laugh – they'd walk about laughing to themselves. Other guys would climb under the table and stay there until morning. Without that . . . Without the drugs and the moonshine they'd have gone totally gaga . . .

They put you on sentry duty and gave you two magazines of cartridges. If something started up then sixty cartridges was thirty seconds of actual combat. The 'spirits'' snipers were so well-trained they could fire at the glow of a cigarette, at the flash of a match.

I realized . . . I'm not telling you about the war any more here – I'm talking about man in general. The kind of man they don't write about much in our books. They're afraid of him. They hide him. About the natural, biological man. Without any ideas. The words 'heroism' and 'spirituality' make me feel sick. They turn my stomach. (*He pauses.*)

All right then, let's go on. I suffered more from our own side. The 'spirits' made a man of you – our guys made shit out of you. It was only in the army that I realized any man can be broken; the only difference is the means and how much time it takes. A 'grand-dad' – he's served all of six months – he's just lying there belly-up in his boots and he calls me over: 'Lick the boots, lick them clean with your tongue. You've got five minutes.' I just stand there. He calls out: 'Come here, Red' – Red is the young guy I went there with, we're friends. And then two assholes come over and start laying into Red, giving it all they've got. I can see they're going to break his back. He looks at me . . . So I start licking the boots, so he can survive and not get crippled. Before the army I didn't know you can hit a man so hard on the kidneys that he'll choke. But if I was alone with no one relying on me . . . then no fucking way could they have broken me.

I had a friend whose nickname was Bear, a great hulking guy almost two metres tall. He came back from Afghanistan and a year later he hanged himself. I don't know . . . He didn't confide in anyone. No one knows why he hanged himself: because of the war, or because he realized what vicious brutes men are. While he was fighting he didn't ask himself these questions; but after the war he started thinking. And he went demented. Another friend of mine turned to the bottle. He wrote to me. I got two letters from him – something like: 'Out there, brother, that was real life, but everything here's absolute shit. Out there we fought and survived, but here nothing makes any fucking sense.' When I called him he was totally assholed. And he was drunk the second time too . . . (*He lights a cigarette.*)

I remember arriving at the Kazan Station in Moscow with Bear. We'd travelled for four days from Tashkent, drinking day and night. We'd forgotten to send telegrams so that someone would meet us. We stepped out on to the platform at five in the morning and all the colours hit us smack in the eye! Everyone dressed in different colours – red, yellow, blue – beautiful young women. Fuck it . . . A completely different world. We were gobsmacked!

I came back on 8 November, and a month later I started at the university; I was reinstated in the second year. I was lucky. I crammed my head full of stuff . . . I didn't have time to go rummaging around inside myself: I had to pass the exams, starting from scratch. In two years I'd forgotten everything. All I could remember was *The Young Soldier's Basic Training Course* – peeling potatoes and eighteen-kilometre runs. Wearing your legs down to the knees. But Bear? He got here, and he had nothing. No qualifications, no job.

The only thing on people's minds here was sausage: the most important thing was that doctor's sausage was two roubles and twenty kopecks and a bottle of vodka was three roubles sixty-two. Nobody was concerned about the boys coming back with their brains all skewed, stumps maybe ten or twelve centimetres long, and bouncing along on their backsides at twenty years old. 'He's not my son, so fine.' That's the system we've got here: they break you in the army *and* in civvy street. Once you're stuck in the system and the gearwheels get a grip on you, you get ground up, no matter how good you were, no matter what dreams you were cherishing deep inside. (*He pauses.*) I haven't got the words for this . . . Nothing like the right ones . . . I'm trying to get my idea across: the most important thing is not to get stuck in the system. But how can you slip through the net? You have to serve the Homeland, with your Komsomol card in your pocket – that's sacred business. It says in the regulations that a soldier must 'staunchly and manfully endure all the rigours of military service'. Staunchly and manfully! Bloody hell – that says it all. (*He stops talking and reaches out to the table for another cigarette, but the pack is already empty.*) Shit! One pack a day isn't enough any more.

We have to start from the fact that we're animals, and this animal nature is overlaid by a thin coating of culture. Touchy-feely stuff. Ah, Rilke! Ah, Pushkin! But the wild beast creeps out of a man in an instant, in less than the blinking of an eye . . . All it takes is for him to feel afraid for himself, for his life. Or get some power. A little bit of power. Just a tiny little bit! The army system of 'ranks': before the oath – a 'spirit'; after the oath – a 'birdie'; after six months – a 'dipper'; after a dipper until one and a half years – a 'granddad'; and from two years on – a 'demobber'. Right at the very beginning you're a disembodied spirit and your life is one big bucket of gash.

But I fired. I fired, like everyone else. That's the most important thing, regardless. Only I don't want to think about it. I don't know how to think about it.

There was heroin lying around everywhere, literally under our feet. Little kids came down from the mountains at night and scattered it about. But we got high on grass. Almost no one took the heroin: it was absolutely pure – try it a couple of times and you were finished. Hooked. I restrained myself. Well, the second rule of survival is: don't think about anything! Eat, sleep, go on the mission. If you see something, forget it immediately, drive it underground, for later ... I saw a man's pupils grow until they filled his eyes completely as the life drained out of him. The pupils expanding. Turning darker ... I saw it and I forgot it immediately. And now I've remembered it with you ...

I fired! Of course I fired. I caught a man in my sights and squeezed ... Now I hope I didn't kill many of them, that's what I'd like to think, because they ... They were defending their Homeland. One of them – I remember him very well. The way I fired and he fell. He threw his hands up and fell. That one I remember. I was afraid of getting into hand-to-hand combat. I'd been told how you had to skewer the man, looking into his eyes ... Fuck it ... Bear opened up to me when he was drunk, when we were travelling for four days from Tashkent to Moscow. He said: 'You can't even imagine the way a man wheezes when the blood rises up through his throat. People should learn how to kill ...' A man who's never killed anyone, who's never even gone hunting, should be taught how to kill another man. Bear told me about this 'spirit' who was lying on the ground, wounded in the stomach, but he was alive, and the commander took out his paratrooper's knife and gave it to Bear: 'Take it and finish him off. Look him in the eyes.' And you know what the point of it is? It's so that afterwards you'll kill without even thinking about it, when you have to save your comrades. And you have to go through all that the first time, make yourself do it ... Bear took the knife and put the blade to the wounded man's throat, then he put it to the man's chest. And he couldn't kill him. How could he do that, just jab the knife into the living ribs?

Where the heart's beating . . . The 'spirit' followed the knife with his eyes. It was a long time before Bear could do it. He took a long time to kill him. When Bear got drunk, he used to cry. He had his place in hell already booked.

After I was demobbed I studied at the university and lived in the student hostel. They drink and shout a lot there. If someone knocked I jumped up like a lunatic and stood behind the door. I took up a defensive position. If there was peal of thunder or the rain started drumming on the windowsill my heart skipped a beat. If I drank a bottle of vodka everything seemed all right. Soon one bottle wasn't enough. Then I got cramps in my liver; it was falling apart. I ended up in hospital and they told me: 'If you want to live at least to forty, son, give up the drink.' I thought: 'I've never even had a woman – all those beautiful girls walking about – and I'll just go and snuff it.' So I gave up drinking. And I got a girlfriend . . .

Love is a supermundane category. I can't say that I love. I'm married now, I have a little daughter, but I don't know whether it's love or something else. Although I'd tear anyone's throat out for them and bury him in the road. I'd give my life for them! But what is love? People profess their love, in the way that they imagine it, but love is bloody tough, arduous work every day. Have I ever loved? To be honest, I can't be sure. I have felt some kind of feelings and had this inner inspiration. I've made some kind of purely spiritual efforts not connected with this shitty life. But is that love or some other damned thing?

When we were at war they taught us: 'You have to love your Homeland.' The Homeland welcomed us back with wide-open arms and a knockout blow in each fist. Why not just ask me if I've been happy? Then I'll answer that I was happy when I walked along my home street towards my own place after Afghanistan . . . It was November . . . It was November, and the smell of the land I hadn't seen for two years hit me in the nose, right in the skull, and it echoed right down to my feet . . . I had a lump in my throat. I couldn't walk, because I wanted to cry. After that I can say that I have been happy in this life. But have I loved? What does that mean – after I've seen death? Death is always ugly . . .

What is love? I was there at the birth when my wife had our daughter. At moments like that you need the person you're closest to beside you to hold your hand. Now I'd force every male bastard to stand beside a woman's head when she's giving birth, when her legs are splayed out and she's covered in blood and shit. Take a look, you sons of bitches, at the way a child comes into this world. Yet you kill so simply. Killing is easy. So simple. I thought I was going to faint. Men come back from the war and they faint at a child's birth. A woman isn't like a door you can just walk in and out of. Two worlds have turned my life upside down – a war and a woman. They've made me think about why a shitty lump of meat like me came into this world.

A man doesn't change when he's at war: he changes after the war. He changes when he takes the eyes that he saw everything with there and looks at what's here. For the first few months it's double vision – you're there and here at the same time. The withdrawal takes place here. Now I'm ready to think about what happened to me there . . . The security guards in the banks, the rich businessmen's bodyguards, the hitmen – they're all our boys. I met them and talked to them, and I realized that they didn't want to come back from the war. To come back here. They liked it better back there. They've still got feelings from that life back there that can't be expressed . . . First of all, it's a contempt for death – there's something higher than death . . . The 'spirits' weren't afraid of death; for instance, if they knew they were going to be shot tomorrow, they laughed as if everything was just fine and carried on talking to each other. They even seemed glad about it. Cheerful and calm. Death is the great transition: you should wait for it like your bride. That's what it says in their Koran.

I'd better tell a joke . . . I've frightened the lady writer. (*He laughs.*) Right then . . . A man dies and goes to hell and looks around. There are people being boiled in a cauldron and some being sawn apart on a table . . . He walks on. And there's a little table with men sitting round it, drinking beer, playing cards and clattering away at dominos. He walks up to them.

'What's that you've got there? Beer?'

'Yup.'

'Can I try it?' He tries it and it really is beer. Cold. 'And what are those, cigarettes?'

'Yup. Fancy a smoke?'

He lights up. 'So what is this place then? Is it hell or not?'

'Of course it's hell. Relax.' They laugh. 'Over there, all that boiling and sawing, that's hell for those who imagine it like that.'

'As thou hast believed, so be it done unto thee.' According to your faith . . . And your inner prayers . . . If you wait for death like a bride she'll come to you as a bride.

I once tried to find a young guy I knew among the dead. The soldiers who took in the dead bodies at the morgue used to be called 'looters'. They took everything out of the pockets. There's a young guy lying there with a hole in his chest, or all his guts spilled out, and they go through his pockets. They used to take everything: a cigarette lighter, nail scissors, a beautiful pen – and then they gave it all to their girlfriends back in the Union. Bloody hell!

I saw so many ruined *kishlaks*. But not a single kindergarten, not a single school that had been built, or tree that had been planted – the ones they wrote about in our newspapers. (*He pauses.*)

You wait and wait for the letters from home . . . Your girlfriend sends a photo of herself up to the waist in flowers – a swimsuit would have been better! A bikini. Or at least full length, so you could look at her legs. In a short skirt . . . At the politics sessions the 'politics pumpers' – our political officers, that is – used to spout about the Homeland and the duty of a soldier . . . But when we were lying in bed at night subject number one was women. What someone's woman was like and what they'd done. The things you could hear! Everyone's hands were in the same place. Bloody hell. Back there . . . for the Afghans buggery's normal. If you go into a *dukan* on your own: 'Comrade, come . . . Come here . . . I'll fuck you up the ass and for that you take whatever you want. Take a shawl for your mother . . .' They didn't bring us enough films – the only thing they delivered regularly was lots of copies of *Frunzenets*, the garrison newspaper. We took it straight to the reading room. Well, to that place. Sometimes we could pick up a music programme. When we heard Ludmila Zykina singing 'The Volga flows from far away, on and on', we all cried. We sat there and cried.

At home I couldn't put a proper phrase together – 'Fuck it' came out straightaway. A string of obscenities. In the beginning my mother asked: 'Why don't you tell me anything about it, son?' I remembered something, but my mother interrupted me: 'Our neighbours arranged alternative service for their son in a hospital. I'd die of shame if my son was carrying old women's bedpans. What kind of man is that?' 'You know what, mother?' I said. 'When I have children I'll do everything I can to make sure they don't serve in our army.' My father and mother looked at me as if I was shell-shocked and raving, and after that they didn't bring up the subject of the war with me, especially in front of their friends.

I ran away from home as quickly as I could. I went away to study. A girl was waiting for me. 'Well,' I thought, 'I'll tumble her the first day . . . I'll screw her the very first day.' But she took my hand off her shoulder. 'It's covered in blood,' she said – and that snipped off my libido for three years. I was afraid to approach a woman for three years. Damn it all! They taught us: 'You've got to defend your Homeland, defend your girl. You're a man . . .' I liked Scandinavian mythology; I liked to read about the Vikings. They considered it shameful for a man to die in bed. They died in battle. From the age of five a boy was accustomed to using weapons. And to death. War is no time for questions: 'Are you a man or a poor, trembling creature?' The purpose of a soldier is to kill: you're an instrument for killing. You have the same purpose as a shell or an automatic rifle. Now I'm getting philosophical. I'm trying to understand myself.

I went to an 'Afghani' club meeting once. I don't go any more. Once was enough. It was a meeting with American Vietnamese War veterans. We sat in a café, one American and three Russians at each table. One of our boys told the American sitting with us: 'I'm angry with Americans because I got blown up by an American mine. I've got one leg missing.' The American answered: 'And I was hit by shrapnel from a Soviet shell in Saigon.' Bloody great! They had a drink and hugged each other – brothers in arms, sort of. And then things went on from there. They boozed Russian-style: 'Here's to brotherhood'; 'One for the road'. But one thing hit me there: a soldier's a soldier everywhere, always the same; meat is meat. It's the meat counter. With only one difference: they have two different types of ice cream for breakfast, and we get nothing but boiled buckwheat for breakfast, lunch and supper. We never saw any fruit and we dreamed about eggs and fresh fish. We used to eat an onion like an apple. I came back from the army with no teeth. It was December, thirty degrees Celsius below freezing. That guy from California, we went to see him back to the hotel. He was wearing a down coat and padded gloves, walking round Moscow muffled up like that, and this Russian Ivan came walking towards us with his sheepskin coat unbuttoned, his singlet hoisted up above his belly button, no cap and no mittens.

'Hi, guys!'

'Hi!'

'Who's this then?'

'An American.'

'Oh, an American!' He shook the American's hand, slapped him on the shoulder and went on his way. We went up into the hotel room and the American wasn't talking any more.

'Hey boss! What's wrong?' we asked him.

'I'm wearing a down coat and gloves, and he's half-naked. But his hand is warm. It's impossible to fight this country.'

'Of course it is,' I answered. 'We'd bombard you with corpses!'

Bloody hell! We drink anything that burns, we screw anything that moves – and if it doesn't move we'll get it moving and screw it anyway.

I haven't talked about Afghanistan for a long time. I'm not interested in those conversations. But if I was given a choice: you'll learn this and that fighting a war, and go through this and that, but there are other possibilities – you can stay a boy and not end up out there – what's your choice? I'd still want to go through it all again and be the person I've become now. Experience it all again. Thanks to Afghanistan I've found friends . . . I met my wife, and I've got such a fantastic little daughter. Over there I learned what shit I've got inside me and just how deep it's hidden. I went back to the Bible and read it with a pencil in my hand. And I reread it all the time. Galich is right when he sings, 'Be afraid of the man who says, "'I know how."' I don't know how. I'm searching. I dream of purple mountains. And swirling columns of prickly sand.

I was born here. Like the woman you love, you don't choose your Homeland: it's given to you. If you were born in this country then find a way to die right in it. You can just croak or you can get killed – but you find a way to die like a man. I want to live in this country. It may be poor and unhappy, but Leskov's Lefty, who can shoe a flea, lives here, and the guys down by the beer kiosk solve all the world's problems. This country deceived us. But I love it.

I've seen . . . I know now that children are born bright and radiant. They're angels.

A private, infantryman

A flash, a fountain of light . . . And that was all. After that came night. Darkness . . . I opened my eyes and crawled along a wall. Where am I? In a hospital. Then I checked to make sure my arms were still there. They were. Then lower down. I touched myself with my hands . . . Where are my legs? My legs! (*He turns away to face the wall and doesn't want to speak for a long time.*)

I forgot everything that had happened before. Severe concussion . . . I forgot my entire life. I opened my passport and read my name. Where was I born? In Voronezh. Thirty years old. Married. Two children. Both boys . . .

I didn't remember a single face. (*He pauses again for a long time, looking at the ceiling.*)

The first to come was my mother. She said: 'I'm your mother.' I looked her over, I couldn't remember, but at the same time this woman wasn't a stranger to me. I realized that she wasn't a stranger. She told me about my childhood, about school . . . Even little details like what a fine coat I'd had in the eighth year, and how I tore it on a fence. What marks I got. There were 'As' and 'Bs', but I got only a 'C' for behaviour. I was a bit of a hooligan. She said I liked pea soup better than anything else. I listened to her and it was like seeing myself from the outside.

The mess attendant called me: 'Get in the wheelchair; I'll take you. Your wife's come to see you.'

A beautiful woman was standing outside the ward. I glanced at her: well, she can stand there if she likes. Where's my wife? But she was my wife. The face seemed familiar, but I didn't recognize her.

She told me about our love. How we met. The first time I kissed her . . . She brought our wedding photos. She talked about when our boys were born. The two boys. I listened and I couldn't remember, but I memorized everything she said. I started getting bad headaches from the strain of it. And the ring – where was my wedding ring? I looked at my hand, and there weren't any fingers.

I remembered my little sons from a photograph. Then they came, and they were different. Mine and not mine. The blond-haired one had turned dark; the little one had grown big. I looked at myself in the mirror: they were like me!

The doctors have promised that my memory could come back. Then I'll have two lives: the one they told me about, and the one that really happened. Come back then, and I'll tell you about the war . . .

A captain, helicopter pilot

The firing kept shifting, wandering across the slope of the mountain for a long time.

Early in the evening a flock of sheep darted out and came towards us. Hoo-ray! A gift from Allah. Allah Akbar! We were hungry and tired after two days on the march. All we had left was rusks. And here was a lost flock. With no owner. We didn't have to buy a sheep or trade tea and soap for it (one sheep cost a kilogramme of tea or ten bars of soap). We didn't have to pillage. The first one we grabbed was the big ram. We tied him to a tree; we knew the other sheep wouldn't go anywhere then. We'd learned that much already. In a bombardment the sheep scatter and then clump back together. They come back to their leader. And after that . . . After that we chose the fattest sheep and led her off . . .

I've observed many times how meekly this animal accepts death. When a pig or a calf is killed it's a different matter. They don't want to die. They try to break free, they squeal. But a sheep doesn't try to run away, it doesn't screech or have a fit of hysterics, it just walks along without making a sound. With its eyes open. Following the man with the knife.

It was never like murder; it always resembled a ritual. A sacrificial ritual.

A private, scout

Day Two

'And another dieth in the bitterness of his soul . . .'

He called again. Fortunately I was at home . . .

'I wasn't going to call. But today I got into a bus and I heard two woman talking:

' "What kind of heroes are they? They killed women and children out there. Are they really right in the head? But they invite them to schools, to talk to our children. And they get social benefits too." I jumped off at the first stop . . .

'We were soldiers and we followed orders. For disobeying orders in wartime they shoot you! You'll get court-martialled. Of course, the generals don't shoot any women and children, but they give the orders. And now we're to blame for everything! Now they try to tell us that carrying out a criminal order is a crime. But I believed the men who gave the orders! I believed them. For as long as I can remember I've been taught to believe. Just believe! No one taught me to think about whether to believe or not, whether to shoot or not! They told me over and over again: "Just have more belief!" And that's the way we were when we left here. But we didn't come back like that.'

'We could meet . . . And talk.'

'I can only talk with men like me. Men from out there. Do you understand? Yes, I killed, I'm soaked in blood . . . But he was lying there: he was my brother. His head over here, his arms over there . . . His skin . . . I asked to go on another raid immediately . . . I saw a funeral in a kishlak. There were a lot of people. They were carrying the body in something white . . . And I gave the order: "Fire!" '

'I wonder how you live with that. How badly does it bother you?'

'Yes, I killed. Because I wanted to live. I wanted to come back home. But now I envy the dead. The dead don't feel pain . . .'

The conversation was broken off again.

The author

It's like a dream. As if I'd just seen it somewhere. In some film or other. I have the feeling now that I didn't kill anyone . . .

I went of my own accord. I asked to be sent. If you ask me whether it was for an idea or to understand who I am, of course it was the second one. I wanted to test myself, see what I was capable of. I wanted to be a hero; I was looking for a chance to be a hero. I left college in the second year. They said . . . I heard people saying it was a kid's war. Boys were fighting there, straight out of the tenth year in school. A war's always like that. That's what the Great Patriotic War was like too. It's like a game for us. Your own vanity and pride were very important. Can I do it or can't I? He could. What about me? That was what we were interested in, not politics. I'd been preparing myself for some kind of test ever since I was a kid. My favourite writer is Jack London. A real man should be strong. Men become strong in war. My girl tried to persuade me not to go: 'Can you imagine Bunin or Mandelstam saying something like that?' None of my friends could understand me. Some had got married; some had got into Eastern philosophy, or into yoga. I was the only one who went to the war.

Sun-scorched mountains up above you. Down below, a little girl calling to the goats, a woman hanging out her laundry . . . Just like in our part of the Caucasus. I was disappointed, actually. At night someone shoots at our campfire: as I pick up the kettle the bullet flies straight under it. War! On the campaign marches the thirst was agonizing, humiliating. Your mouth dries out: you can't gather your spit so that you can swallow. It feels like your mouth's full of sand. We licked the dew; we licked our own sweat. I've got to live. I want to live! I caught a tortoise and stabbed a sharp stone into its throat. And I drank tortoise blood. The others couldn't do it. None of them could. They drank their own urine . . .

I realized that I was capable of killing. I had a gun in my hands . . .

In my first battle I saw men fall into a state of shock. Pass out. Some of them still puke at the mere memory of how they killed. After the action there's an ear hanging on a tree. An eye trickling across a human body . . . but I could take it. One of us was a hunter. He boasted that before the army he used to kill rabbits and bring down wild boar. But he always used to puke up. It's one thing to kill an animal; killing a man's something else altogether. In a battle you go numb, stop feeling. Cold reasoning and calculation. My automatic is my life. Like another arm.

It was a partisan war we were fighting; big battles were rare. Everywhere it was you and him. It gave you the senses of a lynx. You fire a burst and he ducks down. You wait. Now who'll fire? Before you even hear the shot you feel the bullet fly past. You crawl from rock to rock; you hide. You chase after them like a hunter. As taut as a spring. Not even breathing. Waiting for the right moment . . . If you come face to face you can club him to death with your rifle butt. If you kill him you're very keenly aware that you've survived this time. I'm still alive! There's no joy in killing a man. You kill so that you won't be killed. War's not just death, it's something else as well. War even has a smell. Its own smell.

The dead are all different. None of them are the same. Lying there in the water, after the rain, something happens to a dead face; they all have a kind of smile. After the rain they lie there clean. Without water, in the dust, death is more honest. He's wearing a brand new uniform, but instead of a head he has a dry red leaf. It was squashed under a wheel, like a lizard . . . But I'm alive! One sits there by the wall. Beside a house. Cracked nuts lying around him. Sits there with his eyes open. There was no one to close them . . . After someone dies, for ten or fifteen minutes you can still close the eyes. Not after that. The eyes won't close . . . But I'm alive! Another one's bent over, with his fly open. It's still even dripping . . . Whatever way they were living at that moment, whatever they were doing, that was the way they stayed. Still in this world, but already beyond it. Already up above . . . But I'm alive! I can just touch myself to make sure.

The birds aren't afraid of death. They sit and watch. The

children aren't afraid of death. They sit and watch too, calmly and curiously. Like the birds. I've seen an eagle watching a battle. Sitting there like a little sphinx . . . You're eating soup in the mess and you glance at the guy beside you and picture him dead. There was a time when I couldn't look at photographs of my family. When I got back from a mission I couldn't bear to look at children or women. I used to turn my face away. After a while it passes off. I used to run to PT in the morning. I did a lot of weightlifting, thinking about being in good shape for when I got back. I didn't get enough sleep, though. And the lice, especially in winter. They used to sprinkle insecticide powder on the mattresses.

I learned to fear death at home. I came back and I had a son. I felt afraid that, if I died, my son would grow up without me. I remembered my seven bullets. The ones that could have sent me 'to the people upstairs' as we used to say. But they went flying past . . . I even get the feeling I didn't finish the game. Didn't get through all my fighting.

I'm not guilty of anything. I'm not afraid of nightmares. I always chose a fair fight – him and me. Once when I saw them beating a prisoner, two of them beating him, and he was tied up, lying there as limp as a rag, I drove them off, wouldn't let them beat him. I despised their kind. One man took his automatic and fired at an eagle . . . I smashed him in the face . . . What did the bird do to him?

My family and relatives used to ask me: 'What's it like out there?' 'Ah, drop it. I'm sorry. I'll tell you later.'

I graduated from college and I work as an engineer. I want to be just an engineer, not an Afghan War veteran. I don't like remembering. Although I don't know what's going to happen to us, to the generation that survived. We survived a war that no one needed. No one! Not this side or the other. Now I've spoken out at last . . . It's like in a train. People who don't know each other come together, talk for a while and get out at different stations. My hands are shaking. I'm feeling nervous somehow . . . And I thought I'd got off easy from the game. If you write about this don't mention my name.

I'm not afraid, but I don't want to be stuck in all this any longer . . .

An infantry platoon commander

My wedding was planned for December. A month before the wedding, in November, I left for Afghanistan. When I told my fiancé I was going he laughed: 'To defend the southern borders of our Homeland?' But when he realized I wasn't joking he said: 'What is this – haven't you got anyone to sleep with here?'

On the way here I thought: 'I missed the BAM and virgin lands projects. I'm lucky there's still Afghanistan!' I believed the songs that the guys brought back. I used to play them for days on end.

> In the years that have gone by,
> In the land of Afghanistan,
> Russia has scattered across the rocks
> So very many of her sons.

I used to be a bookish, Moscow girl. I thought that real life was somewhere far away. And the men there were all strong, the women were all beautiful. There were lots of adventures. I wanted to break out of the ordinary world . . .

For three nights on the way to Kabul I didn't sleep. At the customs they thought I was high on something. I remember I cried as I tried to prove I wasn't: 'I'm not a drug addict. I'm just short of sleep.' I was lugging a heavy suitcase with my mother's jam and biscuits – and none of the men would help. And they weren't just men, they were young officers, handsome and strong. Boys had always wanted to date me – they adored me. I was genuinely surprised. 'Will someone help?' The way they looked at me!

I was stuck at the transit point for another three nights. The very first day a warrant officer came over. 'If you want to stay in Kabul, come tonight . . .' He was really chubby. His nickname was Balloon.

They took me on at the base as a typist. We used old army typewriters. In the first few weeks I worked my fingers bloody. I typed wearing bandages – the nails were coming off my fingers.

A couple of weeks later a soldier knocked on my door at night. 'The commander wants you.'

'I won't go.'

'Why start acting awkward! You knew where you were coming, didn't you?'

In the morning the commander threatened to send me to Kandahar. And all sorts of other things . . .

What makes Kandahar such a prize?
It's a nightmare of 'spirits' and flies.

After that I was afraid of getting run over or shot in the back . . . Afraid they'd beat me . . .

Two girls shared a room with me in the hostel. One was responsible for the electricity; they called her the Electrician. The other dealt with the chemical water purification – Chlora, they called her. The girls all had the same explanation: 'It's life . . .'

Just at that time they published an article in *Pravda*: 'The Madonnas of Afghanistan'. Girls wrote to us from the Union. They all liked the article; some even went to the military commissariat and asked to come to Afghanistan. They read it in class at school. And we couldn't walk past any soldiers without them laughing at us: 'So, "barrel-busters", you're heroines now! Performing your international duty in bed!' What are 'barrel-busters'? The 'barrels' – they're like trailers – are what the top stars live in, no one lower than a major. The women that they . . . They're called 'barrel-busters'. The boys serving here don't hide what they think: 'If I hear that my girl's been in Afghanistan then she doesn't exist any longer for me.' We've all been through the same illnesses; all the girls have had hepatitis and malaria . . . We've been through the bombardments too . . . But when I meet a boy back in the Union I won't be able to throw my arms round his neck. For them we're all whores or mad-women. Don't sleep with a woman, don't dirty yourself . . . 'And who do I sleep with? I sleep with my automatic . . .' Just try smiling at someone after that . . .

My mother proudly announces to her friends: 'My daughter's in Afghanistan!' My naive mother! I feel like writing to her and saying: 'Mama, shut up, or you'll hear some really terrible things!' Maybe when I get back I'll make sense of it all and I'll recover, thaw out a bit. But right now I'm broken and crushed inside. What have I learned here? How can you learn kindness and compassion here? Or joy?

The *bachata* run after the car and shout: 'Show us the *Khanum* . . .' They might even offer money. They know someone will take it.

I used to think I wouldn't live to get back home. Now I've got over that. There are two dreams that I have here, again and again, by turns.

The first dream. We go into a wealthy *dukan*. The walls are covered with carpets and jewellery. And our boys sell me. A sackful of money is brought out and they count the *afoshkas* . . . Then two 'spirits' wind my hair on to their hands. The alarm clock goes off. I call out in fear and wake up. I've never watched the horrors all the way through.

The second dream. We're flying from Tashkent to Kabul in an Il-76 military plane. Mountains appear outside the window and the bright light fades away. We start falling into some kind of abyss and we end up covered by a thick layer of heavy Afghan earth. I dig away like a mole, but I can't break through to the light. I'm choking. But I keep on digging, digging . . .

If I don't stop myself, there'll be no end to my story. Every day here something happens that shakes your very soul and turns it inside out. Yesterday a boy I know got a letter from the Union, from his girl: 'I don't want to be your friend, you've got blood on your hands . . .' He came running to me, because he knew I'd understand.

We all dream about home, but we don't talk about it much. Out of superstition. We really want to go back, but what will we go back to? We don't talk about that either. We just crack jokes.

'Children, tell me what your fathers do.'

Everyone puts their hand up. 'My father's a doctor.' 'My father's a plumber.' 'My father works in the circus.' Little Vova doesn't say anything.

'Vova, don't you know what your father does?'

'He used to be a pilot, but now he works as a fascist in Afghanistan.'

At home I used to like books about war, but here I carry Dumas around with me. At war you don't want to talk about war. The girls went to see the men who'd been killed. They said they were lying there in nothing but their socks. I won't go . . . I don't like going into town, going to the *dukans* to buy things. There are lots of men with one leg out there in the streets . . . Children on homemade crutches. I can't get used to it. I used to dream of becoming a journalist. But now I know it'll be hard for me to believe in anything. To love anything.

I'll go home and never come back to the South. I can't bear to see mountains any more. When I see mountains I think shelling is about to start. One day they were bombarding us, and one of our girls was kneeling down, crying and praying. She was crossing herself . . . I wonder what she was begging heaven for? All of us here are a bit secretive; no one opens up all the way. Everyone has suffered some kind of disappointment.

And I cry all the time. I cry for that bookish little Moscow girl.

A civilian employee

What did I learn there? That good never wins. There's always just as much evil in the world. Man is terrifying. But nature is beautiful . . . And the dust. Your mouth full of sand all the time. You can't talk . . .

We're combing through a *kishlak*. Me and this young guy walking beside each other. He opens the door into a *duval* – a compound – with his foot and they fire at him point-blank with a machine gun. Nine bullets . . . My mind is flooded with hate. We shot them all, right down to the animals, although shooting an animal is more disturbing. You feel sorry for it. I wouldn't let them shoot the donkeys. What had they done? They had amulets round their necks, the same as the children had . . . With their names on. When we set fire to the wheat field it made me feel sick, because I'm from the country. Out there all I used to remember from the old life were the good things – my childhood, mostly. The way I used to lie in the grass, surrounded by bluebells and daisies . . . The way we used to toast ears of wheat on a fire and eat them . . .

We were surrounded there by a life that we didn't understand.

An alien life. We killed because it was easier than . . . (*He pauses.*) Than if we'd been somewhere more familiar. In places that looked like ours. To be precise, if I talk about my feelings . . . There was revulsion *and* pride – I'd killed someone!

The heat was so bad that the iron sheeting on the roofs of the *dukans* cracked. A field used to break into flames instantly, in an explosion of fire. It smelled of bread. The fire carried the childhood smell of bread up into the air.

Night doesn't come on slowly there, it just drops down on you. A moment ago it was day, and now it's night. The dawn's beautiful . . . You used to be a boy, but now you're a man. That's what war does. Rain falls there – you can see it – but it doesn't reach the ground. You watch satellite broadcasts about the Union and you remember that that other life exists, but it doesn't penetrate into you . . . You can tell them all that. You can print all that. But what's happening right now bothers me – I can't express the real essence of it.

What's it like to live with war, to remember? It means that you're never alone. There are always two of you – you and the war. We don't have much of a choice: keep quiet and forget, or go crazy and scream. No one needs the second option . . . The authorities don't, and neither do our families. The people dear to us. You come here . . . What have you come for? It's just cruel . . . (*He lights a cigarette nervously.*)

Sometimes I want to write about everything I saw. Everything. I have a literary and linguistic education. In the hospital there's a man with one arm and a man with one leg is sitting on his bed, writing a letter to his mother. A little Afghan girl: she took a sweet from a Soviet soldier and the next morning they cut off both her hands . . . To write everything just the way it was, without reflecting on any of it. It was raining . . . Just to write about that – it was raining. No reflecting about it being good or bad, just that it was raining. Rain. Any water there isn't simply water. Water from a flask is almost hot. Bitter to the taste. There's nowhere to hide from the sun . . .

What else would I write about?

Blood. When I saw my first blood, I turned cold, very cold. A chilly shudder. Cold in the forty-degree heat. In the scorching sun.

They brought two prisoners. One had to be killed, because there was no room in the helicopter for both, but we needed one as a 'tongue'. And I couldn't take the decision. Which one?

In the hospital the dead and the living kept swapping places with each other. And I couldn't tell them apart any longer. I once talked to a dead man for half an hour . . .

That's enough! (*He slams his fist down on the table. Then he calms down.*)

I used to think . . . I dreamed about the first night I would sleep at home. After everything. We came back, hoping that they'd be waiting for us at home with wide-open arms. And suddenly we discover that no one's interested in what we've been through. Some young guys I knew were standing in the yard: 'Ah, you're back. It's good that you're back.' I went to a school reunion. The teachers didn't ask about anything either. My conversation with the director of the school went like this.

I say: 'They should put up a monument to the memory of those who died carrying out their international duty.'

She says: 'They were slackers and hooligans. How can we put a memorial plaque up on the school in their honour?' As if to say: 'What have you done that was so heroic? Lost a war. And who needed it? Brezhnev and the army generals? The fanatics of world revolution . . .'

So it turns out that my friends died in vain. And I could have died in vain . . . But my mother saw me from the window and ran the whole length of the street shouting with joy. 'No,' I tell myself. 'They can turn the whole world upside down, but they can't undo this: the men lying in the ground are heroes. Heroes!'

At college an old teacher tried to explain to me. 'You were victims of a political error . . . They made you accomplices to a crime . . .'

'I was eighteen years old then. How old are you? When our skin was bursting in the heat did you not keep quiet about it? When they brought us back in the "black tulips" did you not keep quiet about that? You heard the salvoes of the salutes in the cemeteries and the army bands playing . . . When we were killing out there did you not keep quiet about that? Yet now you've suddenly started talking: "Senseless sacrifices . . . An error . . ."'

But I don't want to be the victim of a political error. I don't want to have fought for that! They can turn the whole world upside down, but they can't ever undo this: the men lying in the ground are heroes. Heroes! I'll write about that myself some day . . . (*After sitting there for a while and calming down, he repeats his own words.*) Man is terrifying . . . But nature is beautiful . . .

It's strange that I should remember the beauty. The death and the beauty.

A private, grenadier

I was lucky. I came back home with my arms, my legs and my eyes. Not burned and not insane. We'd already realized out there that this war wasn't the one we'd come for. But we decided: 'Let's finish the fighting and go back home, and we'll sort things out there.'

We were the first replacements for the men who invaded Afghanistan. We didn't have an idea, but we had orders. Orders are not for discussion: start discussing them, and it's not the army any longer. Read the classics of Marxism-Leninism: 'A soldier has to be like a cartridge, ready to fire at any time.' I remember that very clearly. Men go to war to kill. My profession is killing. That's what I studied. Personal fear: let someone else get killed, but not me. They killed him, but they won't kill me. The mind doesn't accept the slightest possibility of its own extinction. And I didn't go there as a boy – I was thirty.

Out there I got a feeling of what life is. Those were my best years – I tell you that straight. Our life here is grey and small: job – home, home – job. There we tried everything, discovered everything. We experienced genuine manly friendship. We saw exotic sights: the way the morning mist swirls in the narrow ravines, it's like a smokescreen; the *burubakhaikas* – the brightly painted Afghan trucks with great high sides; red buses with people, sheep and cows all jumbled up together and riding inside them; yellow taxis. There are places there like a lunar landscape, something fantastic and cosmic. Nothing but ancient mountains. It seems as if man doesn't exist on this earth, only the stone is alive. And that stone is shooting at you. You just feel the hostility of nature: even for her you're an alien.

We were suspended between life and death, and someone else's life and someone else's death was in our hands too. Is there anything stronger than that feeling? We made whoopee there in a way we'll never make whoopee again anywhere else. Women loved us there in a way they'll never love us again anywhere else. Everything was heightened by the closeness of death; we were always spinning and sparkling, right there alongside death. We had lots of different adventures. I think I know the scent of danger, the way it smells when you see the back of your own head through someone else's eyes . . . Your third eye opens up . . . I tried everything there and I came out unscathed. It was a man's life there. I feel nostalgic. The Afghan syndrome.

Whether it was a just cause or it wasn't, nobody thought about that then. We did what we were ordered to do. Training and habit. Now, of course, everything has been reconsidered, reassessed by time, memory, information and all the truth that's been revealed to us. But that's almost ten years afterwards! Back then there was an image of the enemy, one familiar to us from books, from school, from films about the Basmachis after the Russian Revolution. I watched the movie *The White Sun of the Desert* about five times. And there he was, the enemy! That was enough – that was what I had. We all had a mental picture of war, or revolution. We weren't given any other examples to inspire us.

We replaced the first wave and started merrily hammering in the survey pegs for the future barracks, messes and army clubs. We were issued TT-33 pistols from Second World War times – the political officers used to carry them. Only good for shooting yourself or selling in a *dukan*. We went around dressed like partisans, in whatever we had; a lot of us wore tracksuit pants and trainers. I was like the Good Soldier Švejk. Fifty degrees Celsius, and the command requires a tie and full uniform. As specified by the regulations from Kamchatka to Kabul . . .

Sacks of human meat in the morgue – it comes as a shock! Six months later we're watching a movie and tracer shells start hitting the screen. We carry on watching the movie. We're playing volleyball and shelling starts. We look to see where the shells are coming from, and carry on playing . . . They used to bring us films about war, about Lenin or about an unfaithful wife: he went away, and now she's with someone else. But everyone wanted comedies. They never brought us any comedies. I could have picked up my automatic and emptied it into the screen. The screen was three or four sheets sewn together under the open sky and the audience sat on the sand.

Once a week it was 'bath and glass' day. A bottle of vodka was thirty checks. Worth its weight in gold. People brought it from the Union. According to the customs instructions one man could bring in two bottles of vodka, four bottles of wine and an unlimited amount of beer. You pour out the beer and fill the bottles with vodka. Try a bottle of Borzhomi mineral water and it's 40 per cent alcohol. A jar of jam wrapped up and labelled 'Blueberry' or 'Strawberry' in indelible pencil by somebody's wife. Open it up and it's 40 per cent too. Our dog was called Vermouth. Drinking was 'good for you': 'A red eye won't turn yellow,' they used to say. They used to drink 'skewer' – the de-icing fluid from the planes – and antifreeze, the liquid for stopping the engines freezing.

You warn a new soldier: 'Drink anything, but don't touch the antifreeze.'

A day or two after they arrive the doctor is called. 'What is it?'

'A new boy's poisoned himself with antifreeze . . .'

I smoked drugs. The effects varied. Sometimes I got the willies and went around thinking every bullet in the air had my name on it. If I smoked stuff at night I started getting hallucinations, seeing my family all night long and hugging my wife. Some had hallucinations in colour. Like watching a movie . . . They sold us the drugs in the *dukans* at first, and then they gave them to us for nothing: 'Smoke, Russian! Here, smoke . . .' The *bachata* would run after soldiers and hand it to them.

I feel like laughing. (*He smiles but his eyes are sad.*) I remember funny things as well as the terrifying ones. My favourite jokes . . .

'Comrade lieutenant-colonel, is your rank written as one word or hyphenated?' 'One word of course. The check word is 'table legs'.

'Comrade colonel, where shall we dig?' 'From the fence as far as lunch.'

You don't want to die. It's incomprehensible and you don't want it. Lousy little thoughts. Why did I go to the military academy and not the construction college? Every day we said goodbye to someone . . . Someone caught a tripwire with his heel, heard the click of the detonator and – as always happens – didn't drop and press himself against the ground, but looked round in surprise at the sound and took ten pieces of shrapnel . . . A tank got blown up: the bottom was torn open like a tin can, the rollers and a caterpillar track were ripped off. The driver tried to scramble out through the hatch, but only his hands appeared. He couldn't get any further and he burned up with his tank.

No one wanted to take a dead man's bed in the barracks. When a new man came we called him a 'replacement': 'Sleep here for the time being. On this bed. You didn't know him anyway.' The ones we remembered most often were the ones with children. They'd grow up as orphans. Without any father. But what about the ones who didn't leave any kids? Their girls will find new fiancés, and their mothers will bring up new sons. It'll all happen over and over again.

They paid us incredibly little for a war: about twice basic pay, of which one half was converted into two hundred and seventy checks; and they made deductions for newspapers, taxes and so on. At the same time as an ordinary freelance worker in Salang was paid fifteen hundred checks. Compare that with an officer's pay. Military advisers received from five to ten times as much. The inequality became clear at the customs. When the foreign goods were being taken out. Some had a cassette player and a pair of jeans, and some had a video system and five suitcases the size of mattresses to go with it. They were called 'the foreign invader's dream'. The soldiers could barely even drag them along. The wheels couldn't take the weight. They collapsed.

In Tashkent: 'You from Afghanistan? Want a girl . . . a girl like a peach, my friend?' call the touts from a private brothel.

'No thank you, my friend. I want to go home. To my wife. I need a ticket.'

'For a ticket, you give me baksheesh. Are those sunglasses Italian?'

'Yes . . .' Before I got to Sverdlovsk I'd laid out a hundred roubles and handed over my Italian sunglasses, a Japanese lurex scarf and a French make-up set. But they told me how to deal with the queue: 'What are you standing there for? Slip forty checks in your service passport, and you'll be home a day earlier.'

I took note of that. 'Miss, I need to get to Sverdlovsk.'

'There aren't any tickets. Put your specs on and look at the sign.'

I slipped forty checks in my service passport . . . 'Miss, I need to get to Sverdlovsk . . .'

'I'll take a look. It's fortunate you came when you did: one place has just turned up.'

Coming home on leave is like coming to a different world – your family. For the first few days you don't hear anyone, you only see them. You touch them. How can I tell you what it's like to run your hand over your child's head? In the morning there's a smell of coffee and pancakes in the kitchen. Your wife calls you to breakfast . . .

A month later you have to go away. Where to and what for, you don't understand. You don't think about that, you simply mustn't think about that. You only know that you're going because you have to. It's the job. At night the Afghan sand grates on your teeth, as fine as powdered snow or flour. You've just been lying in the red dust, or on the dry clay, with an armoured vehicle roaring beside you. You come to and jump up – no, you're still at home. You're leaving tomorrow.

My father asked me to stick a piglet. Before, when he killed a piglet, I wouldn't go anywhere near it. I used to stop my ears in order not to hear the squealing. I used to run out of the house.

My father says: 'Come on, help me.' And he gives me the knife.

I say: 'Step back, I'll do it . . . You have to get the heart, here.' I stick it in.

There, everyone was busy saving himself. *You* had to save your-self! I recall . . . Some soldiers are sitting there and an old man and a donkey walk by below them. They blast them with a grenade launcher: zap! No old man, no donkey. 'Guys, are you out of your mind? An old man and a donkey. What did they do to you?'

'Yesterday there was an old man and a donkey too. And there was a soldier walking along. The old man and the donkey walked past him and the soldier was left lying there.'

'Maybe it was a different old man and a different donkey?'

You should never spill the first blood. You'll always be shooting at yesterday's old man and yesterday's donkey.

We did our fighting. We stayed alive and came back home. Now we're trying to figure things out.

A captain, artillery officer

I never used to pray, but I do now. I go to the church service . . .

I sat by the coffin and asked: 'Who's in there? Are you in there, son?' I just kept repeating it: 'Who's there? Answer me, son. You grew up so big, and the coffin's so small.'

Time went by and I wanted to know how my son died. I went to the military commissariat. 'Can you tell me how my son died? And where? I don't believe he was killed. I think all I buried was a metal coffin, but my son is alive somewhere.'

The military commissar turned furious. He even shouted at me: 'That's strictly privileged information. And you're going around telling everyone your son's been killed. I order you not to divulge that!'

I suffered twenty-four hours of torture when I gave birth. When I heard it was a son the pain passed off: I hadn't suffered in vain. I was afraid for him from the very beginning: I didn't have anyone else. We lived in a camp hut and all we had in the room was my bed and a baby buggy, and two chairs as well. I worked as a switchman on the railway and my pay was sixty roubles. When I got back from the hospital I went straight on to the night shift. I travelled to work with the baby buggy. I used to take a little stove with me; when I'd fed him he slept, and I met the trains and saw them on their way. When he'd grown up a bit I used to leave him at home. I tied his leg to the bed and went out. He grew up a good boy.

He got into the construction college in Petrozavodsk. When I went to visit him he just kissed me and ran off somewhere. I was upset. He came back into the room, smiling: 'The girls will come in a minute.'

'What girls?' He'd gone running off to boast to the girls that his mother had come, so that they would come and see what his mother was like.

Whoever gave me any presents? No one did. He came home for Women's Day on 8 March and I met him at the station. 'Here son, let me help you.'

'It's a heavy bag, mama. You take my drawing tube. But be careful with it, there are drawings inside.' So I took it, and he kept checking how I carried it. What kind of drawings did he have in there? At home he took his coat off and I went straight into the kitchen to see how my pies were doing. I looked up and he was standing there holding three red tulips. Where did he get them from, up in the North, in Karelia? He'd wrapped them in a piece of cloth and put them in the tube so they wouldn't get frostbitten. No one had ever given me flowers before.

In the summer he went off to a construction brigade and came back just before my birthday. 'Mama, I'm sorry I didn't send you any birthday wishes. But I brought you this . . .' And he showed me a receipt for a money transfer.

I read it: 'Twelve roubles and fifty kopecks.'

'Mama, you've forgotten big numbers. One thousand, two hundred and fifty roubles . . .'

'I've never held any crazy money like that in my hands – I don't know how it's written.'

He was so delighted. 'Now you're going to rest, and I'm going to work. I'll earn a lot of money. Do you remember when I was little I promised that when I grew up I would really pamper you?'

It's true, he did say that. And he grew up to be a metre and ninety-six centimetres tall. He picked me up and carried me around like a little girl. We probably loved each other so much because we didn't have anyone else. I don't know how I could have given him away to a wife. I'd never have survived it.

They sent him his enlistment notice for the army. He wanted them to put him in the paratroopers. 'Mama, they're taking people into the airborne assault forces, but they won't take me, because I'm too big and strong and I'll break all their cords. The paratroopers have such handsome berets, though . . .'

But he got into the Vitebsk airborne division after all. I came to see him when he took the oath and I didn't even recognize him. He'd straightened up and stopped being shy about his height.

'Mama, why are you so little?'

'Because I miss you and I'm not growing,' I said, trying to make a joke of it.

'Mama, they're sending us to Afghanistan, but they won't take me this time either, because I'm your only child. Why didn't you have a little girl as well?'

When they took the oath there were lots of parents there. I heard someone say:

'Is Zhuravlyov's mother here? Mother, come and congratulate your son.'

I walked over and tried to congratulate him, but he was a metre and ninety-six centimetres, and there was no way I could reach up to him.

The commander ordered him: 'Private Zhuravlyov, bend down and let your mother kiss you.'

He bent down and kissed me and someone photographed us at that moment. It's the only army photo I have.

After the oath they let him out for a few hours and we went to a park. We sat on the grass and he took his boots off. They'd had a fifty-kilometre forced march, and there weren't any size forty-six boots, so they'd given him size forty-four. He didn't complain, on the contrary: 'We ran with rucksacks filled with sand. Where do you think I came?'

'Probably last because of those boots.'

'No, mama, I was first. I took the boots off and ran, and I didn't tip out any sand like the others did.'

I wanted to do something special for him. 'Maybe we could go to a restaurant, son? We've never been to a restaurant.'

'Mama, why don't you just buy me a kilogramme of fruit drops. That would be a great present!'

We said goodbye just before lights out. He waved the bag of fruit drops to me as I left.

They put us parents up at the base, on mats in the sports hall. But we didn't go to bed until early in the morning, because all night long we walked round the barracks where our boys were sleeping. The bugle sounded and I suddenly realized I might see him again, if only from a distance, when they brought them out for PT. They were all running in identical striped singlets and I couldn't spot him. I missed him. They marched in formation to the toilet, in formation to PT, in formation to the mess. They wouldn't let them go on their own, because when the boys found out they were being sent to Afghanistan one hanged himself in the toilet and another slit his wrists. They were keeping an eye on them.

We got into the bus, and I was the only parent who was crying. As if someone had told me I'd just seen him for the last time. Soon he wrote: 'Mama, I saw your bus and I ran so hard to see you one more time.' When we were sitting in the park the radio was playing the song 'How My Dear Mother Saw Me Off'. When I hear that song now . . . (*She holds back her tears.*)

His second letter began: 'Greetings from Kabul . . .' When I read that I started shouting so loudly that the neighbours came running. 'Why doesn't the law protect us?' I banged my head against the wall. 'He's all I have. Even in the tsars' times they didn't take the only breadwinner for the army. And now they've sent him off to war.' For the first time since Sasha was born I regretted that I'd never got married, that there was no one to look after me. Sasha used to tease me:

'Mama, why don't you get married?'

'Because you're so jealous.' That made him laugh and he stopped teasing. We were planning to live together for a long, long time.

There were a few more letters and then silence, such a long silence that I contacted the unit commander. And then Sasha wrote immediately and said: 'Mama, don't write to the unit commander any more. I really caught it hot for that! I couldn't write to you: a wasp stung me on the hand. I didn't want to ask anyone else – you would have been frightened by the strange handwriting.'

He was sparing me, making up fairy tales, as if I didn't watch the television every day and I couldn't guess straight off that he'd been wounded. After that, if there was a day without a letter my legs refused to carry me. He made excuses: 'Well, how can you get letters every day if they only bring us vodka once every ten days?' One letter was full of joy: 'Hoo-rah! We escorted a column to the Union. We reached the border and they wouldn't let us go any further, but at least we got a look at our Homeland from the distance. There's no better country anywhere.' In his last letter he wrote: 'If I survive the summer I'll come back.'

On 29 August I decided that the summer was over and I bought him a suit and a pair of shoes. They're hanging in the wardrobe.

30 August. Before I went to work I took off my earrings and my ring. Somehow I just couldn't wear them.

On 30 August he was killed.

I have my brother to thank for keeping me alive after my son died. For a week he lay beside my sofa at night, like a dog. Guarding me. There was only one thing on my mind: run to the balcony and jump off the seventh floor. I remember they carried the coffin into the room and I lay down on it and kept measuring it and measuring it. One metre, two metres. My son was almost two metres tall . . . I measured with my hands to see if the coffin matched his height. I talked to the coffin like a madwoman: 'Who's in there? Are you in there, son?' They brought him in a closed coffin. 'Here's your son, mother. We're giving him back to you . . .' I couldn't kiss him for the last time. Or stroke him. I didn't even see how he was dressed.

I said I would choose his place in the cemetery myself. They gave me two injections, and I went with my brother. There were already ' "Afghani" graves' on the main avenue. 'Put my son here too, with his own boys, he'll feel more cheerful.'

I don't remember who was with us, some boss or other, but he shook his head. 'It's not allowed to bury them together. We scatter them all over the cemetery.'

Oh, that got me furious. Oh, I was really furious now . . . 'Don't get angry, Sonya. Just don't get angry, Sonya,' my brother begged me. Was I supposed to be all smiles? They showed that Kabul of theirs on the television. But I wanted to take a machine gun and shoot all of them. I used to sit down in front of the television and 'shoot'. It was them who killed my Sasha. Then one time they showed an old woman, probably an Afghan mother. She looked straight at me and I thought: 'Her son's there and perhaps they killed him?' After her I stopped 'shooting'.

I'm not mad, but I'm waiting for him. They tell this story: they brought a mother a coffin, and she buried it. And then a year later her son came back . . . I'm waiting. I'm not mad.

A mother

Right from the beginning. I'll start from the moment when it all collapsed for me. When it all fell apart.

We were advancing on Jalalabad. A little girl about seven years old was standing beside the road. Her smashed arm was hanging by a thread, like a rag doll's. Her black-olive eyes were fixed on me. In shock from the pain . . . I jump down off the vehicle to pick her up and take her to our nurses. She bounds away from me in wild terror, like a little animal, and screams. She bolts, screaming, with her little arm dangling loose, about to fall off . . . I run after her, shouting. I catch her, hold her close and stroke her. She bites and scratches, trembling all over. As if some wild animal has grabbed her, and not a human being. And suddenly I'm struck like lightning by the incredible thought that she doesn't believe I want to save her, she thinks I want to kill her. Russians can't do anything else, they only kill . . .

A stretcher is carried by with an old Afghan woman sitting on it, smiling.

Someone asks: 'Where is she wounded?'

'In the heart,' a nurse says.

Like everyone else I went there with my eyes blazing – someone there needed me. I was willing to give my life for that! The way she ran away from me. The way she trembled! I'll never forget it . . .

I didn't have any dreams about war there. But here I fight battles at night. I catch up with that little girl . . . Those black-olive eyes . . .

'Maybe I should see a psychiatrist?' I asked the guys.

'What?'

'I'm still fighting.'

'We're all still fighting.'

Don't think they were some kind of supermen, sitting on dead bodies with a cigarette in their teeth, opening a tin of bully beef . . . Eating watermelons . . . Rubbish! They were just ordinary guys. Anyone could have ended up in our place – including the very guy who judges us now: 'You killed out there . . .' I'd love to smash that ugly mug in! If you weren't there, don't judge. You'll never be able to stand alongside us. And no one has any right to judge us. At least understand that. Try to . . . We've been left alone, face to face with this war: 'Sort out the mess for yourselves.' We feel guilty all the time; we have to make excuses all the time. Or keep quiet. Who do we have to make our excuses to? They stuck us out there; we trusted them. And guys died with that belief out there. Don't put the ones who were out there on the same level as the ones who sent them. A friend of mine was killed . . . Major Sasha Kravets. Tell his mother that he's guilty. Tell his wife. And his children. 'You're in good shape,' the doctor told me. What kind of good shape are we all in? We brought so much back inside us . . .

The way we felt about the Homeland out there was quite different. We called it 'the Union'. When we saw off the 'demobbers' it was: 'Be sure to give our greetings to the Union.' We thought we had something big and powerful watching our backs and it would always protect us. But I remember coming out of a battle with casualties – killed and seriously wounded. And that evening we switched on the television to distract ourselves, wondering what was going on back in the Union. A gigantic new factory has been built in Siberia. The Queen of England has held a dinner in honour of some high-ranking guest. In Voronezh teenagers have raped two little schoolgirls, out of sheer boredom. A prince has been killed in Africa . . . And we just feel like nobody needs us; the country just carries on with its own life . . . The first one to blow a fuse was Sasha Kuchinsky: 'Turn it off! Or I'll shoot that television right now.'

After action you report over the radio: 'Note down: six three-hundreds, four zero-twenty-ones.' The 'three-hundreds' are the wounded, the 'zero-twenty-ones' are the dead. You look at a dead man and think about his mother. I know that her son has been killed, but she doesn't know yet. Have they sent her the news? It's even worse if he fell into a river or a ravine and they didn't find the body. They tell his mother he's missing in action.

Whose war was it? The mothers' war – they fought it. And they'll carry on fighting it until they die. Nursing us and praying for us. For our souls. But the people as a whole didn't suffer. The people don't know. They were told we were fighting against 'armed gangs'. So in nine years a regular army of a hundred thousand men can't defeat scattered little groups of bandits? An army with the latest equipment . . . God help you if you get caught in one of our artillery bombardments when the Grad or Uragan rocket launchers are pounding a target. The telegraph poles are sent flying. You want to crawl into the ground, like an earthworm . . . And the 'bandits' had Maxim machine guns that we'd only seen in the movies. The Stinger missiles and Japanese recoilless shoulder-launched weapons – they got hold of those later . . . When prisoners were brought in they were thin, haggard men with work-worn peasants' hands. What sort of 'bandits' were these? This was a people!

We realized that out there: they didn't want this. And even if they did, what did *we* want it for? You ride past abandoned *kishlaks* . . . The smoke from a campfire is still floating in the air; there's a smell of food. A camel walks along trailing its guts behind it, as if its humps are unravelling. I have to shoot it . . . . But my mind is still programmed for a life of peace. I can't finish it off. I just don't have the heart. Someone else might go straight ahead and shoot the camel. Just like that! With enthusiasm, with wild abandon. Back in the Union he'd be put away for that; but here he's a hero. Taking revenge on the 'bandits'. Why do eighteen- and nineteen-year-olds kill so much more easily than thirty-year-olds, for instance? They feel no pity. After the war I suddenly discovered how terrifying children's fairy tales are. Someone's always being killed in them. The witch Baba Yaga actually roasts people in her oven, but children aren't frightened by that. They don't cry very often.

But I wanted to remain normal. A singer came to perform for us. A beautiful woman, with really soulful songs. And out there you long to see a woman; you wait for her like someone really close and dear to you. She came out on to the stage. 'On my way here, they let me fire a machine gun. I had so much fun firing it . . .' She started singing and at the chorus she said: 'Come on, boys, clap! Clap, boys!'

No one clapped. They didn't say anything. And she left, the concert fell through. The supergirl came to visit the supermen. But every day there were eight, nine or ten empty beds in those boys' barracks. The boys who used to sleep on them were already in the freezer. In the morgue. And in the barracks there were just letters laid out diagonally across the beds . . . From his mother, from his girl: 'Fly with a greeting – speed back with your answer . . .'

The most important thing in that war was to survive. Not to get blown up by a mine, not to get burned up in an armoured personnel carrier, not to become a target for a sniper. For some the important thing was not only to survive but to bring a few things home: a television, a sheepskin coat, a really fancy cassette player . . . There was this joke going round that people in the Union only learned about the war in the commission sales shops. From the new goods. In the winter I went back to our Smolensk and the girls were all wearing Afghan sheepskin coats. It was the fashion!

Every soldier has a little amulet hanging round his neck. 'What's that you've got there?' I ask.

'A little prayer my mother gave me.'

When I got back my mother confessed. 'Tolya, you don't know, but I put a spell on you; that's why you're alive and unhurt.'

When we went out on a raid, I put a note in the upper part of my clothes and another one in the lower part. If I got blown up, one part would be left, either the upper or the lower one. Or some used to wear bracelets with their name, blood group, rhesus factor and military service number. They never said 'I'll go' – it was 'I've been sent'. They never spoke the word 'last'. 'Let's go in one last time . . .' 'Have you totally lost it or what?' There's no such word . . . In a queue it's 'at the end', or 'fourth' or 'fifth'. But no one uses that word here.

War has mean, lousy laws: get your photo taken before you go out on a combat mission, and you get killed; shave, and you get killed. And the first to get killed were the ones who came aiming to be heroes – the blue-eyed boys. I met one who told me: 'I'm going to be a hero!' He was killed just like that, out of hand. Out on an operation we lie there, relieving ourselves – begging your pardon! – right there. It's a soldiers' saying: 'Better to wallow in your own shit than let the mines make shit of you.' We developed our own slang: a 'craft' was an aeroplane: a 'bulletproof' was an armoured vest; 'the bush' was bushes and thickets of reeds; a 'spinner' was a helicopter; 'glitches' meant he did drugs, saw things, jumped on a mine and blew himself up; a 'swapper' was someone who was leaving and going home. We made up enough slang to fill an *Afghan Soldier's Dictionary*.

Guys were killed most often during their first months and their last ones. During their first months they were too curious, and during their final months their defence centres switched off and they started acting stupid. At night they couldn't understand where they were, who they were, what it was all for. Was all this really happening to them? The 'swappers' don't sleep for six weeks or two months. They have their own way of calculating dates: '43 March' or '56 February' means 'I should be replaced at the end of March or the end of February'. They wait really hard, with all their hearts and souls. The menu in the mess: 'red fish' is sprats in tomato sauce, 'white fish' is sprats in oil. They're irritated by the flower-beds in the middle of the garrison. They're irritated by the jokes that just recently made them split their sides with laughter: they don't like them. It's strange that only yesterday and the day before, that seemed funny. What's so funny about it?

An officer comes to the Union on an assignment. He goes into a hairdresser's and the girl sits him in the chair. 'How's the situation in Afghanistan?'

'It's normalizing . . .'

A few minutes later: 'How's the situation in Afghanistan?'

'It's normalizing . . .'

After another little while: 'How's the situation in Afghanistan?'

'It's normalizing . . .'

He gets his haircut and leaves. The people in the hairdresser's are all scratching their heads. 'Why did you torment the man like that?'

'The moment I ask about Afghanistan his hair stands up on end. It's easier to cut like that.'

I like jokes. Little pieces of nonsense. But thinking seriously about things is frightening.

A Soviet pilot is shot down over Vietnam – we can change that to 'over Afghanistan' . . . The American CIA men show him parts of the plane that was shot down: 'Tell us what part this is. And this one? And this one?' He doesn't say anything. They beat him. He still doesn't say anything. And then there's an exchange of prisoners and he goes back to his own unit and they ask him: 'What's it like being a prisoner? Tough?' And he answers: 'No, it's not all that tough. But you have to learn all the equipment components off by heart. Or else they beat you badly.'

What draws me back there isn't the war, but the people. You wait and wait. And then on the last day it seems a shame to leave. You think you ought to have taken everybody's address. Everybody's . . .

Buttercup – that's what we used to call Valerka Shirokov, a delicate elegant guy. At the drop of a hat someone might sing out: 'Hands like buttercups . . .' But he was as tough as nails. Never said a single unnecessary word. We had this money grubber; he hoarded everything, used to buy stuff and swap stuff. Valerka stood right in front of him, took two hundred checks out of his own wallet, showed them to guy and then, right in front of his stupefied eyes, tore them into little pieces. And then he walked out without saying a word.

Sasha Rudik – the two of us saw in the New Year on a raid. For a New Year tree we set our automatics in a pyramid and hung grenades on them for toys. And we wrote 'Happy New Year!!!' on a

Grad rocket launcher with toothpaste. Three exclamation marks for some reason. Sasha was a good painter. I brought home a bedsheet with one of his landscapes on it. He didn't paint mountains. We stopped liking mountains out there. Ask anyone: 'What's making you so blue?' and the answer was 'I want to go in the forest . . . Swim in a river . . . Drink a big mug of milk . . .'

In a restaurant in Tashkent a waitress came up to us. 'Will you have milk, my darlings?'

'Two glasses each of plain water. We'll drink milk tomorrow. We've only just arrived.'

Everyone took a suitcase of jam and a birch-twig broom out there with them. They sell eucalyptus ones there, fantastic brooms. But no, we took our own birch-twig ones.

Sashik Lashchuk – he was a nice clean boy. He used to write home often. 'My parents are getting on a bit. They don't know I'm here. I make things up for them about Mongolia.' He came with a guitar and left with a guitar too.

There were all sorts of people there. Don't imagine we were all the same. First they said nothing at all about us, then they started imagining we were all heroes, and now they're debunking us, so they can forget about us later. Out there one guy might fling himself on a mine and save other guys that he didn't even know, but another might come up to you and say: 'If you like, I'll wash your laundry, just don't send me out on combat missions.'

The KamAZ trucks there would drive along with place names in big letters on their sun visors: 'Kostroma', 'Dubna', 'Leningrad', 'Naberezhnye Chelny'. Or 'I want to go to Alma-Ata!' If a Leningrader found another Leningrader, or a Kostroman found another Kostroman, they embraced like brothers. And in the Union we're still like brothers. Well, if a young guy's walking down the street with a crutch and a brand new medal, who else can it be but one of us? My brother . . . Our brother . . . We'll embrace, and sometimes we'll just sit on a bench and smoke a cigarette, and it feels like we've talked all day. We suffer from wasting disease . . . Out there it was a disparity between weight and height, but here it's a disparity between feelings and the ability to pour everything out, to spill it out in words and actions. We're all dystrophic in this life here.

We were travelling from the airport to a hotel. Our first few hours at home. We weren't talking, we'd gone quiet. Then at the same moment our nerves gave out and we all shouted to the driver: 'The ruts! The ruts! Stay in the ruts!' And then we laughed. And we felt happy: we're in the Union! We can drive along the shoulder of the road, or straight along the middle. Right across the whole world. The thought of it was enough to make us feel drunk.

A few days later we discovered something. 'Guys! We've all got a stoop.' We couldn't walk standing up straight; we'd forgotten how. For six months I used to tie myself to the bed at night to straighten myself out.

A meeting at the officers' club: 'Tell us about the romance of serving in Afghanistan.' 'Did you personally kill anyone?' The girls are particularly fond of bloodthirsty questions. It gives them a thrill. They ask: 'Could you have decided not to go to Afghanistan?' Me? I . . .

We only had one man who refused, a battery commander, Major Bondarenko: 'I'll defend my Homeland. I won't go to Afghanistan.' That was a military court of honour straightaway – they despised him for cowardice! What sort of male vanity was that? Was he supposed to put a noose round his neck or a pistol to his temple? He was immediately demoted or, as we say, they 'scattered his stars'. From being a major he became a captain. And he was sent to a construction battalion. Who'd want to go through that? They threw him out of the Party. Or through that? They threw him out of the army. Or through that? That's more terrible than ending up at war. Forty-five years old. Thirty-five of them spent in the army: the Suvorov College, the military academy. What can he do in civilian life? Start from scratch?

'What can you do?' they ask an officer.

'I can command a company or a platoon or a battery.'

'What else can you do?'

'I can dig.'

'What else?'

'I can not dig . . .'

In the customs on my way back they wiped my cassettes of a concert by Rosenbaum.

'Guys, these are great songs!'

'But we've got a list,' they said, showing me. 'It says which songs can be brought in and which can't.'

I arrived in Smolensk and Rosenbaum's songs were coming out of the windows of all the student hostels.

This policeman comes up to us. He needs to frighten some racketeers: 'Come on boys, give us a hand.' Or disband an unofficial gathering: 'Let's call the "Afghanis".' Supposedly an 'Afghani' is well used to all this, it's nothing to him: hard fists and a soft head. Everybody's afraid of us. Everybody loathes us. But when your arm hurts you don't go and cut it off. You take care of it to heal it. You nurse it.

Why do we get together? Together we try to save each other . . . But we still go home alone.

A major, artillery regiment propaganda officer

Every night I have exactly the same dream. It plays over and over again. Everybody shoots – I shoot too. Everybody runs – I run too. Then I fall, and wake up.

I'm in a hospital bed . . . I wake and I try to jump up off the bed, so I can go out into the corridor for a smoke. But I remember I haven't got any legs . . . And then I come back to reality . . .

I don't want to hear about any 'political error'! I don't want to know! If it was a mistake then give me back my legs . . . (*He flings away his crutches in despair.*) I'm sorry . . . I'm sorry. (*He sits there for a while and calms down.*)

What about you? Have you ever taken the unsent letters from a dead man's pocket? 'My dear darling . . .' 'Dearest . . .' 'My love . . .' Have you ever seen a soldier shot simultaneously by a matchlock arquebus and a Chinese automatic rifle?

They sent us there, and we followed orders. In the army you have to carry out an order first; only then can you appeal against it. If they tell you 'Forward!' – then it's forward. Otherwise you can hand in your Party card. Did you swear an oath? You did. It's no good switching to mineral water after your kidneys have already failed. 'We didn't send you out there.' Then who did?

I had a friend out there. When I went on a mission he used to see me off. When I got back he used to hug me. He was a real live wire! I'll never have a friend like that here . . .

I don't go outside very often. I still feel embarrassed. Have you ever fastened on our artificial legs, or seen them from close up? Walking on them you're afraid of breaking your neck. They say that in other countries men with artificial limbs go skiing, play tennis and dance. So buy those with our foreign currency, instead of French cosmetics. Instead of Cuban sugar. Or Moroccan oranges and Italian furniture.

I'm twenty-two. I have my whole life ahead of me. I have to look for a wife. I used to have a girl. I told her 'I hate you' – to make her go away. She pitied me. But I want someone to *love* me.

> At night I dream of my own dear home,
> And the edge of a forest with rowan trees.
> Thirty, fifty, ninety, a hundred times . . .
> Cuckoo, how long will you call to me?

Of all our songs that's my favourite. But sometimes I don't even want to live through the day.

Even now I still dream of catching sight of it, just out of the corner of my eye: that patch of land. That biblical desert. We all feel drawn there. The way you feel when you stand on the edge of a precipice or somewhere high above water. The feeling's so strong it makes you dizzy.

The war's over. Now they'll try to forget about us – try to hide us somewhere well out of sight. Try to push us aside. That's the way it was with the Winter War in Finland. All those books that have been written about the Great Patriotic War, and nothing about the Winter War. No one likes to remember a war that was lost. In ten years' time I'll get used to that. And I won't give a damn.

Did I kill anyone there? Yes, I killed! Did you think we could all stay angels out there? Were you expecting angels to come back?

A senior lieutenant, commander of a mortar platoon

I was serving in the Soviet Far East. I was summoned to the unit command. The duty telephone operator handed me a telegram: 'Send Senior Lieutenant Ivanov to army HQ for consideration of his transfer to the Turkestan military region in order to continue his service.' Date and time. I'd been expecting to be sent to Cuba, because when I had the medical exam they talked about a country with a hot climate.

They asked me: 'You don't object if we send you on a tour of duty abroad, do you?'

'No, I don't mind, sir.'

'You're going to Afghanistan.'

'Yes, sir.'

'You know they shoot people and kill them out there . . .'

'Yes, sir.'

What kind of life do army sappers have in the Union? They dig things with spades and smash things with picks. But I wanted to use what I'd been taught at the military academy. Sappers are always needed in a war. I went to learn how to fight . . .

Out of everyone who was summoned only one refused. He was summoned three times.

'You don't object if we send you on a tour of duty abroad, do you?'

'Yes, I do object, sir.'

I wouldn't want to be in his boots. They gave him an immediate reprimand, and now there's a stain on his name as an officer – he'll never get a promotion again. He refused because of his health; it was either gastritis he had, or peptic ulcers. But they didn't take any notice of that. Whether the climate's hot or not, if they suggest it you've got to go. The lists have already been printed.

It took me six days to get from Khabarovsk to Moscow by train. All the way across Russia, crossing the Siberian rivers, travelling along the shore of Lake Baikal. After the first day and night the attendant ran out of tea, and on the second day the boiler broke down. My family met me and they cried a bit. But you have to do what you have to do.

The plane's hatch opened and there was a bright blue sky. In Russia it's only above a river that we have a sky as blue as it is there. There was bustling and shouting, but they were all our people. Some meeting a 'replacement', some meeting friends, some waiting for a parcel from their family in the Union. All of them tanned and jolly. I couldn't believe any more that somewhere it was minus thirty-five degrees Celsius and the armour plating was freezing cold. I saw my first Afghan at the transit point, over the top of the barbed-wire fence. I was interested, but I didn't have any other feelings. Just a man like any other.

I got my papers for Bagram as the commander of a road-building platoon in an engineering battalion. We got up early in the morning and set out as if we were going to a regular job: a tank with a mine flail, a group of snipers, a mine sniffer dog and two armoured personnel carriers as our escort. For the first few kilometres we rode on the armour plating. We had a good view of the track marks from there: the road was dusty and the dust was a layer of fine powder, like snow. If a bird landed it left a track mark. If a tank had passed that way the day before we had to keep our eyes skinned: they could bury a mine in the impressions left by a caterpillar track. They imitated the patterns, using their fingers, and swept their own tracks clean with a sack or a turban.

The road twisted past two dead *kishlaks*; there were no people here, nothing but scorched clay. An excellent hiding-place. We always had to be on the lookout. When we'd passed the *kishlaks* we climbed down off the armour plating. And now we did things this way: the dog ran on ahead, weaving to and fro, and the sappers followed it with a probe, walking along and stabbing the ground. Doing this you had to rely on God, your intuition, your experience and your gut instinct. A broken branch here; a lump of iron, which wasn't there yesterday; and a rock over that way. They used to leave signs for themselves so they wouldn't get blown up.

One lump of metal, then another, some kind of bolt. They seem to be just lying in the dust. But under the ground there are batteries. And a wire to a bomb or a crate of TNT . . . An anti-tank mine can't feel a man. It detonates under a load of two hundred and fifty or three hundred kilogrammes. The first time someone got blown up I was the only one left sitting on the tank. My place was beside the gun barrel and the turret protected me. The others were swept away by the blast. I immediately felt myself to check that my head was still there. Were my arms and legs still there? They were, and we moved on.

Up ahead there was another blast. A lightly armoured articulated truck had run on to a powerful landmine. The truck had split in half, and the crater was three metres long and as deep as the height of a man. The truck had been carrying mortar bombs, about two hundred of them. The bombs were lying in the bushes and at the side of the road, fanned right out. There had been five soldiers in the truck, and a senior lieutenant. The two of us had spent the evening together a few times, smoking and talking. No one was left alive.

The dogs were a great help. They're like people: some are talented, some aren't; some have good intuition – some don't. A sentry will fall asleep, but a dog won't. I loved one especially. He used to fawn on our men and bark at the Afghan soldiers. Their uniform was brighter green than ours, yellowish. But how could he tell the difference? He could smell mines from several paces away and he used to brace himself against the ground: don't come close!

There were various kinds of booby traps. The most dangerous were the homemade mines. They were never the same twice; you couldn't spot any pattern to them. Or any technical standards! An old rusty kettle filled with explosive. Or a cassette player, or a clock. A tin can . . . If someone went anywhere without a sapper we called him a 'suicide pilot'. Mines on a road, mines on a mountain track, mines in a house. The sappers went first, like scouts.

We were stuck in this entrenchment. There'd already been one detonation in it, but we'd done a bit of looting and we'd been hanging around there for two days. I jumped down and there was this explosion! I didn't lose consciousness. I looked up at the sky. It was glowing . . . A sapper's first reaction after a blast is to look at the sky. To see if his eyes are intact. I used to carry a tourniquet around my rifle butt. They used that tourniquet to tie me off above the knee. I already knew that they amputated three to five centimetres above the place where the tourniquet was applied.

'Where are you putting that tourniquet?' I shouted at the soldier.

'It's right up to your knee, comrade senior lieutenant.'

And then they drove me fifteen kilometres to the field hospital. It took an hour and a half. They washed my wounds there and gave me a procaine nerve block. The first day, as they cut my leg off, the saw buzzed like a sawmill: I blacked out. The second day they operated on my eyes. The flame from the blast had hit me in the face. You could say they patched my eyes back together – there were twenty-two sutures. They took them out two or three each day, so that the eyeball wouldn't fall apart. They used to come up and shine a little torch at me from the left and then from the right, to see if there was any sensitivity to light in the site of the retina. The light of that little torch was red. It has to be the strongest light possible.

I could write a story about an officer being transformed into a home-based worker. I assemble light sockets . . . A hundred a day. I rivet on the little wires. What wires? Red, black, white – I don't know. I can't see. I'm almost blind. Not totally, but I guess and figure things out more than I see them. I crochet nets. I glue little boxes together. I used to think only madmen did this kind of work . . . Thirteen nets a day. I already match the normal quota.

Sappers didn't have much chance of coming back unhurt, or even coming back at all – especially the ones in the mine-clearing and special mine-clearing companies. They were either wounded or killed. When we set out on an operation we never shook hands as we left. The day I got blown up the new company commander shook my hand. He did it from the heart; no one had warned him yet. And I went flying . . . Believe it or not – please yourself. There was this belief that, if you'd asked to come to Afghanistan, then things would end badly; but if you'd been sent, it was a soldier's duty, and maybe you'd get through it okay. And go back home.

What do I dream about now? A long minefield. I'm filling out the record form: the number of mines, a drawing of the rows and reference-points for finding them. But my form has got lost. They often used to get lost. Or you could take a form where the reference-point was a tree, but it had burned down. Or it was a group of rocks, but they'd been blown up. No one used to go and check. They were afraid. They could get blown up by their own mines. In my dream I see children running about beside my minefield. They don't know that there are mines there. I have to shout to them: 'There are mines! Don't go that way!' I have to get there before them. I run. I have both my legs again . . . And I see . . .

But that's only at night, only in my dreams . . .

A senior lieutenant, sapper

I can't do everything like everyone else. I can't live that way. Maybe it's all ridiculous. With that war. But I'm a romantic kind of person. I think that I've never really lived, and I'm not living now. I'm always dreaming about life. Inventing it, picturing it.

The very first day after I got there, the head of the hospital summoned me and asked: 'What made you come here?' He didn't understand . . . A man. I had to tell him my entire life story. Tell an absolute stranger, a man I didn't know. A soldier. Like on the parade ground. That was the most painful and humiliating thing for me there. There's nothing secret or intimate, everything's dragged into the open and exposed. Have you seen the film *Zapredel*, about convict life in a prison camp? We lived according to the same laws. The same barbed wire, the same little patch of ground.

My circle was the serving women and the cooks. The conversations were about roubles, checks, meat with bones and without, smoked sausage and Bulgarian biscuits. To my way of understanding it was self-sacrifice, a woman's duty – to protect our boys, to save them! I had an exalted view of everything. Men were bleeding to death, so I would give my blood. I'd already realized at the transit point in Tashkent that I was going to the wrong place. I got into the plane and I cried, I couldn't stop. It was the same there as it is here, the same things that I was running away from, that I wanted to turn my back on. At the transit point the vodka flowed like a river. 'And we dream of the grass at the cosmodrome . . . The green, green grass . . .' It was as if I'd flown out into space.

Here in the Union, everyone has their own home, their own castle. But out there . . . There were four of us in one room. A girl who worked as a cook used to bring meat from the mess and stick it under her bed.

'Wash the floor,' she said.

'I washed it yesterday. It's your turn today.'

'Wash it, I'll give you a hundred roubles.'

I didn't say anything.

'I'll give you some meat.'

I didn't say anything. So she took the bucket of water and poured it over my bed.

'Ha, ha, ha, ha.' Everybody laughed.

Another girl, a serving woman, used to swear like a trooper but liked the poems of Marina Tsvetaeva. After her shift she sat there playing patience. 'Yes there will be, no there won't . . . Yes there will be, no there won't be . . .'

'What will there be or won't there be?'

'Love – what else?'

And there were weddings there. Genuine weddings! And love. But not often. Love only lasted as far as Tashkent: he turned left from there and she turned right. Like in the song: 'She's going the other way'.

Tanya Betzer (tall and large) liked to sit up late and talk. She only drank neat alcohol.

'How can you do that?'

'What do you mean? Vodka's too weak. It doesn't do anything for me.'

She took home five or six hundred postcards of movie stars. They're expensive in the *dukans*. She used to flaunt them: 'I don't begrudge money for art.'

I remember Verochka Kharkova sitting in front of a mirror and sticking her tongue out. She was afraid of typhoid fever and someone had told her that you had to look in a mirror every morning. If you had typhoid there would be impressions from your incisors on your tongue.

They didn't accept me. What a stupid fool, carrying around test tubes with microbes! I worked as a medical bacteriologist. I was always talking about the same things: typhoid, hepatitis or paratyphoid. The wounded didn't get into hospital straightaway. They used to lie up in the mountains, in the sand, for five to ten hours, or a day, or even two. Their wounds were invaded by microbes: 'wound infection' it's called. A man might be in intensive care for his wounds and I would discover he had typhoid fever as well.

They died without saying anything. I only once saw an officer burst into tears. A Moldavian. A surgeon who was Moldavian went over and asked him in his own language: 'What's bothering you, my friend? Where does it hurt?'

And the officer burst into tears. 'Save me. I must live. I have a wife and a daughter and I love them. I must go back . . .'

He would have died without saying anything, but he burst into tears because he heard his own native tongue.

I couldn't go into the morgue. They used to bring in human flesh ground up with soil. And then there was that meat under the girls' beds. They used to put their frying pans on the table and cry 'Ruba! Ruba!' That means 'Forward!' in Afghan. The heat . . . Their sweat used to drip into the frying pans. I only saw wounded men and dealt with microbes. But I couldn't go and sell the microbes, could I? In the canteen shop you could buy caramels for hard currency checks. I fantasized about them!

'Afghanistan, What a Lovely Place!' – that was a song they used to sing. I was always afraid, to be quite honest. I'm not brave. When I went there I couldn't even make sense of all the stars on the shoulder straps, the ranks. I used to speak respectfully to everyone. I don't remember who, but someone in the hospital kitchen gave me two raw eggs, because doctors were always half-starved. Our diet was potato paste, and frozen meat that had been stored in army food depots since time immemorial – from the old reserves, it was as hard as wood, colourless, odourless . . . I grabbed those two eggs and wrapped them in a napkin, thinking I'd eat them at home with onions. All day long I thought about the supper I was going to have. Then they brought in a boy on a trolley, who was being evacuated to Tashkent. I couldn't see what there was under the sheet; all I saw was his handsome head lolling about on the pillow. He looked up at me. 'I'm hungry.' It was just before lunch, but they hadn't brought the mess kettles yet. They were taking him away – and who knew when his plane would take off and they would feed him? 'Here,' I said, and gave him the two eggs. I turned and walked away without asking if he had any arms or legs. I put the eggs on his pillow. I didn't break them and I didn't feed him. What if he'd really had no arms?

Another time I spent two hours riding in a truck with dead bodies right there beside me. Four bodies. They were lying there in tracksuits.

I came back home. I couldn't listen to music, or talk in the street or the trolleybus. I just wanted to close the door of my room and be alone with the television. The day before I flew back to the Union the chief medical officer of our hospital, Yury Yefimovich Zhibkov, shot himself. Why? What was going on in his soul? Some people couldn't understand, but I do . . . I understand, in fact I know. Out there it's always close by . . . that darkness.

In Afghanistan I copied this from one of the officers: 'A foreigner, who happens to find himself in Afghanistan, will be under the special protection of heaven if he comes out of there well, unharmed and with his head still on his shoulders' – the words of a Frenchman called Fourier. You had to survive not just physically. A human being is a creature with a complex filling. A puff pastry pie, as the girls used to say. They started philosophizing a bit towards the end of the war. Before they came home . . .

I see a young man in the street and there's something touching and familiar about him. He must be an 'Afghani'! But I don't call to him, so as not to look ridiculous. I'm not brave. I've got a soft character. I was frightened when I found myself thinking that I might be turning into an aggressive, cruel creature. Man is a dependent being, after all. He doesn't even completely understand how much he's governed by his own past actions and by what has been done to him. He's afraid . . . When we were getting ready to discharge boys they hid in the attics and the basement areas of the hospital. They didn't want to be discharged to their units. We used to catch them and drag them out. At the transit point the young girls taught me who I should give a bottle of vodka to in order to get a cushy spot . . . They taught me. They were eighteen or twenty, and I was forty-five.

In the customs, when I was on the way back home, they made me undress right down to my bra. 'Who are you?'

'A medical bacteriologist.'

'Show us your documents.' They took the documents. 'Open the suitcases, we're going to frisk them.' I was taking back my old coat, a blanket, a bedspread, hairpins and other bits and bobs. Everything that I'd brought from home. They tipped it out on to the table. 'Are you some kind of crazy woman? I suppose you write poetry, do you?'

I can't bear it here. It's more frightening here than it is out there. When someone went back out there from the Union, and brought something to drink, we all sat down at one table. The third toast was silent – for those who had been killed. We sat there at the table, with the mice strolling about, climbing into our shoes. At four in the morning there was a howl . . . The first time we jumped up: 'It's wolves, girls.' The girls laughed: 'It's the mullah making the call to prayer.' For a long time at home I used to wake up at four in the morning.

I wanted to carry on with that work, so I've asked to go to Nicaragua. Somewhere where there's a war going on. Here . . . I don't know how to live here any longer . . .

A medical bacteriologist

I chose him first. A tall, handsome boy, standing there. 'Girls,' I said, 'he's mine.' I walked over and invited him to the ladies' waltz – that's when the girls invite boys. But I was inviting my destiny.

I really wanted a son. We agreed that if it was a girl I'd name her. She would be Olechka. If it was a boy then he would name him. He'd be Artyom or Denis. So Olechka was born.

'And will we have a little son?'

'Yes. Just let Olechka grow up a bit.' I would have given him a son too.

'Lyuba, don't be frightened. You'll lose your milk' – I was breast-feeding the little baby – 'They're sending me to Afghanistan.'

'Why you? You've got a little child.'

'If not me then someone else will get the short straw. The Party has given the order and the Komsomol has replied "Yes, sir."'

He was a dedicated army man. 'Orders,' he used to say, 'are not for discussion.' In their family his mother had a very strong character; he was used to doing as he was told, obeying orders. Being in the army was easy for him.

How did we see him off? The men smoked. His mother didn't say anything. I cried: 'Who needs this war?' Our daughter slept in her cot.

Outside in the street I met the local idiot, a deranged girl who often used to show up at the market or in the shop in our garrison. People said she had been raped when she was young, and since then she didn't even recognize her mother. She stopped beside me. 'Now they'll bring your husband back in a box,' she laughed and ran off.

I didn't know what would happen, but I knew that something would.

I waited for him, like in that poem by Konstantin Simonov: 'Wait for me, and I'll return . . .' I could write three or four letters a day and post them all. It seemed to me that, when I thought about him and longed for him, I was taking care of him. He wrote to say that there, at the war, everyone did his own job. They followed orders. But everyone had his own destiny. Don't worry and wait.

When I visited his parents no one ever mentioned Afghanistan. Neither his mother nor his father. It wasn't a definite decision, but everyone was afraid of that word.

I dressed our little girl to take her to kindergarten, and kissed her. I opened the door and there were soldiers standing outside. One of them was holding my husband's suitcase, the small brown one that I had packed. Something happened to me . . . 'If I let them in, they'll bring something terrible into our home,' I thought. 'I won't let them in, and everything will stay the way it is.'

'Is he wounded?' I still had that hope – that he'd only been wounded.

The military commissar came in first. 'Ludmila Iosifovna, it is with profound sorrow that I must inform you that your husband . . .'

I had no tears. I screamed. I saw a friend of his and leaped at him. 'Tolik, if you tell me, I'll believe you. Why don't you say anything?'

He brought over the warrant officer who had accompanied the coffin. 'Tell her . . .' But the warrant officer was trembling. He didn't say anything either.

Some woman came up to me and kissed me. 'Calm down. Give us his family's phone numbers.'

I sat down and immediately blurted out all the addresses and phone numbers, dozens of addresses and phone numbers that I usually never remembered. They checked them afterwards in my address book – they were all exactly right.

We had only a small, one-room flat, so they left the coffin in the unit's club. I put my arms round it and shouted: 'Why you? When did you ever do anything bad to anyone?'

When I regained consciousness I looked at that box: 'They'll bring your husband back in a box . . .' And I shouted out again. 'I don't believe my husband is in there. Prove to me that he is. There isn't even a little window. What have you brought me? Who have you brought me?'

They called his friend. 'Tolik,' I said, 'swear to me that my husband is in there.'

'I swear on my daughter that your husband is in there. He died immediately, without suffering. I can't tell you any more than that.'

His own words had come true: 'If you have to die, it's best to go without suffering.' And we were left behind . . .

There's a big photograph of him hanging on the wall. 'Get papa down for me,' my daughter asks. 'I'm going to play with papa.' She surrounds the photograph with her toys and talks to him. I'm putting her to bed at night and she asks: 'Which part of papa did they shoot at? Why did they choose our papa?' I take her to kindergarten. In the evening, when I have to take her home, she bawls: 'I won't leave until papa comes to get me. Where's my papa?'

I don't know how to answer her. How can I explain? I'm only twenty-one myself. This summer I took her to my mother in the country. Perhaps she'll forget him there . . . I don't have the strength to cry every day. And every minute. If I see a husband and wife walking along together, with a child – I cry. My heart screams out, my body screams out . . . I remember our love. Pardon me for being so frank. I can only confide in you, someone I don't know. It's hard to talk to anyone close to you. 'If you could just come back for one minute . . . and see how your daughter has grown!' I tell him at night. 'For you that senseless war is over. But not for me. And for our daughter? Our children are the most unfortunate ones – they'll bear the brunt of everything. Do you hear me . . .'

Who am I shouting to? Who will hear me?

A wife

I used to dream that I would have a son . . . I would bear for myself a man whom I would love and who would love me.

My husband and I separated. He left me for a young woman and she had his child immediately after she left school. I suppose I must have loved him, because there hasn't been anyone else. And I haven't looked.

I raised my son with my mother: two women and a little boy. I used to get up quietly and watch from the door of the building to see who he was spending his time with. 'Mama,' he used to say when he came back home, 'I'm grown-up now, but you're still keeping an eye on me.'

He was as small as a girl, white and fragile; he was born at eight months and bottle-fed. Our generation couldn't produce healthy children; we grew up during the war – with the shelling, the shooting and the hunger . . . the fear . . . He always used to play with the girls – the girls accepted him, he didn't fight. He liked cats and used to tie ribbons on them.

'Buy us a hamster, mama. They've got warm fur; it feels wet.' The hamster was bought. And a fish tank. And little fish. When we went to the market he would say: 'Buy me a live chicken. A speckled hen.'

I wonder about it: did he really fire a gun out there? My home-loving boy . . . He wasn't made for war. We loved him very much; we cherished him.

We went to visit him at the training camp in Ashkhabad.

'Andriusha, I want to go and talk to the commanding officer. You're my only child. And the border's very close here.'

'Don't you dare, mama. They'll laugh at me and call me a little mother's boy. They already call me "flimsy, mimsy and timid" as it is.'

'How are things for you here?'

'We've got a good lieutenant; he treats us like equals. But the captain can slap you in the face.'

'What? Your granny and I never hit you, even when you were little.'

'It's a man's life here, mama. I'd better not tell you and granny anything about it.'

He was only all mine when he was little. I used to wash him in the bath and he climbed out into the puddles of water like a little imp; I wrapped him in a sheet and hugged him. I thought no one would ever take him away from me. I wouldn't let anyone have him. But they took him away from me after all.

After the eighth year in school I persuaded him to go to the building trade school. I thought it would be easier for him in the army with a qualification like that. And after he'd served his time he could go on to a college. He wanted to be a forest ranger. He was always so happy in the forest. He could recognize birds from their songs and he showed me where all the different flowers were. In that way he reminded me of his father. He was a Siberian; he loved nature so much that he wouldn't let them cut the grass in the courtyard: 'Let everything grow!' Andriusha liked the forest ranger's uniform and the peaked cap: 'Mama, it's like an army uniform.'

And now I wonder if he really fired a gun out there.

He often used to write from Ashkhabad to me and his granny. I learned one letter off by heart – I held it in my hands a thousand times:

'Hello, my dear mama and granny! I've been in the army now for more than three months. Things are going well for me here. So far I've coped with all the assignments I've been set and I haven't had any reprimands from the command. Not long ago our company went to visit the field training camp eighty kilometres from Ashkhabad, up in the mountains. They all did two weeks of mountain training, studying tactics and firing small arms. Three of the men and I didn't go to the camp – we were helping out at the base. They kept us here because we're working at a furniture factory, building a workshop. And for that the factory will make tables for our company. We do bricklaying and plastering there.

'Mama, you asked about your letter. I got it, and I also got the parcel and the ten roubles that you put in it. My friend and I used the money to eat in the canteen a few times and we bought sweets . . .'

I comforted myself with the hope that, if he was doing plastering work and laying bricks, he was needed as a builder. Let him build their personal dachas and garages, as long as they didn't send him off anywhere. He wrote later that he was working for some general out in the country.

It was 1981. There were rumours going round, but not many people knew that Afghanistan was a bloody massacre, a slaughterhouse. On the television we saw Soviet and Afghan soldiers fraternizing, flowers on our armoured personnel carriers, peasants kissing the land they had been given. Only one thing made me feel frightened. When I went to see him in Ashkhabad, I met a woman there. At the hotel they told me first of all: 'We don't have any places.'

'I'll sleep on the floor then. I've come a long way to see my son, a soldier. And I won't leave.'

'Well, all right then; we'll let you into a four-bed room. There's one mother in it already, she's visiting her son too.'

That woman was the first to tell me that they were planning a new levy for Afghanistan; she said she had brought a lot of money to save her son. She was going away satisfied, and when we parted she gave me this advice: 'Don't be a naive idiot.' When I told my mother about this she started crying: 'Why didn't you throw yourself at their feet? Why didn't you beg? You could have taken your earrings off and given those to them.' Those cheap earrings were the most expensive things in our home. They didn't even have any diamonds in them! But my mother had lived an extremely modest life, and to her they seemed like a fortune. My God! The things they do to us! If he hadn't gone someone else would have. And that boy has a mother too.

Even to Andriusha it came as a surprise that he'd been put in an airborne assault battalion and was flying out to Afghanistan. He was bursting with boyish pride. And he didn't try to hide it.

I'm a woman and strictly a civilian. Perhaps there are things I don't understand. But let them explain to me why my son was doing plastering work and laying bricks at the time when he should have been training for battle. They knew where they were sending them. The newspapers published pictures of the mujahedeen. Thirty- or forty-year-old men. On their own land. With their families and children nearby. And tell me how, just one week before he flew out there, he was suddenly moved from a combat services unit to an airborne assault battalion? Even I know what airborne assault forces are and what strong young men they need. They have to be specially trained. And the commander of the training camp told me: 'Your son was an outstanding student in military and political training.' When did that happen? Where? At the furniture factory? At the general's dacha? Who did I give my son to? Who did I trust him to? They didn't even try to make a soldier of him.

There was only one letter from Afghanistan: 'Don't worry, it's beautiful here and calm. Lots of flowers that we don't have, trees in blossom and birds singing. Lots of fish.' Paradise, not a war. He was reassuring us in case, God forbid, we might start making a fuss, trying to get him out of there. Boys who had never faced bullets. Almost children. They were thrown into the fire and they took it as an honour. That was the way we raised them.

He was killed in the very first month. My boy. My darling. What did he look like, lying there? I'll never know.

They brought him back ten days later. For all those ten days I'd dreamed that I'd lost something and I couldn't find it. For all those ten days the kettle wailed in the kitchen. I put it on to make tea and it sang in different voices. I like houseplants: I have lots of them on the windowsills, on the wardrobe, on the bookshelves. Every morning when I watered them, I dropped the pots. They slid out of my hands and broke. The air was filled with the smell of damp earth.

Three cars stopped in front of the building: two army jeeps and an ambulance. I guessed immediately that they were coming to us, to our home. I went to the door myself and opened it. 'Don't tell me! Don't tell me anything! I hate you! Just give me my son's body. I'll bury him my way. Alone. I don't want any military honours . . .'

Write it! Write the truth! The whole truth! I'm not afraid of anything any more. I've been afraid all my life. I've had enough.

A mother

The truth? Only a reckless man will tell you the truth. A reckless man will tell you absolutely everything.

Nobody knows the truth. Apart from us. The truth is too terrible; the truth will never be told. Nobody will want to be the first; nobody will take the risk. Who's going to tell you how they transported drugs in the coffins? And fur coats. Who's going to show you a string of dried human ears? Have you heard about that already, or is it news to you? War trophies. They used to keep them in matchboxes. They curled up into these little leaves. Impossible? Is it embarrassing to hear things like that about our glorious Soviet young men? Well, it is possible! It happened! That's another truth that none of you can get away from. It can't just be blanked out, painted over. And you thought: 'We'll just put up some monuments and that will be it. We'll just give out some medals'?

I didn't go there to kill; I was a normal human being. They impressed on us that it was bandits we were fighting there; we'd be heroes, everyone would thank us. I remember the posters very clearly: 'Soldiers, let us strengthen the southern borders of our Homeland!' 'We will not shame the honour of our forces!' 'Flourish, Homeland of Lenin!' 'Glory to the Communist Party of the Soviet Union!' And then I came back. Out there I only had a little mirror all the time, but I have a big mirror here. When I looked into it I didn't recognize myself. There was someone else looking out at me. New eyes, a new face. My entire appearance had changed.

I was serving in Czechoslovakia when I heard they were sending me to Afghanistan.

'Why me?'

'You're a bachelor.'

I packed as if I was going on a business trip. What should I take with me? No one knew. We didn't have any 'Afghanis' with us. Someone advised me to take rubber boots, but I never had any use for them in two years. I left them in Kabul. We flew from Tashkent sitting on crates of cartridges. We landed in Shindand. The *Tsarandoi*, their police, had Russian automatic rifles from the time of the Great Patriotic War and their soldiers were filthy, with tattered uniforms, as if they'd just climbed out of the trenches. A sharp contrast with what I was used to in Czechoslovakia. They were loading wounded men into a helicopter, and one man had a piece of shrapnel in his stomach. 'He's a goner, he'll die on the way,' I heard one of the helicopter crew say. I was staggered by how calmly they spoke about death.

Probably that was the most inscrutable thing out there – the attitude to death. And again, if you want the whole truth . . . that's impossible. What's unthinkable here is commonplace there. Killing is terrifying and repellent. But very soon you start thinking that although killing right up close *is* terrifying and repellent, killing together, en masse, is exciting and sometimes – I saw it – even fun. In peacetime the guns are stacked in pyramids, every pyramid with its own lock, and the armoury has an acoustic alarm system. But there you had your weapon with you all the time – you got used to it. In the evening we used to fire a pistol at the lightbulb from bed. We were too lazy to get up and turn the light off. When the heat drove us crazy we used to empty our automatics into the air, just to fire at something ... We surround a caravan and it resists, with machine gun fire. The order's given: wipe the caravan out ... We switch into extermination mode. The air's filled with the wild roaring of wounded camels. So is that what they gave us medals on behalf of the grateful Afghan people for?

War is war: you have to kill. They didn't give us deadly weapons so we could play at soldiers with the other kids in our class, did they? Or so we could fix tractors and seed drills and such? We were being killed, and we killed too. We killed where we could. We killed where we wanted. But this wasn't the war that we knew from books and films, with battle fronts, no-man's-land, front lines. It was *kirgiz* war. The *kirgizes* were underground channels that had been built at some time for irrigation. Men appeared out of them day and night, like ghosts. With automatic rifles, with rocks in their hands. It's quite possible that not long ago you were haggling with this ghost in a *dukan*, but here he's beyond the bounds of your fellow-feeling. He's just killed your friend. What's lying there instead of your friend isn't a man any more. It's only half-human. His last words were: 'Don't write to my mother about this, I beg you; she mustn't ever find out.' And you, *shuravi*, Soviet man, you're beyond the bounds of his fellow-feeling too. Your artillery raked his *kishlak* and he could hardly find anything left of his mother or his wife or his children. And if you fall into his hands he'll make mincemeat cutlets out of you. Modern weapons increase the gravity of our crimes. With a knife I could kill one man, or two. With a bomb it's dozens. But I'm a soldier: killing is my profession. How does it go in that fairy tale? 'I am the slave of Aladdin's magic lamp ...' I am the slave of the Ministry of Defence. I'll shoot at whatever they tell me to shoot at. Shooting is my profession.

But I didn't come here to kill. I didn't want to kill. How did it happen? Why didn't the Afghan people take us for who we really were? The *bachata* stand there in the frost with rubber galoshes on their bare feet, and our boys give them their dry rations. I saw that with my own eyes. A tattered little kid runs up to the personnel carrier.

He doesn't ask for anything; like the others he just looks. I had twenty afghanis in my pocket and I gave them to him. He went down on his knees in the sand and didn't get up again until we got into the personnel carrier and drove away. But nearby something different was happening. Our patrols were taking money from the water boys. What kind of money was that? Miserable kopecks. No, I don't want to go there, not even as a tourist. I'll never go there. I told you: 'The truth is too terrible; the truth will never be told.' Nobody needs it. Neither you who stayed here, nor us who were out there. There are more of you, mind. Our children will grow up and hide the fact that their fathers fought out there.

I've met frauds: 'I was out in Afghanistan. We did this out there, I did that . . .'

'Where did you serve?'

'In Kabul.'

'What unit?'

'I was in the special forces . . .'

In the Kolyma prison camps, in the huts where they kept the madmen, people used to shout 'I'm Stalin! I'm Stalin!' But now normal young guys shout 'I was in Afghanistan!' They're insane. They should put them in the funny farm!

I remember it when I'm on my own. I have a drink and just sit. I like to listen to the 'Afghani' songs. But on my own. It happened . . . Those pages. They may be smeared with filth, but there's no getting away from them. The guys get together and they feel bitter and cheated. It's hard for them to find themselves, to acquire any kind of moral values. One confessed to me: 'If I knew nothing would happen to me I could kill a man. Just like that. For nothing. I wouldn't care.' Afghanistan happened, and now it's over. I'm not going to spend the rest of my life praying and repenting. I want to get married. I want a son. The sooner we shut up about it the better it will be for everyone. Who needs this truth? The rabble! So that they can revile us: 'Ah, those bastards! They killed people out there, they looted, and here they get special benefits?' And we'll be left as the only ones to blame, with everything we went through down the drain. But I'd like to preserve it, if only for myself.

What was it all for? What for?

I went into the toilet at a railway station in Moscow and I saw it belonged to a cooperative company. A young guy was sitting there, counting the money, with a sign above his head that said: 'Entrance free for children up to seven years of age, invalids, veterans of the Great Patriotic War and internationalist soldiers'.

I was staggered. 'Did you think that up yourself?'

'Yes,' he said proudly. 'Show your ID and go in.'

'My father went right through the war, and I spent two years swallowing foreign sand, just so that you would let me urinate for free?'

I never felt so much hate for anyone in Afghanistan as I did for that young guy. He decided he could pay us . . .

A senior lieutenant, artillery crew commander

I flew back to the Union on leave and went into a bathhouse. People were groaning in pleasure on the bunks, and to me it sounded like wounded men . . .

At home I used to miss my friends in Afghanistan. But after a few days in Kabul I was dreaming of home. I come from Simferopol and I graduated from music school. Happy people don't come here. All the women here are lonely and needy. You try living on a hundred and twenty roubles a month – that's my pay – and I want to dress well, and take interesting holidays. They ask me: 'Did you come here to find a fiancé?' Well, so what if it's true . . . ? Well, yes, it's true. I'm thirty-two and I'm single . . .

Here I learned that the most terrible mine is the 'Italian'. After one of those they collect a man up in a bucket. A young guy came to me and kept telling me things, going on and on. I thought he would never stop. I got frightened. Then he said: 'Sorry, got to go.' A young guy I didn't know. That's normal. He just saw a woman and he wanted to confide in her. He'd seen what was left of boys after a burst of machine gun fire: half a boot, and that's all. Boys that he knew . . . I thought he would never stop. Who did he go on to next?

We've got two women's hostels here. They call one the

'Cat-House'; that's where the ones who have been in Afghanistan for two or three years live. The other one's the 'Daisy'; that's where the new girls are, the ones who are still clean, so to speak – 'He loves me, he loves me not, he'll cherish my heart or tear it apart.' Saturday is the soldiers' day at the bathhouse and Sunday is the women's day. They don't let women into the officers' bathhouse, because women are dirty. And those officers only come to us for one thing . . . for you know what. They knock on the door at night, with a bottle of wine. They've got photos of their children and their wives in their wallets; they show them to us. That's normal.

The shelling starts. A shell flies through the air with this whistling sound. Something inside you snaps. It hurts inside. Two soldiers and a dog went off on a mission. The dog came back, but they didn't . . . (*She pauses for a moment.*) The shelling starts and we run to hide in a trench. But the Afghan children dance for joy on the rooftops. One of our men is brought back dead . . . The children laugh and clap their hands. We take presents for them to the *kishlaks*: flour, mattresses, cuddly toys. Teddy bears and rabbits . . . But they dance (*She pauses.*) The shelling starts and they're happy . . .

The first questions in the Union are 'Did you get married? What special benefits will they give you?' The only benefit we get (the civilian employees, that is) is a thousand roubles for our family, if we get killed. When they deliver goods to the canteen shop the men go to the front of the queue: 'Who are you? We've got to buy presents for our wives.' But at night they come knocking on our doors. That's normal. It's the way things are here. They perform their 'international duty' and make money. They have a price list: a jar of dried milk goes for fifty *afoshkas*, an army cap with a peak is four hundred *afoshkas*, a mirror off a truck is a thousand, a wheel from a KamAZ truck is eighteen to twenty thousand, a Makarov pistol is thirty thousand, a Kalashnikov automatic is a hundred thousand, a truckload of rubbish from the garrison (depending on the kind of rubbish, if there are tin cans in it and how many) is from seven hundred to two thousand *afoshkas*. That's normal . . . The women who live best here are the ones who sleep with the warrant officers. Who's higher than a warrant officer? Only a senior warrant officer. But the boys in the outposts have scurvy. They live on rotten cabbage.

The nurses tell me that in the wards the men with missing legs talk about everything but the future. No one here likes to talk about the future. And they don't talk about love. Probably it's terrifying to die if you're happy. More terrifying, that is. But I feel sorry for my mother.

A cat creeps between the dead men, looking for something to eat; it's afraid. The boys lie there as if they were alive. The cat probably doesn't know if they're alive or dead . . .

You stop me yourself. I'll just go on and on. And I haven't killed anybody . . .

A civilian employee

Sometimes I start wondering . . . What if I'd never got into this war? I'd be happy. I'd never have felt disappointed in myself and I'd never have found out things about myself that it's best not to know. As Zarathustra said: 'And if you gaze long into an abyss, the abyss also gazes into you.'

I was a second-year student at a radio engineering college, but I was attracted to music and books about art. That world was closer to me. I started feeling frustrated and caged in, and during that period I got my call-up papers. I'm a weak-willed kind of person; I try not to interfere with my own destiny. If you interfere you'll lose anyway; and that way you're to blame, no matter what happens. Of course, I wasn't ready for the army. On the hop – it caught me on the hop.

They didn't say so outright, but it was clear enough: we were going to Afghanistan. I didn't interfere with my destiny . . . They lined us up on the parade ground and read out the order, about us being internationalist soldiers. It all went over very calmly – you can't say 'I'm afraid! I don't want to go!' We were going to perform our international duty; it was all laid out very neatly. But at the transit point in Gardez it began . . . The old hands took everything valuable: boots, striped singlets, berets. Everything cost money to buy back: a beret was ten checks, a set of badges was valued at twenty-five. (A paratrooper had to have five of them: a guardsman's badge, an 'airborne elite' badge , a parachutist's badge, a proficiency badge and a military sportsman's badge – we called it a 'runner'.) They took our dress uniform shirts – they used to swap those with the Afghans for drugs. A group of 'granddads' comes up to you. 'Where's your kitbag?' They rummage about in it and take what they like – and that's it. In our company they took everybody's new uniforms and gave them old ones. They called you to the stores and said: 'What do want new things for here? Those boys are going back to the Union.' I wrote home and said how beautiful the sky was in Mongolia, that the food was good and the sun was shining. But this was a war.

We went out to a *kishlak* for the first time. The battalion commander had taught us how to behave with the local population. 'All Afghans, no matter what age they might be, are *bacha* to you. Have you got that? I'll show you all the rest.'

We met an old man on the road and the order was given: 'Stop the vehicle. Inspect everything!' The battalion commander went up to the old man, took off his turban and rummaged about in his beard. 'Right, on your way, *bacha*.' It was an unexpected incident.

At the *kishlak* we threw slabs of barley porridge to the children. They ran away – they thought we were tossing grenades.

My first combat outing was to escort a column. Inside I was excited and curious: the war was right here beside me! I was holding a gun and I had grenades on my belt – just like I'd only seen before on posters. As the gunlayer, as we approached the green zone I was watching very carefully through the sight. This turban appeared . . . 'Seryoga,' I shouted to the gunner, 'I see a turban! What should I do?'

'Shoot.'

'Shoot, just like that?'

'What did you expect?' He fired a shot.

'I see another turban! A white turban. What should I do?'

'Shoot!' We fired half the vehicle's supply of ammunition. We fired from the main gun and the machine gun.

'Where did you see a white turban? That's a snowdrift.'

'Seryoga, your "snowdrift" is running! Your snowman's got an automatic!' We jumped down off the vehicle and blasted away with our own automatics.

The point wasn't that I wanted to kill a man or not. I was always hungry and sleepy. There was only one thing I wanted – for it all to end as soon as possible. To stop shooting and go ... And what about riding on red-hot armour plate? Breathing acrid dry sand? Bullets whistling over our heads, while we sleep ... To kill or not to kill – that's a question for after the war. The actual psychology of war is simpler than that. Out there you mustn't see your enemy as a human being. You can't kill him then. We blockaded this *dushman kishlak*. We stayed there for a day, two days. The heat and the fatigue drove me berserk. And we became even more cruel than the 'greens'. At least they were from this place; they grew up in these *kishlaks*. But we didn't even think for a moment. It wasn't our life. It was easier for us just to toss a grenade ...

One time we were coming back with seven of our boys wounded and two shell-shocked. The *kishlaks* along the road looked dead and empty; some of the people had gone to the mountains, some were sitting it out in their *duvals*, or compounds. Suddenly this old Afghan woman came dashing out, weeping and shouting, and started hammering on the armour plate with her fists. She had a son. She cursed us ... We all felt the same way about her: 'What's she yelling and making threats about? Get her off the road!' We didn't kill her, but we could have. We knocked her down into the dust and drove on. We were carrying seven wounded ...

We didn't know very much. We were soldiers – we fought. Our military life was entirely separate from the Afghans; they were forbidden to show their faces on the base. All we knew was that they killed us. But we all wanted to live. I accepted that I might get wounded. I even wanted to be lightly wounded, so that I could lie down for a while and catch up on my sleep. But nobody wanted to die. When three of our soldiers went into a *dukan*, shot the owner's family and looted the place, an investigation was set up. At first it was denied by the unit; it wasn't us, not our men. They brought us our bullets, which had been extracted from the dead victims. Then they started looking: who did it? They found three men: an officer, a warrant officer and a private. But I remember that when the search was going on in the company, and they were looking for the stolen money and goods, there was a feeling of resentment: how come they were searching here because of them, because of some Afghans who had been killed? There was a court martial. Two of them, the warrant officer and the private, were sentenced to be shot. Everyone felt sorry for them, dying because of a piece of nonsense like that. They called it 'stupid nonsense', not a crime. It was as if the shopkeeper's murdered family didn't even exist. Everything was all very neat and tidy. It was them and us. Friend and enemy. I've only started thinking about it now, when the stereotypes have crumbled. And I'm the one who could never read Turgenev's story about Mumu the dog without shedding tears!

In a war something happens to a man. In a war he's the same man and not the same. We were never taught 'Thou shalt not kill', were we? War veterans used to come to our school or college and tell us how they killed. They all had rows of medal ribbons pinned to their best suits. I never heard anyone say that it's wrong to kill in a war. They only put people who kill in peacetime on trial – they're 'murderers'. But in war they call it something different: 'the filial duty to the Homeland' – 'a man's sacred cause' – 'defending the Fatherland'. They explained to us that we were repeating the heroic deeds of the soldiers of the Great Patriotic War. How could we have had any doubt? We had always been told that we were the best. If we were the best, why should I bother to think, if there was nothing wrong with us? Later on I pondered a lot about things. I looked for someone to talk to about it . . . My friends told me: 'You've either gone crazy or you want to go crazy.' And I . . . I was brought up by my mother, a strong, dominant person. I never wanted to interfere with my own destiny.

At the training camp scouts from the special forces told us thrilling stories. Cruel and beautiful stories. I wanted to be strong, like they were. And not be afraid of anything. I probably suffer from an inferiority complex: I like music and books, but I also wanted to crash into a *kishlak*, slit everybody's throats and then boast flippantly about it afterwards. But I remember something different: I remember feeling terror and panic . . . Like when we were riding along and they started shelling us. The vehicles stopped and the command was given: 'Take up defensive positions.' We started jumping down. I stood up and another man moved into the spot where I had been. A grenade hit him full on. I felt myself flying away from the vehicle, face down. I landed slowly, like in a cartoon film. But the pieces of the other man's body fell faster than I did. For some reason I flew more slowly . . . And my mind recorded all of this, that's the strange thing. You can probably remember your own death like that, as you follow it through. That's weird. I landed, and scuttled into an irrigation ditch. I lay down and lifted up my wounded arm. I could see that I was only lightly wounded, but I held my arm and didn't move.

No, I didn't turn out to be a strong man . . . The kind who can crash into a *kishlak* and slit someone's throat. A year later I ended up in hospital. With exhaustion. I was the only 'youngster' in the platoon; ten 'granddads', and I was the only 'youngster'. I was sleeping three hours a day. I washed everybody's dishes, chopped firewood and kept the general area tidy. I brought the water. It was about twenty metres to the river. Walking there one morning I got the feeling: 'Don't go that way, there's a mine!' But I was afraid they would beat me up again. They'd wake up and there'd be no water, nothing to wash with. So I went, and I did get blown up. But thank God I only tripped a signal mine. The flare zoomed into the air, lighting up everything. I dropped to the ground and sat there for a while, then crawled on. Just one bucket of water. Otherwise there wasn't even any to brush our teeth with. They wouldn't care what had happened; they'd just beat me. In one year I was reduced from being a normal young guy to a muscular dystrophy case. I couldn't walk across the ward without a nurse; I was simply streaming with sweat. I went back to the unit and they started beating me again. They beat me so badly that they damaged my leg and I had to have an operation.

The battalion commander came to see me in the hospital: 'Who beat you?' Although they used to beat me at night I knew who did it anyway. But I couldn't admit that, it would make me an informer. That was a law that couldn't be broken. 'Why don't you say anything? Tell me who it was, and I'll have the bastard court-martialled.'

I kept quiet. External authority was powerless against the internal rules of the soldier's life, and it was those rules that decided my destiny. Anyone who tried to go against them always suffered defeat. I'd seen that. I didn't interfere with my own destiny . . . At the end of my time in the army I tried to beat someone myself, but I couldn't do it. The 'granddad' system doesn't depend on the individual, it's dictated by herd instinct. First they beat you, then you have to do the beating. I hid the fact that I couldn't beat anyone from the 'demobbers'. They would all have despised me – both the guys who were beaten and the guys who beat them.

When I came back home I went to the military commissariat. They'd just brought in a zinc coffin. It was our senior lieutenant. The notification of death said: 'Killed while performing his international duty.' And at that moment I recalled how he used to get drunk, walk along the corridor and smash the orderlies on the jaw. He used to amuse himself like that on a weekly basis. If you didn't hide you ended up spitting teeth . . . A man has no more than a drop of humanity in him – I realized that at the war. If there's nothing to eat he's cruel; if he's not feeling good he's cruel. So how much of him is truly human?

I only went to a cemetery once. The headstones said 'Died heroically', 'Displayed courage and valour'. There were some heroes, of course, if you take the word 'hero' in a narrow sense; for instance, someone who shielded a friend during combat or carried a wounded commander out to a place of safety . . . But I know that one of our men killed himself doing drugs and another was shot by the sentry when he was sneaking into the food depot. We all used to sneak into the food depot. We dreamed of condensed milk and biscuits. But you won't write about that. No one will ever say that a truth like that is lying there, under the ground. Medals for the living, legends for the dead – and that's great for everyone.

War is like the life here. Everything's just the same, except that there's more death. Thank God I have a different world now; it has blanked out that one. It's a world of books and music, and it has saved me. It was here, not out there, that I started figuring out where I'd been and what had happened to me. But I think about it on my own; I don't go to the 'Afghani' clubs. I can't even imagine going to a school and telling them about the war, and how an immature, unformed individual like me was moulded into a killer, and other stuff like that. That all we wanted to do was eat and sleep. I hate our 'Afghanis'. Their clubs are like the army. The same old army tricks: 'We don't like metalheads: let's smash their faces in! Let's give the queers a drubbing!' That's a piece of my life I want to separate myself from, not identify with. We have a cruel society; it lives by cruel laws . . . I hadn't noticed that before.

We once stole a load of phenazepam. They use it for treating psychological problems. The dose is one or two tablets. Some of us swallowed ten, some swallowed twenty . . . At three o'clock in the morning some of us went to the kitchen to wash the dishes. But they were already clean. Others just sat there morosely, playing cards . . . And one did his business on his pillow. Absolutely ludicrous. The nurse fled in horror and called the guard.

That's the way the war is recorded in my memory. On the one hand it was absolutely ludicrous . . . (*He pauses.*) But on the other, after what we did out there, we'll never get into heaven . . .

A private, gunlayer

I gave birth to twins, two boys. But only one of them survived. Until he became a legal adult at the age of eighteen, and the army call-up papers arrived, we were registered for support with the Institute for the Protection of Motherhood and Childhood. What point was there in sending soldiers like that to Afghanistan? My neighbour was right to reproach me: 'Couldn't you have got a couple of thousand together and paid a bribe?' Someone paid and saved their son. And my son was sent instead of him. But I didn't understand that I had to save my son with money. I tried to save him with my heart.

I went to see him take the oath and I saw that he wasn't prepared for war, he was bewildered. We had always been frank with each other. 'You're not ready, Kolya. I'm going to put in a plea for you.'

'Mama, don't make a fuss and don't demean yourself. Do you think it bothers anyone that I'm not prepared? Who takes any notice of things like that here?'

But I managed to get a meeting with the battalion commander anyway and started pleading with him. 'He's my only son. If anything happens to him, I won't be able to carry on living. And he's not prepared. I can see he's not ready.'

He was sympathetic. 'Go to your military commissariat. If they send me an official request, I'll assign him to the Union.'

My plane arrived at night, and at nine in the morning I ran to the commissariat. Our military commissar was Comrade Goryachev. He was sitting there, talking on the phone. So I stood there.

'What's your business?' I told him. Then the phone rang again. He picked it up and said to me: 'I won't sign any request.'

I implored him, I went down on my knees. I was ready to kiss his hand. 'He's my only family.' He didn't even get up from his desk.

When I left I asked him to write down my name anyway. I was still hoping. He might think about it and take a look at my son's file. He's not made of stone, is he?

Four months went by. They have three-month intensive training courses, and my son was already writing from Afghanistan. Just four months. Only one summer . . .

I was on my way to work in the morning. As I walked down the stairs they were coming up towards me. Three soldiers and a woman. The military men were in front, and they were all carrying their peaked caps on their bent left arms. I knew from somewhere that that meant mourning. It was a sign of mourning . . . Instead of going down I ran back up. And they obviously realized that I was the mother. They came up after me. Then I got in the lift and went down. I wanted to dash out into the street and run off! Escape! Not hear anything! When I reached the ground floor the lift stopped to let people get in – and *they* were already there, waiting for me. I pressed the button and went up to my own floor. I heard them come in and I hid in the bedroom. They followed me . . . With their caps on their arms.

One of them was the military commissar, Goryachev. While I still had some strength left I pounced on him like a cat and yelled: 'You're soaked in my son's blood! You're soaked in my son's blood!' He didn't say anything, even though I was about to hit him. He didn't say anything. And I don't remember anything after that.

I didn't feel drawn to people again until a year later. Before that I kept myself absolutely to myself, like a leper. I was wrong. People weren't to blame. But at that time it seemed to me that they were guilty of my son's death. A shop assistant I knew in the bakery, a taxi driver who was just a stranger, and Military Commissar Goryachev – they were all to blame. But I wasn't drawn to people like that, only to other people like me. We used to meet at the cemetery, beside the little graves. In the early evening, after work, one mother comes hurrying from the bus, another is already sitting beside her headstone and crying, another is painting the little fence round a grave. They only talk about one thing . . . their children. They're all we talk about, as if they're still alive. I remember all those conversations by heart . . .

'I went out on to the balcony. There were two officers and a doctor, and they walked in the front entrance. I watched through the spyhole to see which way they would go. They stopped on our landing and turned right . . . To the neighbours' place? They had a son in the army too. The bell rang and I opened the door: "What is it? Has my son been killed?" "Take courage, mother."'

'They told me straight off: "The coffin's by the entrance, mother. Where do you want us to put it?" My husband and I were getting ready to go to work. There were eggs frying on the cooker. The kettle was boiling.'

'They took him and cropped his hair. And five months later they brought his coffin.'

'They brought me mine after four months.'

'And mine after nine . . .'

'I asked the man who accompanied the coffin: "Is there anything in there?" "I saw them put him in the coffin. He's there." I looked at him and saw him lower his head: "There's something in there." '

'Was there any smell? We had a smell.'

'And we did too. There were even white worms that fell on the floor . . .'

'I didn't have any smell. Except of fresh wood. Raw planks . . .'

'If a helicopter burned out, they collected them up in pieces. They found an arm here, a leg there . . . They identified them from a watch, from their socks . . .'

'Our coffin stood in the courtyard for an hour. Our son was two metres tall, a paratrooper. They brought a sarcophagus – a little wooden coffin – and a zinc coffin too. It was too awkward to manoeuvre easily through our hallways . . . Seven men could hardly lift it.'

'They took eighteen days to bring my son. They collected a full plane-load first. For a "black tulip". They took them to the Urals, and then to Leningrad. And only after that to Minsk . . .'

'They didn't send back a single little thing. At least I'd have had something to remember him by. He used to smoke – at least his lighter could have been left to me . . .'

'It's good that they don't open the coffin. We didn't see what they'd done to our sons. In my mind's eye I always see him alive. Unhurt.'

We sit there like that until the sun sets. We feel all right there, because we remember our children.

How long will we live? People don't live long with pain like that in their hearts. Or with bitterness like that.

At the District Soviet executive committee they promised us: 'We'll give you a new flat. Choose any building in our district.'

We found a brick building, not one of the prefabricated panel ones. It was convenient for getting to the cemetery. A direct route, without any changes. I told them the address.

'Are you crazy? That's a Central Committee building, for the Party elite.'

'Is my son's blood that cheap, then?'

The secretary of the Party committee at our institute is a good man, he's honest. I don't know how he ended up on the Central Committee. He went to appeal for me and he told me afterwards what happened. 'You should have heard what they said to me. "She's grief-stricken," they said. "But what's it to you?" They almost threw me out of the Party.'

I ought to have gone myself. What would they have said to me?

I'm going to visit my son today. I'll meet one of my friends. The men do their fighting during the war; the women do their fighting after it . . . Our fight comes after the war . . .

A mother

I was a fool . . . Eighteen years old . . . What did I understand? (*He sings.*)

> From Tambov to Vienna,
> From Bordeaux to Kostroma,
> The women all love soldiers . . .

A hussar's song. I liked the way I looked in uniform; it suited me. Women always like a man in military uniform. That's the way it was a hundred years ago, two hundred. And it's the same now.

When they showed the war on television I used to sit there, fascinated. I was excited by the shooting, excited by the death – yes, I was excited. Excited, and that's all there is to it. When I ended up in the war, for the first few months I wanted some killing to happen right in front of my eyes, so that I could write to my friend about it. I was a fool . . . Eighteen years old.

The military oath says: '. . . I am always ready to come to the defence of my Homeland, the Union of Soviet Socialist Republics, at the order of the Soviet government and, as a fighting man of the armed forces, I swear that I will defend it courageously, skilfully and with dignity and honour, sparing neither blood nor life itself to achieve complete victory over enemies . . .'

Afghanistan seemed like heaven to me. I'd only ever seen anything like it in *Film Travellers' Club* on television. The clay houses and strange birds. The garlands of mountains. I'd never seen mountains before. Or camels. I saw oranges growing . . . I only found out later that they hung mines on the trees, like oranges (if an aerial catches on the branch they detonate). If the wind comes up everything beyond your outstretched hand is black, complete darkness – you're blind. When they bring the boiled grain the cooking pot's half full of sand . . . A few hours later it's sunny and you can see the mountain peaks. A burst from a machine gun, or a shot from a grenade launcher, and two of you are gone. You stand there and fire for a while. Then you move on. And there's sunshine and mountains again. A snake glinting as it disappears into the sand. The glint of a fish . . . (*He ponders for a moment.*) I'm usually a poor talker. Inarticulate. I'm trying hard today . . .

I wasn't an outstanding student in school and I wasn't a hero in the war. Just a simple city kid. I grew up in the courtyard of our block; our parents didn't have any time to spend on raising us. We grew up at school and in the courtyard. I don't know how to answer your questions. I can't answer them . . . I'm an average kind of person. I've never thought much about the big things. There's one thing I remember, though: even if the bullets are whistling by really close you still don't have any idea of what death is. A man lies there in the sand, and you call to him . . . You still haven't understood what death is . . . Look, that's what it's like . . .

I was wounded in the leg, not too badly. I thought: 'Seems like I'm wounded.' I thought it with surprise. Abstractly. My leg hurt, but I still didn't believe that it had happened to me. I was still a new boy there: I wanted to do a bit of shooting. The boys took a knife and cut open the top of my boot. My vein was shot through. They put on a tourniquet. That hurt, but I couldn't show that it did; I had to keep my dignity as a man. I put up with it. I ran from one tank to another – an obvious target – for about a hundred metres. There was shelling and the rocks were crumbling, but I couldn't say I wouldn't run or I wouldn't crawl. I had to keep my self-respect. I crossed myself and ran . . . I hobbled . . . There was blood in my boots, blood everywhere.

The fighting went on for more than an hour after that. We went out at four in the morning, the action ended at four in the afternoon, and we hadn't eaten anything in all that time. My hands were covered in my own blood, but that didn't stop me: I ate white bread with those hands. Then they told me that my friend had passed away in the hospital – he'd caught a bullet in the head. I imagined that, after he'd been killed, in a few days' time at the evening rollcall someone might answer for him: 'Igor Dashko was killed in the performance of his international duty.' He was quiet, like I was, no hero – he didn't push himself forward – but even so they shouldn't have just forgotten about him and immediately struck him out of the lists. I was the only one who remembered him . . . I decided to say goodbye to him . . . He was lying in his coffin. I looked at him for a long time. I looked hard, so that I'd remember him afterwards.

The ticket offices in Tashkent didn't have any tickets, but in the evening we struck a deal with the conductors on a train: we each gave them fifty roubles, then got in and off we went. There were only four of us in the carriage, and two conductors. They got two hundred roubles each. Those guys got a good deal, but we didn't give a damn. We laughed for no reason at all – the feeling bubbled up inside: 'We're alive! We're alive!'

At home I opened the door. Then I took a bucket and went across the yard to get water. Across my own yard!

A military award – a medal – was handed to me at my college. There was an article in the newspaper: 'An Award Finds Its Hero'. I thought that was funny, as if Red Army sleuths had been searching for me for forty years since the war had ended. I didn't say that we went there so that the dawn of the April Revolution would rise over the land of Afghanistan. But they wrote it . . .

Before the army I used to like hunting. I dreamed of serving my time, then going off to Siberia and being a huntsman there, or a forest ranger. I was a fool . . . Eighteen years old. And now? I went hunting with a friend. He shot a goose, and then we saw that he'd winged the bird. I ran to get it. My friend fired, but I ran to catch it alive. I didn't want to kill it . . .

I was just a kid. What did I understand? I've read lots of books about war that describe it beautifully. But I've got nothing to tell you about it. (*I was already getting ready to leave. Suddenly he opens the fridge, takes out a bottle of vodka, pours half a glass and gulps it down.)*

To hell with this fucking life! And this war! My wife said: 'You're a fascist!' and she left. She took our daughter. All that twaddle I just span you is rubbish! Fairy tales! I'm no expert on women and putting the world to rights . . . At the war I used to think: 'I'll come back and I'll get married.' Well, I came back and I got married. *(He pours himself more vodka.)* Vodka . . . Books and vodka. That's where the secret of the Russian soul is hidden – look for the basis of Russian patriotism there. We believe words, those little squiggles on paper . . . 'You're a fascist!' and she left.

Damn those mummies in the Kremlin! They wanted a world revolution . . . But I've only got one life. One life! I remember the eyes of a dog that was sitting beside a soldier who'd been killed. A-a-a-agh! Those cursed mummies! Yesterday I had a dream. People flying along as fast as artillery shells and having the same effect. Bombs falling . . . I don't know what kind of bombs they were. All the people were dead, but the bus and the things in it were all safe and sound . . . Absolutely! A-a-a-agh! I love her! I love her . . . I haven't had any other women. I couldn't give a damn for the war! Heroes? Heroes are the same kind of people as all the rest: deceitful, greedy boozers. Don't invent any heroes. Don't make them up. Write about love instead . . .

What does war smell of? A-a-a-agh . . . It smells of killing, not death. Death has a different smell. *(He pours more vodka.)* I won't offer a lady vodka, and I don't have any wine, damn it. I don't drink wine. Here's to love! The Afghans themselves weren't afraid of death. If people aren't afraid of death, then why kill them? What's the point? Kids from Ryazan, or from remote villages in Siberia . . . We decided that, if they didn't have toilets and toilet paper in their houses (because they wipe themselves with stones), then they were inferior to us. We made all that up, so it would be easier for us to kill them.

I told her about all this. Maybe that was a mistake? Of course it was. I should have played the hero. But I told her that killing a man was as easy as killing a duck when you go hunting. Catch him in the sight, take good aim and squeeze the trigger. At first I used to close my eyes when I fired, but later I used to look. I'm drunk already. I can . . . A-a-a-agh . . . I'll tell you . . . I wanted a woman all the time. It's unpredictable, damn it. In a war a man behaves unpredictably . . . If I'd come back as a hero my wife wouldn't have left me. We lost the war. The country fell apart. Why should the women respect the men?

Damn it. I've got drunk . . . Pardon me, madam writer. You wanted the truth? Here's the truth for you . . . Dying's easy and living's hard. That is, in the sense . . . Well, take this . . . A man's lying there dead, and a heap of checks has fallen out of his pocket. He collected them for life, for a beautiful life. I was a fool . . . a fool . . . But war . . . there's a lot of beauty in it. Fire's beautiful. A burning *kishlak* – it burns down: the people have run away, they untied all the animals and let them go. Then they come back. Their houses are gone. But the animals run out of the clay ruins and the people hug them and weep and call their names: 'You're alive! You're alive!' (*He tries to put the glass down on the table and it falls over.*)

As you were! Attention! Stand to attention, fuck it! I beg your pardon, madam. I drink – as you can see, I drink. I'll keep on drinking until I forget. I won't forget the war . . . My wife . . . I'm not a serious drinker . . . The more I drink the less serious I get . . . So she left. She put up with me for five years. I used to bring her flowers, a bunch of snowdrops in every pocket. The very first ones! I'm drunk . . . A-a-a-agh . . . They nailed the coffins together with chinks in them, like crates for fruit. In the barracks . . . with a poster on the wall about indestructible Soviet-Afghan friendship . . . Right! But maybe my wife will come back? I'll stop drinking . . . (*He picks up the bottle.*) Books and vodka. The two Russian mysteries . . . I read a lot now. When you live without love suddenly there's lots of time. And I don't watch the television. It's bullshit!

Write, madam. Write . . . But why are women writing about the war? Where are all the men? Fuck it all! You have to know war . . . It's not knowledge from books, it's not from what I've seen – it was inside me before that. From somewhere or other. But I don't understand anything about love: a woman is more mysterious to me than war. There's nothing more terrifying than love.

A private, tank crewman

Who told you that people don't love war? Who told you that?

I didn't go to Afghanistan alone. I went with my dog Chara. If I shouted 'Die!' she dropped. 'Close your eyes!' and she put her paws over her face and eyes. If I was feeling bad, really upset, she used to sit beside me and cry. For the first few days I was numb with delight at being there. I was seriously ill as a child – so at first they wouldn't take me into the army. But I couldn't have that! A young guy who hasn't served in the army? It's shameful. People would laugh at me. The army is a school of life. It's where boys become men. I got in to the army. And I started writing applications to be sent to Afghanistan.

'You'll croak after two days out there,' they said, trying to frighten me.

'No, I have to be there.' I wanted to prove that I was the same as everyone else.

I hid where I was serving from my parents. From the age of twelve I'd had an inflammation of the lymph nodes, so of course they would have got all the doctors together. I wrote that I was being sent to East Germany. I only told them the number of the field post office, said it was a secret unit and I couldn't give the name of the town.

I took my dog and my guitar with me. In the special section they asked me: 'How did you end up here?'

'Well, like this . . .' and I told them how many applications I'd put in.

'You couldn't have *wanted* to come. Are you insane or something?'

I'd never smoked, but I wanted to take up smoking there.

I got my first look at men who'd been killed: legs sliced off right at the crotch, holes in their heads . . . I walked away and fell down. Yeah, right . . . Some hero! Sand and more sand all around. Nothing growing but camelthorn bushes. In the beginning I used to remember home and my mother, but later I only thought about water. Fifty degrees Celsius, your skin melts on your automatic. I went around with my hands scorched red. My favourite memory was like a hallucination. How back in the Union we used to take a leave pass and guzzle ice cream until our throats turned numb. After action there's a smell of roasted meat . . .

Everyone says: 'The soul! The soul!' In a war the soul is something abstract; a man is transposed into a different state there. The dreams . . . I used to wake up all the time hooting with wild laughter. Sometimes someone would even call my name . . . Then I'd open my eyes and remember: war! I'm at war! The morning . . . The guys are getting washed and shaved . . . Jokes, quips and pranks. Water poured into someone's trousers . . . Out in the field you don't sleep long, only two or three hours. The best thing is to get into a guard detail at the beginning of the night, because the soundest sleep is in the morning. And the morning shift also has to brew the tea. In the field we used to cook our food on the campfire. Field rations were a couple of two-hundred-gramme tins of boiled grain with meat, a little jar of pâté, rusks or crackers, two little packets of sugar (like on a train) and two tea bags. Occasionally they issued tinned meat, one tin for several men. If I got friendly with someone we heated up two lots of boiled grain in his mess tin and brewed the tea in mine.

Someone stole a dead man's automatic rifle at night. They found him. One of our men. He sold it at a *dukan* for eighty thousand afghanis. He showed us what he'd bought: two cassette players and some denim stuff. We would have killed him ourselves, torn him to pieces, but he was under guard. At the trial he sat there without saying anything. And cried.

In the newspapers they wrote about 'feats of heroism'. We were outraged. But the mysterious thing is: I came home two years ago, and when I read a newspaper looking for 'feats of heroism' now I believe it.

Out there it seemed like I would come back home and revamp everything in my life. Change it all. A lot of men come back, get divorced, get married again and go away somewhere. Some go to Siberia to build a pipeline, some join the fire brigade. Wherever there's some risk. They can't feel satisfied any longer with existing instead of living. I saw roasted guys out there. At first they're yellow, with just the eyes gleaming, then the skin comes off and they're pink . . . A climb up into the mountains? It's like this: an automatic rifle – that goes without saying; a double issue of ammunition – about ten kilogrammes of cartridges; a grenade that weighs kilogrammes, plus a mine for every man – that's another ten kilogrammes or so; a bulletproof vest; dry rations. Basically you've got about forty kilogrammes hung all over you, if not more. I've seen a man soaking wet with sweat, as if he'd got caught in a cloudburst. I saw the orange crust on a dead man's stiff, frozen face . . . For some reason it was orange . . . I saw friendship and cowardice. Meanness . . . But please don't just take a wild swipe with this. Be careful with it. There's a lot of . . . vituperation around just now. Although why hasn't anyone handed in their Party card? No one put a bullet through their head when we were out there, did they? And what about you, the famous writer? What were you doing when we were out there? (*He's about to end the conversation, but then he changes his mind.*) You wrote a book, right? And watched the television . . .

I came back. My mother undressed me like a little child and felt me all over: 'Safe and unharmed, my little darling.' Unharmed on the surface, but burning inside. Everything bothered me: bright sunlight bothered me, a cheerful song bothered me, someone laughing bothered me. I was afraid to stay at home alone. I slept with my eyes half-open. The books, photos, cassette player and guitar in my room were the same. But the person I used to be was gone. I couldn't walk through a park without glancing back. In a café a waiter stood behind me and asked: 'What will you order?' And I was ready to jump up and run, I couldn't bear anyone standing behind me. If I saw some nasty son of a bitch all I thought was 'Shoot him!' Out there I could go up to anyone and kill him, like a chicken . . . And the war would just write it all off. Out there we had to do the exact opposite of what's required by life in peacetime. Now we have to forget all the skills acquired in the war. I'm an excellent shot; I can fling grenades and hit the target. Who needs that here? Out there it seemed like there was something to defend. We were defending our Homeland, our life. But here, a friend can't lend you three roubles. His wife won't let him. What kind of friend is that?

I realized that we aren't needed at home. What we went through isn't needed. It's superfluous, inconvenient. Immediately after Afghanistan I worked as a mechanic, repairing cars, and as an instructor at the district committee of the Komsomol. But I left. It's the same morass everywhere. People busy with earning money, with their dachas, cars and smoked sausage. Nobody has any time for us. If we didn't stand up for our rights ourselves, it would be an unknown war. If there weren't so many of us, hundreds of thousands, they would have hushed us up, the same way they hushed up Vietnam and Egypt in their time . . . Out there we all hated the 'spirits' together. Who can I hate now, so that I can have friends again?

I went to the military commissariat and asked to be sent to some hotspot. And there were plenty more like me there – with their brains screwed up by the war.

I wake up in the morning and I'm glad if I don't remember my dreams. I don't tell anyone my dreams, but they keep coming back to me . . . The same dreams, over and over. It's as if I'm asleep and I see a great ocean of people . . . All around our house . . . I look round, but for some reason I can't get up. Then I realize that I'm lying in a coffin. It's a wooden coffin without any zinc covering it. I remember that clearly . . . But I'm alive – I remember that I'm alive, but I'm lying in a coffin. The gates open, everyone goes out into the road and they carry me out into the road too. Crowds of people, all their faces filled with grief and some kind of mysterious exaltation. I can't understand it . . . What's happened? Why am I in a coffin? Suddenly the procession stops and I hear someone say: 'Give me the hammer.' Then I get the idea that I'm having a dream. Someone says it again: 'Give me the hammer.' It's like it's reality and a dream at the same time. And then someone says 'Give me the hammer' for a third time. I hear the lid slam shut and the hammer starts tapping, one nail hits me in the finger. I start banging my head against the lid, and my feet. Bang – the lid goes flying off and falls on the ground. The people watch as I rise up and sit there, exposed to the waist. I try to shout out: 'That hurts! Why are you nailing me in? I've got nothing to breathe in there.' They cry, but they don't say anything to me. They all seem to be dumb ... faces filled with exaltation. Mysterious exaltation ... Invisible ... And then I see it ... I get an idea of what it is. And I don't know how I can speak to them so that they'll hear me. I think I'm shouting, but my lips are pressed tight together, I can't open them. I really am dead, and I have to keep quiet. Someone says it again: 'Give me the hammer' ...

A private, logistics driver

Day Three

'Regard not them that have familiar spirits, neither seek after wizards . . .'

'In the beginning God created the heaven and the earth . . .

And God called the light Day, and the darkness he called Night. And the evening and the morning were the first day.

And God said, Let there be a firmament in the midst of the waters, and let it divide the waters from the waters . . .

And God called the firmament Heaven. And the evening and the morning were the second day.

And God said, Let the waters under the heaven be gathered together unto one place, and let the dry land appear: and it was so . . .

And the earth brought forth grass, and herb yielding seed after his kind, and the tree yielding fruit, whose seed was in itself, after his kind . . .

And the evening and the morning were the third day . . .'

What do I seek in the Scriptures? Questions or answers? What questions and what answers? How much humanity is there in a human being? Some think there's a lot, others say there isn't much. Below the thin layer of culture the beast is immediately apparent. So how much?

He could have helped me, my main character . . . But he has been silent for a long time.

Suddenly one evening the phone rings.

'It was all stupid, then? Right? Is that it? Do you understand what it meant for me? For us? I went there as a normal young Soviet guy. The Homeland wouldn't betray us! You can't forbid a madman's insanity . . . Some say we came through purgatory; others say it was a rubbish tip. A plague on both your houses! I want to live! I want to love! I'm going to have a son soon . . . I'm going to call him Alyoshka – that's the name of my

friend who was killed. And afterwards there'll be a little girl – I want a girl as well – she'll be Alyonka . . .

'We didn't turn into cowards! We didn't deceive you! That's enough, no more. I won't call again . . . This story's over for me. I'm getting out of it. I'm not going to shoot myself. I won't fling myself head first off the balcony. I want to live! I've survived for a second time . . . The first time was out there, at the war, and the second time was here. That's all! Goodbye!'

He hung up. But I've carried on talking to him for a long time . . . Listening to him . . .

The author

Put plaques up on the graves, carve it into the headstones, that it was all in vain. Carve it into the stone, to last for centuries . . .

They killed us out there, then they judged us back here. They brought the wounded to the Union and unloaded them at the back of the airport, so people wouldn't notice. I didn't know . . . None of you bothered to think why young men who had served in the army came back into peacetime with an Order of the Red Star and medals 'For Valour' and 'For Services in Battle'. They brought back the coffins and the cripples. But nobody asked those questions . . . I didn't hear them . . . I heard something different. In '86, when I came back on leave, they asked me: 'Do you go sunbathing and fishing out there and earn tons of money?' The newspapers said nothing or they lied. And the television too. We were invaders, they write now. If we were invaders why did we feed them and hand out medicine? When we entered a *kishlak* they were delighted . . . And when we left they were delighted. I never did understand why they were always delighted.

There's a bus driving along, with women and children – some of them even sitting on the roof. We stop it for a check. A dry crack from a pistol, and one of my soldiers falls face down in the sand. We turn him over on his back: the bullet went straight into his heart. I could have blasted them all with a grenade launcher. We searched them and we didn't find a pistol or any other kind of weapon. Baskets of fruit, copper kettles for sale. No one in the bus but women and *bachata*, like gipsy kids. And my soldier falls face down in the sand . . .

Put plaques up on the graves, carve it into the headstones, that it was all in vain!

We were walking along as usual and I was suddenly struck dumb for a few minutes. I couldn't speak. It was some kind of presentiment . . . I wanted to shout out 'Stop!' but I couldn't. I carried on walking. A flash! For a little while, just for an instant, I lost consciousness. Then I saw that I was on the bottom of a crater and I started crawling. I didn't feel any pain. I just didn't have the strength to crawl – everyone was overtaking me. About four hundred metres left to crawl, and everyone was overtaking me. About four hundred metres. And then someone spoke at last: 'Let's sit here, we're out of danger.' I tried to sit up like everyone else, and that was when I saw I didn't have any legs . . . I jerked up my automatic and I was going to shoot myself. They grabbed it out of my hands . . . Someone said: 'The major's lost his legs. I feel so sorry for him.' The moment I heard him say 'I feel so sorry for him' I got this pain right through all my body . . . It was so terrible that I started howling.

To this day I usually only walk along a road. On the asphalt. I won't go along a path into the forest. I'm afraid of walking across grass. There's soft new spring grass beside our building, but I'm still afraid anyway.

In the hospital everyone with both legs missing was dumped in the same ward. There were four of us. Two wooden legs beside each bed. Eight wooden legs altogether. On 23 February a teacher brought some little schoolgirls with flowers to see us. To wish us a happy Soviet Army Day. They just stood there and cried. No one in the ward touched any food for two days. No one said anything.

Someone's relative turned up to see him and treated us all to cake: 'It was all pointless, boys. Pointless! But never mind: they'll give you a pension and you can watch television all day long.'

'You go to hell!' Four crutches were flung at him.

They took one of us down from a noose in the toilet. He wound a sheet round his neck and tried to hang himself on the handle of the window. He'd got a letter from his girl: 'You know "Afghanis" are out of fashion now . . .' And he'd lost both his legs . . .

Put plaques up on the graves, carve it into the headstones, that it was all in vain! Tell the dead about it . . .

A major, commander of a mountain warfare company

I came back from there with the feeling that I wanted to sit in front of the mirror for a long time, and brush my hair . . .

I wanted to have a child. To wash nappies and hear a baby crying. The doctors told me I couldn't. 'Your heart won't stand the strain.' I didn't listen to them. It was a difficult birth when I had my daughter. They gave me a Caesarean section, because I started having a heart attack. 'No one will understand,' a friend of mine wrote in a letter to the hospital, 'that we came back sick. They'll say: "That's not an injury" . . .'

And now probably no one will believe how it all started for me. In spring 1982 . . . I was an extramural university student (in my third year at the philology faculty) when I was summoned to the military commissariat.

'We need nurses in Afghanistan. How do you feel about that? You'd get one and a half times the basic rate of pay. Plus checks.'

'But I'm studying.' After I graduated from medical college I'd worked as a nurse. But I dreamed of a new profession: I wanted to be a teacher. Some find their calling straightaway, but I made a mistake the first time round.

'Are you a member of the Komsomol?'

'Yes.'

'Think about it.'

'I want to study.'

'I advise you to think about it. If not, we'll call the university and tell them what kind of Komsomol member you are. The Homeland requires it . . .'

In the plane from Tashkent to Kabul the girl sitting next to me was going back out there from leave. 'Did you bring an iron? An electric heater?'

'I'm going to the war.'

'Ah, I get it. One more romantic fool who's read too many books about war.'

'I don't like books about war.'

'Then what are you going for?'

That cursed question 'What for?' would dog my footsteps right through the two years I spent there.

But really: what did I go for?

What they called the transit point I remember as a row of tents. In the 'canteen' they fed people buckwheat that was in short supply out here and Undevit vitamins.

'You're a beautiful girl. What have you come here for?' an elderly officer asked me. I burst into tears.

'Who's upset you?'

'You've upset me.'

'I have?'

'You're the fifth person who asked me what I'm here for.'

From Kabul to Kunduz by plane, from Kunduz to Faizabad by helicopter. Everyone I spoke to about Faizabad said: 'You're crazy. They shoot people and kill them there.' So – it's goodbye! I looked at Afghanistan from high up in the air: a big beautiful country, mountains like ours, mountain rivers like ours (I've been to the Caucasus), wide expanses like ours. I fell in love with it!

In Faizabad I was a theatre nurse. My territory was the 'operating theatre' tent. The entire field hospital was in tents. They used to joke about it: 'Swing your feet down off the camp bed, and you're already at work.' My first operation was on an old Afghan woman with an injury to her subclavian artery. Where were the vascular clamps? There weren't enough clamps. We held the artery closed with our fingers. We needed suture material . . . We took one reel of silk, then another, and immediately they just crumbled into dust. They'd obviously been lying in the stores since the last war, since 1941.

But we saved the Afghan woman. That evening the surgeon and I looked into the clinic. We wanted to find out how she was feeling. She was lying there with her eyes open . . . When she saw us she started moving her lips. I thought she wanted to say something. To thank us. But she was trying to spit at us . . . I didn't understand then that they had a right to hate us. For some reason I was expecting love. I just stood there, turned to stone. We'd saved her life and she . . .

They brought the wounded in helicopters. The moment I heard a helicopter there, I ran.

The mercury in the thermometer stuck at forty degrees. Forty degrees Celsius! Sometimes it was fifty . . . There was no air to breathe in the operating tent. I could barely manage to wipe away the surgeons' sweat in time with a napkin, and they were standing over open wounds. One of the non-sterile medics used to give them something to drink through a drip tube pushed in under their masks. There wasn't enough blood substitute. We used to call a soldier and he would lie down on the table and give blood right there. Two surgeons. Two tables. And I was the only theatre nurse. The general physicians assisted at operations. But they didn't have a clue about sterile conditions. I was running to and fro between the tables. Suddenly the lightbulb went out above one table. Someone unscrewed it with sterile gloves.

'Get out of here!'

'What's the problem?'

'Get out!' There was a man lying on the table with his rib cage open. 'Get out!'

We used to stand at the operating table all day and night. Sometimes for two days and two nights. Sometimes they brought the wounded in from combat missions, sometimes there was a sudden rush of self-inflicted injuries – they shot themselves in the knee or damaged their fingers . . . Seas of blood. And there wasn't enough cotton wool.

The men who decided to shoot themselves were despised. Even we medics used to abuse them. I used to tell them: 'Boys are being killed, and you want to go home to mama? He's hurt his knee. He's snagged his finger. Were you hoping they'd send you back to the Union? Why didn't you shoot yourself in the temple? If I were you I'd have shot myself in the temple.' I swear I used to say that! At the time they seemed like despicable cowards to me; it's only now I understand that perhaps it was a protest, a reluctance to kill. But I'm only just beginning to understand that.

In '84 I came back home. A boy I know asked me uncertainly: 'What do you think: should we be out there?'

I was indignant. 'If we weren't there, the Americans would be. We're internationalists.' As if I could prove that somehow.

It's amazing how little we thought about things out there. We saw our boys being mutilated and burned. We saw them like that and we learned to hate. We didn't learn to think. We used to go up in a helicopter and the beauty took our breath away! The desert has its own beauty: the sand isn't dead, it moves, it's alive. The mountains were spread out below, covered with red poppies or some other flowers I didn't know . . . But I couldn't take any pleasure in that beauty any more. It didn't really move my heart. I liked May best, with its searing heat. I used to look at the dry empty land with a feeling of vengeful satisfaction: 'That's just what you deserve! You're the reason we're suffering and being killed here.' I hated it!

I don't remember days. I remember wounds. Gunshot wounds, wounds from landmines. The helicopters just kept on and on arriving. They brought them in on stretchers. They lay there, covered in sheets with red blotches creeping across them.

I wonder . . . I ask myself . . . Why do I only remember the terrible things? There was friendship; people gave each other a helping hand. And there was heroism. Maybe it's that old Afghan woman who stops me? Maybe she's the one who throws me off . . . We saved her life and she wanted to spit in our faces. I found out later that she came from a *kishlak* that our special forces had been through. No one was left alive, apart from her. Out of the whole *kishlak*. But it all started when they fired from that *kishlak* and brought down two of our helicopters. They stabbed the burned-out helicopters with pitchforks. And ultimately, in the end . . . we didn't bother to think about who started it first and responded. We only felt pity for our own kind.

They sent one of our doctors on combat missions. The first time he came back in tears: 'All my life I've been taught to heal, but today I killed . . . What did I kill them for?' A month later he could analyse his feelings calmly: 'You start firing and get carried away: "There, take that!"'

At night the rats used to attack us . . . We covered our beds with netting canopies. The flies were as big as teaspoons. But we got used to the flies too. Any animal is more fastidious than a human being. Any of them!

The girls used to dry scorpions as souvenirs. Big fat creatures stuck on pins, like brooches, or hanging on threads. I was a 'weaver'. I used to take the aircrews' parachute harnesses and pull threads out of them. Then I sterilized the threads and we used them for stitching and closing wounds. When I came back from leave I brought back a whole suitcase of needles, clamps and suture material. I was crazy! I brought an iron so I wouldn't have to dry my wet medical gown on my own body in winter. And an electric heater.

At night everyone in the ward made cotton wool balls and washed and dried the gauze swabs. We lived like a single family. We already sensed that when we went back we would be a lost generation. Superfluous. When the cleaners, librarians and hotel managers started arriving we were puzzled at first: who needed a cleaner for two or three sets of living quarters or a librarian for about twenty tattered books? Why have thousands of women in this war? Well, you understand . . . I can't explain it genteelly. In cultured language. It was simply for one reason. So the men wouldn't go crazy . . . We used to avoid those women, although they hadn't done anything to offend us.

But I loved someone there. I had a boyfriend . . . He's still alive. But I deceived my husband: when I got married I told him the man I used to love had been killed. He wasn't killed. We were the ones who killed our love . . .

'Did you ever meet a real, live "spirit"?' they asked me at home. 'I mean, with a bandit's face and a dagger in his hand, of course?'

'I did. Although he was a handsome young man. He'd graduated from the Moscow Polytechnical Institute.' But my younger brother imagined something out of Tolstoy's *Hadji Murad*.

'But why did you work for two or three days at a time? You could have worked eight hours and taken a rest.'

'What on earth do you mean? Don't you understand?'

They don't understand. But I know that I'll never be needed as much as I was out there. I go to work, read books and do the laundry. I listen to music. But there was a meaning to life out there, and that's missing here. Everything here is half-hearted . . . a half-whisper . . .

A nurse

I had two sons, two dear little boys . . . They grew up. One was big and the other was small. The older one, Sasha, went into the army when the younger one, Yura, was in the sixth year at school.

'Sasha, where are they sending you?'

'Wherever the Homeland commands, that's where I'll go.'

I used to tell my younger son: 'Just look what a brother you have, Yura!'

A letter from Sasha arrived and Yura came running to me with it. 'Are they sending our Sasha to war?'

'They kill people in a war, son.'

'You don't understand, mama. He'll come back with a medal "For Valour".'

That evening he played in the yard with his friends – they were fighting the 'spirits'. 'Ta-ta . . . ta-ta . . . ta-ta . . .' He came back indoors. 'What do you think, mama, will the war be over before I turn eighteen?'

'I hope it will be sooner than that.'

'Our Sasha's lucky, he'll be a hero. If only you'd had me first and him later.'

They brought Sasha's little suitcase, with his blue swimming trunks, toothbrush, a piece of half-used soap and a soap dish. And an identification certificate.

'Your son died in hospital.'

What he said – it's like a record playing in my head: 'Wherever the Homeland commands, that's where I'll go . . . Wherever the Homeland commands, that's where I'll go . . .'

They carried the box in and set it down as if there was nothing in it.

When they were little I used to call 'Sasha!' and they both came running. If I called 'Yura!' both of them answered.

All night long I sat there calling to him: 'Sasha!'

The box didn't say anything. It was heavy, made of zinc. In the morning I looked up and saw my younger boy. 'Yurochka, where have you been?'

'Mama, when you cry I want to run away to the end of the world.' He'd been hiding at the neighbours' place. He ran away from the cemetery too, and we had a really hard time finding him.

They brought Sasha's decorations: two orders and a medal 'For Valour'. 'Yura, look what a fine medal!'

'I can see it, mama, but our Sasha can't . . .'

My son's been gone for three years now, and I haven't dreamed about him once. I put his trousers under my pillow, and his vest: 'Come in my dream, son. Come to see me.' But he doesn't come. What have I done to offend him?

From the window of our apartment we can see a school with its yard. The children there play at fighting the 'spirits'. I hear it all the time: 'Ta-ta . . . Ta-ta . . . Ta-ta . . .'

At night I lie there and beg him: 'Come in my dream, son. Come to see me.'

Once I dreamed of a coffin. With a large opening where the head is. I lean down to kiss him . . . But who's this lying there? It's not my son . . . Someone dark-skinned. Some Afghan boy who looks like Sasha . . . At first I thought he was the one who killed my son. Then I realized that he was dead too. And someone had killed him. I leaned down and kissed him through the opening. And I woke up feeling afraid. 'Where am I? What's happening to me?'

Who was it that came . . . ? What news did they bring . . . ?

A mother

Two years . . . I had it right up to here . . . I want to forget it. Like a bad dream. I wasn't there. I wasn't!

But I was there, after all . . .

I graduated from the military academy. And after I took the leave I was entitled to, in the summer of '86 I came to Moscow and did as it said in my travel order: I reported to the headquarters of an important military institution. It wasn't that easy to find. I walked into the pass and registration office and dialled a three-digit number.

'Colonel Sazonov here,' a voice answered.

'Good morning to you, comrade colonel! I'm reporting and at your service. I'm in the pass and registration office.'

'Ah yes, I know, I know. Are you already aware where they're sending you?'

'To the Democratic Republic of Afghanistan. According to provisional information, to the city of Kabul.'

'Is that a surprise to you?'

'Not at all, comrade colonel.'

For five years they'd impressed it on us: 'You'll all end up there.' So without any dissembling at all I could honestly tell the colonel: 'I've been expecting this for five whole years.'

If anyone imagines that an officer's departure for Afghanistan consists of a single phone call, followed by rapid packing, a restrained and manly farewell to your wife and children, and boarding a roaring plane in the murky light before dawn – then they're wrong. The road to war has acquired an inescapable bureaucratic procedure: it's not just orders, an automatic rifle and dry rations, you also have to have medical certificates, performance reports – 'Possesses a correct understanding of the policy of the Party and the government' – service passports, visas, personal testimonials and travel orders, vaccination certificates, customs declarations and boarding passes. And only after all that can you get in the plane, take off and hear the drunken pilot shout out: 'Forward! To the landmines!'

The newspapers told us: 'The military and political situation in the Democratic Republic of Afghanistan remains complex and contradictory.' The military assured us that the withdrawal of the first six regiments should be regarded as no more than a propaganda move. There could be no question at all of a total withdrawal of Soviet forces. 'This war will see us all out.' None of the men who flew with me had any doubt about that. 'Forward! To the landmines!' the drunken captain shouted through my sleep.

So, I'm a paratrooper. I was immediately informed that the army was divided into two parts: paratroopers and *solyara*. I never did establish the correct etymology of that word *solyara*. A lot of the soldiers and warrant officers, and some of the officers, got tattoos on their arms. There wasn't much variety: more often than not it was just an Il-76 plane with a parachute canopy underneath it. There were some variations, though. For instance, I came across this lyrical composition: clouds, little birds, a parachutist hanging under a canopy and the touching inscription 'Love the sky'. The paratroopers' unofficial code decrees that 'A paratrooper only goes down on his knees in two cases: beside the body of a friend and in order to drink water from a stream.'

My war began . . .

'Fall in! Attention!' I give the orders to follow the planned route of march: 'The permanent base is the district Party committee of Bagrami, in the *kishlak* Shevani. Speed along the route is set by the lead vehicle. Spacing depends on the speed. Call signs are: for me, "Cutter"; for everyone else, the side numbers of the vehicles. At ease!' The usual ritual before our propaganda detachment sets out.

I jump up on to my BRDM, a nippy little armoured car. I heard its nickname from our Afghan advisers – *bali-bali*. Translated from Afghan, *bali* means 'yes'. When Afghans are testing a microphone, in addition to our traditional 'one-two, one-two', they say '*bali-bali*'. As an interpreter I'm interested in everything to do with language.

'Salto! Salto! This is Cutter. Let's go!'

Behind a low stone wall there are two small single-storey brick houses, whitewashed on the outside. A red plaque: 'District Party Committee'. Comrade Laghman is waiting for us on the porch. He's dressed in Soviet Army cotton.

'Salaam alaikum, rafik Laghman.'

'Salaam alaikum. Chetogur asti! Khud asti! Djor asti! Khair khairat asti?' he says in a volley of traditional Afghan greetings, all of which indicate that the speaker is enquiring after your health. There's no need to answer these questions, you can simply repeat them.

The commander seizes the chance to show off his favourite phrase: 'Chetogur asti? Khud asti? In Afghanistan through stupidity.'

Hearing something he doesn't understand, Comrade Laghman looks at me in bewilderment. 'A Russian folk-saying,' I explain.

We are invited into the office. They bring us tea in little teapots. For the Afghans tea is a compulsory element of hospitality. Without tea the work won't start and the business discussion won't happen. To refuse tea is like not holding out your hand when you meet someone.

In the *kishlak* we are met by the elders and the *bachata*, who are permanently unclean (they don't wash the really little ones at all; according to Sharia law a layer of dirt protects against the mischief of evil) and dressed any old way. Since I'm speaking Farsi everyone considers it necessary to check my knowledge. The inevitable question follows: 'What time is it?' I reply, provoking a storm of delight. (If I can reply that must mean I really do know Farsi, I'm not just pretending.)

'Are you a Muslim?'

'Yes, I am,' I joke.

They require proof.

'Do you know the Kalima?' The Kalima is a special verbal formula; by pronouncing it you become a Muslim.

'La ilah illa miah va Muhammad rasul Allah,' I declaim. 'There is no God but Allah, and Muhammad is his prophet.'

'Dost! Dost! Friend! Friend!' the *bachata* babble, reaching out their thin little arms in a gesture of acknowledgement. They'll ask me to repeat those words again several times, bringing their friends and whispering, spellbound: 'He knows the Kalima.'

Our sound system, which the Afghans themselves have nicknamed 'Alla Pugacheva', is already churning out Afghan folk melodies. The soldiers set out the visual propaganda on the vehicles: flags, posters and political slogans. They unroll a screen; we're going to show a film now. The doctors set up tables and lay out boxes of medicine.

The meeting opens. A mullah in a long white cape and white

turban comes to the front. He reads a surah from the Koran. After the surah he appeals to Allah to protect all true believers against universal evil. He bends his arms at the elbows and raises his hands to heaven. Everybody, including us, repeats these movements after him. After the mullah, Comrade Laghman speaks. He gives a very long speech. That's one of the Afghans' distinguishing qualities. They all know how to talk and they like doing it. Linguistics has a term, 'emotional colouration'. Well, Afghan speech is more than simply coloured, it's brightly daubed with metaphors, similes and epithets. Afghan officers repeatedly told me how surprised they were that our political workers conducted their sessions using pieces of papers, all with the same words and phrases: 'in the vanguard of the broad communist movement', 'to serve as a constant example', 'some comrades fail to understand'.

A long time before I arrived in Afghanistan meetings like these ones of ours had become merely a routine chore. People came to them to have a medical examination or get a bag of flour. The loud ovations were all long gone, together with the friendly cries of 'Zaido bod! Long live!' with arms upraised, which accompanied all the speeches in the days when the people believed what we were telling them about: the radiant peaks of the April Revolution and the bright communist future.

The *bachata* don't listen to the speeches. They're interested in what the film will be. As usual we have cartoons in English, and two documentaries in Farsi and Pashto. They like Indian films here, with lots of fighting and shooting.

After the films the gifts are given out. We've brought sacks of flour and children's toys. We hand them over to the chairman of the *kishlak*, to be divided among the poorest people and the families of those who have been killed. After swearing publicly that everything will be done in due order he and his son start lugging the sacks home.

'What do you think? Will he hand it all out?' the brigade commander asks anxiously.

'I don't think so. Some of the locals came up and warned me that he's light-fingered. Tomorrow it will all be in the *dukans*.'

The command is given: 'Everyone form up. Prepare to move out.'

'One-one-two ready to move out . . . Three-zero-five ready . . . Three-zero-seven ready . . .'

The *bachata* see us on our way with a shower of stones. One of them hits me. 'From the grateful Afghan people,' I think.

We go back to the unit via Kabul. The windows of some of the *dukans* are decorated with signs in Russian: 'The cheapest vodka', 'Any goods at any price', 'The "Little Brother" shop for Russian friends'. The shopkeepers tout their wares in Russian: 'Slimline shirts', 'Stonewashed denim', ' "Earl Grey" tea set for six', 'Trainers with velcro fasteners', 'White and blue striped lurex'. The stalls sell our condensed milk and green peas, our thermos flasks, electric kettles, mattresses, blankets . . .

I've been home for a long time now. I still have dreams about Kabul. Little clay houses clinging to the mountain slopes: it gets dark and lights come on in them. From a distance it's as if you're looking at a magnificent skyscraper. If I'd never been there it would take me a while to realize that it's only an optical illusion.

I came back from out there and left the army a year later. Have you ever seen the way a bayonet glints in the moonlight? No? I couldn't bear to see that any longer.

I left the army and entered the faculty of journalism. I want to write . . . I read what others write.

'Do you know the Kalima?' . . . 'La ilah illa miah va Muhammad . . .' 'Dost! Dost!' . . . Hungry soldiers . . . Men suffering from muscular dystrophy. Their entire bodies covered with boils. Vitamin deficiency. And *dukans* piled high with Russian food . . . The frantically swivelling eyes of a man dying from a stray piece of shrapnel . . . One of our officers beside a hanged Afghan. Smiling . . .

What am I supposed to do with this? I was there . . . I saw it, but no one's writing about it. It's a kind of optical illusion. If it isn't written it's as if it never happened. Did it happen or didn't it?

A senior lieutenant, interpreter

I don't remember many specific things, personal things of my own.

About two hundred of us flew there in the plane. Two hundred men. A man in a crowd, a group or a herd, and a man on his own, are different people. As I flew out I thought about what I would see there . . . What I would learn . . . War was a new world.

From our commander's parting words: 'On a mountain ascent, if you fall don't call out. Fall in silence, like a living stone. It's the only way you can save your comrades.'

When you're looking out from a high cliff the sun seems so close that you can touch it, take hold of it.

Before the army I read Alexander Fersman's book *A Memoir of Stone*. I remember I was astounded by phrases like: 'the life of stone', 'the memory of stone', 'the voice of stone', 'the body of stone', 'the name of stone' . . . I didn't understand that you could talk about stone as an animate object. But out there I discovered for myself that you can watch stone for a long time, like water or fire.

From the teachings of a sergeant: 'You have to fire a little bit ahead of an animal, otherwise it will slip past your bullet. It's the same for a running man . . . The one who stays alive is the one who fires first. First, fuck it! Have you got that? If you have then you'll come back home and all the women will be yours!'

Was there fear? There was. Sappers felt it for the first five minutes. The helicopter crews felt it as they ran to their choppers. In the infantry we felt it until someone fired the first shot.

We climb up into the mountains . . . We climb from early morning until late at night. We're so tired we feel sick, we puke. First your legs turn to lead, then your arms. Your arms start trembling at the joints.

One man fell. 'I can't. I can't get up!' Three of us grab him and drag him along. 'Leave me, guys! Shoot me!'

'You bastard, we would shoot you, but you've got a mother at home . . .'

'Shoot me!'

Water! Water! The thirst is torture. Halfway there and everyone's flask is already empty. Your tongue flops out of your mouth and dangles there; you can't stick it back in. Somehow we still manage to smoke. We went up the mountains to the snow and looked for places with melt water – we drank from puddles and gnawed ice with our teeth. We forgot all about the chlorine tablets: 'Damn the ampoule of potassium permanganate!' You crawl to the snow and lick it . . . There's a machine gun stammering behind you, and you're drinking out of a puddle . . . You splutter and choke, hurrying in case they kill you before you've drunk your fill. A dead man lies there, face down in the water, as if he's drinking.

I'm like an outside observer now . . . I look back in that direction. What was I like? I haven't answered the most important question for you: how did I end up in Afghanistan? I asked to be sent in order to support the revolutionary will of the Afghan people. Back then they were showing the revolution on the television, talking about it on the radio, writing about it in the newspapers. 'A red star is glowing in the East! We must help, lend the hand of brotherhood . . .' I prepared for the war well in advance. I played sports. I learned karate. It's not easy hitting someone in the face the first time. So that it crunches. You have to step over that line, and then – crunch!

My first dead Afghan . . . A boy about seven years old. Lying there with his arms flung out, as if he was asleep. With the ripped-open belly of a motionless horse beside him . . . I got over it somehow, probably because I'd read so many books about war.

I remember our 'Afghani' songs. I'm hurrying to work and I suddenly start muttering:

Tell me, for whom did they all give their lives and why?
Why did the platoon go in facing machine gun fire?

I look round, hoping that no one has heard me! They'll think I came back from there gaga or shell-shocked. (*He sings.*)

Afghanistan, a mountain country beautiful and wild,
The order's simple: 'Up on your feet now, go and die' . . .

I came back, and for two years I dreamed that I was at my own funeral. Or I woke up in terror, thinking I had nothing to shoot myself with!

My friends asked me if I had any decorations. Or if I was

wounded. Did I fire a gun? I tried to share what I'd felt there, but they weren't interested at all. I started drinking. I drank alone . . . The third toast is for those who were killed. For Yurka. I could have saved him. Kept him alive . . . We were in hospital in Kabul together. I had a scratch on my shoulder and concussion, but his leg had been torn off. There were lots of guys there with legs and arms missing. They smoked and cracked jokes. They were okay there. But they didn't want to come back to the Union. To the bitter end they kept asking to be left there. In the Union a new life would begin . . . On the day they were sending us to the airport, Yurka slashed his wrists in the toilet.

I'd tried to change his way of thinking, when we played chess in the evenings: 'Yurka, don't get downhearted. What about Alexei Meresiev? Have you read *The Story of a Real Man*?'

'I've got a really beautiful girl waiting for me . . .'

Sometimes I hate everyone I meet in the street. It's a good thing they take away your gun and grenades at the border. We did our job, so now we can just be ignored, right? And Yurka can be forgotten?

When I wake up at night I can't tell if I'm here or I'm there. Here I live like a passive onlooker. I have a wife and a child. I hug them, but I don't feel anything; I kiss them, but I don't feel anything. I used to love pigeons. I used to love the morning. I'd give anything at all if only I could get my joy back.

A private, infantryman

My daughter came back from school and said: 'Mama, no one believes that you were in Afghanistan.'

'Why not?'

They'd asked her: 'Who sent your mother there?'

I haven't got used to a life of peace yet – I'm still revelling in it . . . I haven't got used to having no one shooting and no one shelling, to being able to turn a tap and drink a glass of water without it smelling of chlorine. Out there the bread smells of chlorine, and so do the macaroni, the buckwheat, the meat and the compote. I've been back home for two years now. I remember meeting my daughter, but nothing else sticks in my memory; it's all so small and insignificant compared with what I went through out there. So we've bought a new table for the kitchen, and a television: what else has happened here? Nothing. My daughter's growing up . . . She wrote to the commander of my unit in Afghanistan: 'Send me back my mama as soon as possible. I miss her very much.' Apart from my daughter nothing else interests me after Afghanistan.

The rivers there are a fabulous bright blue. Sky-blue water! I never thought water could be such a heavenly colour. Red poppies grow the way daisies do here: bonfires of poppies at the foot of the mountains. The tall haughty camels gaze at it all calmly, like old men. A donkey was blown up by an antipersonnel mine as it was pulling a cartload of oranges to the market. It lay there crying from the pain. One of our nurses bandaged it up.

Curse you, Afghanistan!

I can't sleep quietly after that place. Or live like everyone else. I came back and at first my neighbours and friends often used to ask if they could come round. 'Valya, we'll just drop in to see you for a minute. Tell us what kind of dishes they use out there. What are the carpets like? Is it true that there are heaps of clothes and video equipment? Cassette players and CD players? What did you bring back? Maybe you could sell us something?'

They brought more coffins back from there than cassette players. But they've been forgotten.

Curse you, Afghanistan!

My daughter's growing up. And my flat's very small, only one room. Out there they promised us: 'When you go back home they'll thank you for everything.' I went to the district Party committee and they took my documents. 'Were you wounded?'

'No, I came back unhurt. Unhurt on the outside, but you can't see what's inside.'

'Well, carry on living like everyone else. We didn't send you there.'

Standing in the queue for sugar: 'They brought back lots of stuff from out there and here they get pushy about their rights.'

We set out six coffins together: Major Yashchenko, a lieutenant and four privates . . . They lay there, wrapped in white sheets. We couldn't see their heads: they didn't have any. I never thought that men could sob and wail like that . . . I still have the photographs. They put up cairns made of bomb fragments at the spot where they were killed and carved their names on rocks. The 'spirits' flung the rocks over a cliff. They shot up the monuments or blew them up, so that nothing would be left of us.

Curse you, Afghanistan!

My daughter grew up without me. Two years in a boarding school. I got back and the teacher complained that her marks were all 'Cs'. How could I talk to her about it? She was a big girl already.

'Mama, what did you do out there?'

'The women there helped the men. I knew a woman who told a man: "You're going to live." And he did. "You're going to walk." And he did. Before that she took away from him a letter that he'd written to his wife: "What good am I to anyone with no legs? Forget about me." She told him: "Write 'Hello, my dear wife and dear Allochka and Alyoshka . . .'"'

How did I end up going there? I was summoned by the commander and he said: 'You have to do it!' We're raised on that phrase. At the transit point there was a young girl lying on a bare mattress and crying: 'I've got everything at home: a four-room flat, a fiancé, parents who love me.'

'Why did you come here?'

'They told me things were difficult here. That I had to come.'

I didn't bring anything back except my memories.

Curse you, Afghanistan!

That war will never be over for me . . . Yesterday my daughter came back from being with her friends. 'Mama, when I said that you were in Afghanistan, one girl laughed for some reason.'

What answer can I give her to that?

A warrant officer, security service head of department

Death is a terrible thing, but there are things that are far more terrible. Don't say in my presence that we were victims, that it was a mistake. Don't utter those words in my presence. I won't permit it.

We fought well and bravely. Why do you attack us? I kissed the banner tenderly, like a woman. With reverence. We were brought up to believe that it was sacred if you kissed the banner. We love our Homeland; we believe in it. Right, right, right . . . (*He drums his fingers on the table nervously.*) Out there I still . . . If an exhaust pipe backfires under my window I feel this sickening fear. A jangle of broken glass . . . and immediately my head's totally empty, there's just this jangling emptiness in my head. The ring of the long-distance telephone is like someone firing somewhere . . . I don't want to blot all this out. I can't just discard my sleepless nights. My agony. I can't forget the chilly shiver down my spine in fifty degrees Celsius.

We used to drive along, yelling songs at the tops of our voices. We called out to the girls, teasing them; from a truck they all look beautiful. We were happy driving along. There were occasional cowards, though.

'I'm going to refuse. Better prison than war.'

'Right then, take that!' We used to beat them. We taunted them, they even bolted from the unit.

I pulled my first dead man out of a hatch. He said: 'I want to live' – and he died. Right, right, right . . . After a battle it's impossible to look at the beauty. At the mountains or a lilac-coloured gorge filled with mist. An elegant bird . . . You want to shoot it all up! I used to shoot . . . I shot up into the sky! Or you just stand there, ever so quietly and gently. A young guy I knew took a long time to die. He lay there like a child who has only just learned to talk, repeating the names of everything his eyes came across: 'Mountains . . . tree . . . bird . . . sky . . .' And so on, right to the very end.

A young *Tsarandoi* – that's one of their policemen – said: 'When I die, Allah will take me up into heaven. But where will you end up?'

Where will I end up? I ended up in hospital. My father came to see me in Tashkent. 'Now you've been wounded you can stay in the Union.'

'How can I stay, if my friends are out there?'

He's a communist, but he went to the church and lit a candle.

'Why did you do that, father?'

'I have to put my faith in something. Who else can I ask to make sure you come back?'

There was a young guy lying beside me. His mother came from Dushanbe to see him. She brought fruit and cognac: 'I want to keep my son at home. Who can I ask?'

'Mother, why don't we just keep your cognac and drink to our own health?'

'But I want to keep my son at home.'

We drank her cognac. A whole crate of it. On my last day in the ward we heard they'd discovered that one of our group had an ulcer; they were putting him in a medical and sanitary battalion. The bastard! We erased his face from our memory.

For me it's either black or white. There's no grey. No half-tones.

Out there we couldn't believe that somewhere it rained all day long, with rain and sunshine at the same time. With our Arkhangelsk mosquitoes buzzing over the water . . . Nothing but scorched, rugged mountains . . . Roasting, prickly sand . . . Right, right, right . . . And our bloodied soldiers lying on it, like on a big sheet . . . All their male parts have been cut off . . . A message to us: 'Your women will never have sons from them' . . .

And you tell us to forget?

We came back: some with Japanese cassette players, some clicking musical cigarette lighters and some in threadbare, washed-out cotton army gear, with empty briefcases.

We fought well and bravely. We were rewarded with medals. They say you can recognize us 'Afghanis' without the medals, just from the eyes.

'Hey are you from Afghanistan?'

But I just walk along in my shabby Soviet coat and Soviet shoes . . .

A private, logistics driver

But what if she's alive? Maybe my little girl's alive, but somewhere far away . . . I'd be glad anyway, wherever she was, as long as she was alive. That's what I think, that's what I want, what I really want!

I had this dream too . . . that she came home. She took a chair and sat down in the middle of the room. She had her long hair, very beautiful, tumbling over her shoulders. She tossed it back with her hand, like that, and said: 'Mama, why do you keep on calling me all the time, when you know I can't come to you? I've got a husband here, and two children . . . I've got a family . . .'

And then, in the dream, I remembered that after we buried her, maybe a month later, I got the thought that she wasn't dead, that she'd been kidnapped. That was my consolation. When we walked along the street people always used to look round at her. She's tall, with long flowing hair . . . And then I received this confirmation that I'd guessed right. She's alive somewhere . . .

I work in medicine. All my life I've believed that medicine is a sacred profession. I loved it so very much that I enticed my daughter into it too. But now I curse myself. If she hadn't joined my profession she'd have stayed at home and she'd still be alive. Now there's just my husband and me; we don't have anyone else. Life's empty, terribly empty. The evening comes and we sit down and watch the television. We sit there without talking. Sometimes we might not say a single word the whole evening. Only, when they start singing I start crying, and my husband groans and goes out. You can't even imagine what's in here, inside my chest . . . In the morning I have to go to work and I can't get up. Such terrible pain! Sometimes I think I won't get up, I won't go. I'll just lie there and wait until I'm taken to her. Until I'm called . . .

I have a tendency to imagine things. I'm with her all the time – even in my dreams nothing is ever repeated. She's even with me when I read. Although now I read books about plants and animals, about stars. I don't like to read about people, about human affairs . . . When spring came I thought nature would help me. We went out into the country . . . The violets were blooming. There were little baby leaves on the trees. And I started screaming. That was how the beauty of nature and the joy of living things affected me . . . Now I've started feeling afraid of time passing by: it's taking her, the memory of her, away from me. The details are disappearing. The words. What she said, the way she smiled . . . I collected the hairs from her suit and put them in a little box.

'What are you doing?' my husband asked me.

'I'm keeping this. She's gone.'

Sometimes I'm sitting at home, thinking, and I hear a voice say, quite clearly: 'Mama, don't cry.' I look round and there's no one there. I carry on remembering. She's lying there. The grave has already been dug and the earth is ready to receive her. And I go down on my knees in front of her: 'My darling little daughter! My darling little daughter! How did this happen? Where are you? Where have you gone to?' She's still with me, although she's lying in the coffin. But soon she'll be in the ground.

I remember that day when she came back from work and said: 'The chief physician called me in today.' Then she stopped.

'And?' Even before I heard the answer to my question I got a bad feeling.

'Our hospital has been given a quota to send one person to Afghanistan.'

'And?'

'They want a theatre nurse.' She worked as a theatre nurse in cardiology.

'And?' I'd forgotten all the other words; I just kept repeating the same thing.

'I agreed.'

'And?'

'Someone has to go, in any case. And I want to be where things are hard.'

Like everyone else I already knew there was a war on and blood was being spilled. I started crying, but I couldn't say no. She would just have given me a stern look and asked: 'Mama, what about the Hippocratic oath?'

It took her a few months to collect all the documents. She brought her character reference and showed it to me. It said: 'She possesses a correct understanding of the policy of the Party and the government.' But I still didn't believe it all.

When I talk about her I feel better. As if she's here and I'm going to bury her tomorrow . . . She's still with me. Or maybe she's alive somewhere? All I'd like to know is how she is now. Is her hair still long? And what kind of blouse is she wearing? I'm interested in everything . . .

My soul has snapped shut. I don't want to see people. I like to be alone ... Then I'm with her, my little Svetochka, and I talk. The moment anyone comes in it all breaks down. I don't want to let anyone into that world. My mother comes from the village to see me, but I don't even want to confide in her. Only, once a woman came see me. Someone from work. I wouldn't let her go; we sat here into the night. Her husband was afraid that the metro would close ... Her son came back from Afghanistan and he was just like a little child: 'Mama, I'll bake the pies with you ... Mama, I'll go to the laundry with you.' He's afraid of men; his only friends are little girls. She went running to the doctor, and he told her: 'Give it time, it'll pass off.' People like that are closer and dearer to me now. I could have been friends with that woman, but she didn't come to see me again. She kept looking at Svetochka's photograph and crying all the time.

But there was something else I wanted to remember. What was it I wanted to remember? Ah! When she came back on leave the first time ... No, before that, when we saw her off, when she was going away. Her school friends and colleagues from work came to the railway station. And one old surgeon leaned down and kissed her hands: 'I'll never see hands like these again.'

She came back on leave, looking thin and small. She slept for three days. She got up, ate and slept. Got up again, ate and slept.

'Svetochka, how are things there for you?'

'Everything's fine, mama. Everything's fine.' She sat there without saying anything else, smiling quietly to herself.

'Svetochka, what's wrong with your hands?' Her hands had changed – I didn't recognize them. They looked like the hands of a fifty-year-old woman.

'There's a lot of work there, mama. How can I think about my hands? Just imagine, when we're preparing to operate we wash our hands with formic acid. One doctor came over to me and asked: "Don't you have any pity for your kidneys?" He's thinking about his kidneys. And men are dying right there beside him. But don't you worry. I'm happy there. I'm needed.'

She left three days earlier than she had to. 'I'm sorry, mama, there are only two nurses left in our field hospital. We have enough doctors, but not enough nurses. The girls will be totally swamped. I just have to go.'

Her granny will be ninety soon. Svetochka really loved her a lot and used to tell her: 'Don't you die, now. Wait for me.' We went to see her granny at the dacha. She was standing beside a big rose bush and Svetochka told her: 'Don't you die, now. Wait for me.' Her granny went and cut all the roses for her. She took that bouquet with her when she went away.

We had to get up at five in the morning. When I woke her up she said: 'Mama, I still haven't had enough sleep. I think I'll never get enough sleep now.' In the taxi she opened her handbag and gasped: 'I've forgotten the keys to our flat. I haven't got any keys. What if I come back and you're not at home?' I found the keys later, in an old skirt of hers. I was going to send them in a parcel, so she wouldn't worry. So she would have keys for our home.

But what if she's alive? Walking around somewhere and laughing . . . Enjoying the flowers. She loved roses. I go to visit our granny now. She's still alive, because Svetochka told her: 'Don't you die, now. Wait for me.' I get up in the night and there's a bouquet of roses on the table – she cut them that evening . . . and two cups of tea. 'Why aren't you sleeping?' I ask her.

'I'm having tea with Svetlanka.' She always used to call her Svetlanka.

I dream about her, and in my dream I tell myself: 'I'll go up and kiss her, and if she's warm that means she's alive.' Then I walk up and kiss her, and she is warm. So she *is* alive!

What if she's living somewhere? Somewhere else . . .

I was sitting by her little grave in the cemetery. Two soldiers walking along stopped. 'Oh! Our Sveta. Just look . . .' Then he noticed me: 'Are you her mother?'

I flung myself on him. 'Did you know Svetochka?'

But he turned to his friend and said: 'Both her legs were blown off in the shelling. And she died.'

I screamed really loudly at that and he got frightened. 'Didn't you know anything? Oh, I'm so sorry! Forgive me!' And he ran away.

I never saw him again. And I didn't try to find him.

I was sitting by the little grave when a mother walked by with her children. I heard what she said. 'What kind of mother is that? How could she let her only daughter go to war these days?' (It was carved on the headstone: 'To our only daughter'.) 'How could she give away her little girl?'

How dare they? How can they? She swore an oath. She was a nurse. Surgeons kissed her hands. She went to save the men, their sons.

'People!' I cry out in my soul. 'Don't turn away from me! Stand by the grave with me. Don't leave me here alone . . .'

A mother

'Afghanistan, fuck it! Afghanistan!' My friend picks up the newspaper and reads: 'Soviet soldiers freed from captivity . . . They gave an interview to Western journalists . . .' And then a stream of obscenities.

'What's your problem?'

'Why, I'd put every last one of them up against the wall. And shoot them myself.'

'You want even more bloodshed? Haven't you seen enough of that already?'

'I've no pity for traitors. We got our arms and legs torn off, and they flattened skyscrapers in New York . . . And they spoke on Voice of America.'

Out there he was my friend . . . We used to sing 'and we go halves on a crust of bread as well'. (*He pauses.*) I hate them! I hate them!

'Who?'

That's clear enough, isn't it? I lost my friend – here, not in the war . . . (*He searches for the right words.*) I don't have anyone else. I don't have any other friends. They've all scattered now. They're all sitting in their burrows, making money.

Afghanistan, fuck it! It would be better if I'd been killed. They'd have put a memorial plaque up at my school, made me into a hero. Kids dream of being heroes. I didn't want to be one. Our forces had already been moved into Afghanistan, but I didn't know anything about it. I wasn't interested. That was the time of my first love; I was going crazy. But now I'm afraid to touch a woman, even when

I squeeze into a crowded trolleybus in the morning. Do you understand? Nothing works out for me with women . . . My girlfriend
left me. The woman I loved. We'd lived together for two years . . .
I burned the kettle that day. I just sat there and watched as it burned.
That sort of thing happens to me sometimes; I completely switch
off, lose touch with reality. She came back from work and smelled
it. 'What did you burn?'

'The kettle.'

'That's the third one.'

'Do you know what blood smells like? After two or three hours
it smells the same as sweaty armpits do. The smell of burning is
better.'

She left and locked the door behind her. And didn't come back
for a year. I started feeling afraid of them. They're . . . Women are
a completely different species. Completely different. That's why
they're unhappy with us. They'll listen to you, agree with everything you say and not understand a single thing.

'What do you mean, "Good morning"? You were screaming again.
You screamed all night again,' she used to weep in the morning.

I didn't tell her everything. I didn't tell her about the rush of ela-
tion in the helicopters when they were bombing. The boys used to
boast about how beautiful a burning *kishlak* was. Especially at
night. A wounded man lying there, one of our soldiers. He's dying.
And he calls for his mother or his girlfriend. A wounded 'spirit'
lying beside him is dying too. And he calls for his mother or his girl.
An Afghan name here, a Russian name there . . .

'What do you mean, "Good morning"? You were screaming
again. I'm afraid of you.'

She doesn't know . . . She doesn't know how our lieutenant was
killed. We saw water and stopped the vehicles. 'Halt! All halt!' the
lieutenant shouted and pointed to a dirty bundle lying beside the
stream. 'Is that a mine?'

The sappers went first. They picked up the 'mine' and it started
whimpering. It was a child. Afghanistan, fuck it! What could we
do? Leave it or take it with us? No one made the lieutenant do it – it
was his own idea: 'We can't abandon it. It'll starve to death. I'll take

it to the *kishlak*. It's close by.' We waited for them for an hour; it was only twenty minutes there and back.

They were lying in the sand. The lieutenant and his driver. In the middle of the *kishlak* . . . The women had killed them with hoes.

'What do you mean, "Good morning"? You were screaming again. And then you started punching me and twisted my arms.'

Sometimes I can't remember my own name and address or everything that happened to me. I come back to my senses . . . And then it's like I start living again. But uncertainly. I walk out of the building and immediately start wondering if I locked the door or not, if I turned off the gas or not. I go to bed and then sit up to check whether I set the alarm clock for the morning or not. On my way to work I meet my neighbours and wonder if I've already said good morning to them or not.

Kipling said:

> Oh, East is East, and West is West, and never the twain shall
>   meet,
> Till Earth and Sky stand presently at God's great Judgment
>   Seat;
> But there is neither East nor West, Border, nor Breed, nor
>   Birth,
> When two strong men stand face to face, though they come
>   from the ends of the earth!

I remember . . . she used to love me. She cried and said: 'You've been through hell . . . I'll save you.' But what I went through was a rubbish tip . . . When I left for Afghanistan women were wearing long dresses; when I came back they were all wearing short ones. They looked strange to me. I asked her to put on a long one. She laughed, and then she took offence. She started hating me . . . (*He closes his eyes and repeats the lines of verse.*)

> But there is neither East nor West, Border, nor Breed, nor
>   Birth,
> When two strong men stand face to face, though they come
>   from the ends of the earth!

What was I talking about? Eh? My girl's long dresses . . . They're hanging in the wardrobe; she didn't take them with her. And I write poems to her . . .

Afghanistan, fuck it! I like talking to myself . . .

A sergeant, scout

I've been a military man all my life . . . All I know about any other life is what I've been told.

Professional military men have their own psychology: it doesn't matter if a war is just or not. Wherever they send us it's a just war, a necessary war. When they sent me that meant it was a just war. That was what we all thought. I myself stood in front of the soldiers and talked about defending our southern borders. I trained them ideologically. Political awareness sessions twice a week. I couldn't tell them 'I have my doubts', could I? The army doesn't tolerate free thinking. Once they fall you in you don't do anything unless you're ordered to. From morning till night.

The command is 'Reveille! Get up!' You get up. The command is 'Fall in for PT! Left turn! Run!' You do your PT. 'Spread out through the wood! Five minutes to move your bowels!' You spread out. The command is 'Fall in!'

In the barracks I never came across a portrait of . . . Well, who, for instance? Let's say Tsiolkovsky or Leo Tolstoy. I never saw a single one. There are portraits of Nikolai Gastello and Alexander Matrosov – heroes of the Great Patriotic War. Once, when I was still a young lieutenant, I hung up a portrait of Romain Rolland in my room (I'd cut it out of some magazine or other). The unit commander walked in. 'Who's that?'

'Romain Rolland, a French writer, comrade colonel.'

'Take that Frenchman down immediately! We've got enough heroes of our own, haven't we?'

'Comrade colonel . . .'

'About turn! Quick march to the stores and come back with Karl Marx!'

'But he's a German, isn't he?'

'Silence! Two days under arrest!'

What has Karl Marx got to do with it? I myself used to stand in front of a group of soldiers and say: 'What's this lathe good for? It's foreign. What's this foreign make of car good for? It falls to pieces on our roads. Everything that's best in the world is ours.' And it's only now that I've started thinking: 'Why couldn't the best lathe be in Japan, and the best nylon stockings in France and the best girls in Taiwan?' And I'm fifty years old . . .

I dreamed that I'd killed a man. He went down on his knees. Then on all fours. He didn't raise his head. I couldn't see his face; their faces are all the same . . . I shot him quite calmly, looked at his blood quite calmly. But I shouted out loud when I woke up and remembered that dream.

They've already written about the war as 'a political error' and called it 'Brezhnev's reckless gamble' and 'a crime', but we had to fight and die. And kill. They write that here, but we died out there. 'Judge not, that ye be not judged!' What were we defending? A revolution? No, I didn't think that any longer; I was already breaking up inside. But I tried to convince myself that we were defending our garrisons, our men.

Rice fields burning. Tracer bullets set them on fire. The rice crackles and burns quickly. The war is helped by the heat too. The peasants come running and gather up the scorched and roasted remains off the ground. I never saw Afghan children cry. They whimpered and whined. The children are light and small. You can't tell how old they are. Wide trousers with little legs sticking out from them.

All the time I had the feeling that someone wanted to kill me. Stupid bullets . . . I still don't know if you can get used to that. But the melons and watermelons there are as big as stools. Stick a bayonet in one and it bursts apart. Dying is so simple. Killing is harder. We didn't talk about the dead men. Those were the rules of the game, if you can put it like that. When I went out on a raid I left a letter to my wife at the bottom of my suitcase. A farewell letter. I wrote: 'Deactivate my pistol and give it to my son.'

When the action started the cassette player was still bawling. Vladimir Vysotsky's voice:

In hot and yellow Africa,
In its very central part,
Disaster struck unscheduled,
Like a bolt out of the blue.
The Elephant was bewildered:
'Looks like there's going to be a flood.'
But what exactly happened there?
Why, a Giraffe and an Antelope
Went and fell in love.

The *dushmans* used to play Vysotsky too. Lots of them had studied in the Union and graduated from Soviet colleges. They had Soviet diplomas. Waiting in ambush at night we used to hear him singing from their positions too:

My friend has gone to Magadan,
Doff your hats now, all doff your hats!
He didn't go there under guard,
But of his own free will, just like that.

Up in the mountains they watched our films. About Kotovsky and Kovpak. They learned from us how to fight against us. How to fight a partisan war . . .

I took the letters from the pockets of our boys who were killed. And the photographs – Tanya from Chernigov, Mashenka from Pskov. Photographs taken in provincial studios. All exactly the same. With naive inscriptions: 'Awaiting your reply as a nightingale waits for summer' – 'Fly with a greeting – speed back with your answer'. They used to lie on my desk like a deck of cards. The faces of simple Russian girls . . .

I can't come back to this world. Living here . . . It's too cramped for me, living here. The adrenalin in my blood rebels. There's no edge to the sensations, not enough contempt for life. I've started getting ill. The doctors have diagnosed narrowing of the arteries. But I've got my own diagnosis: Afghanistan . . . I miss the rhythm. That rhythm, the one for hurling myself into a fight. For taking risks, for defending something. Even now I want to go back, but I don't know what I'd feel there . . . I'd be swamped by the visions. The scenes . . . The smashed and burned-out military vehicles on the roads. Tanks and personnel carriers . . . Is that really all that's left of us out there?

I went to the cemetery . . . I wanted to walk round the 'Afghani' graves, and I met someone's mother. 'Go away, commander! You're alive, even if you do have grey hair. But my son's lying in the ground. My son had never even shaved.'

A friend of mine died recently; he was fighting in Ethiopia. In that heat out there he damaged his kidneys. Everything he had learned went with him. Another comrade told me about how he ended up in Vietnam. And I've met men who were sent to Angola, Egypt, Hungary in '56, Czechoslovakia in '68. We all used to talk to each other . . . Now they're all growing radishes at their dachas. They go fishing. And I'm on a pension now, because of the state of my health. I had one of my lungs removed in the hospital in Kabul. And now the other one's started acting up. I need to have a rhythm! I need things to do!

I heard that there's a hospital near Khmelnitsky where they have all the men who have been rejected by their families and the ones who didn't want to go back home. One young man wrote to me from there: 'I lie here with no arms and no legs. When I wake up in the morning, I don't know if I'm a man or an animal. Sometimes I feel like miaowing or barking. I grit my teeth . . .' I want to go and visit him. I'm looking for something to occupy myself with.

I need a rhythm, the rhythm that goes with fighting. But I don't know who I can fight. I can't just stand there with my boys any longer and feed them propaganda: 'We're the best. We're the most just.' But I do maintain that's what we wanted to be. Only it didn't work out. 'Why' is a different question. Why things didn't work out right yet again . . .

A major, battalion commander

Our consciences are clear before our Homeland . . . I carried out my duty as a soldier honestly. So don't any of you here go shouting about that . . . Don't go standing things on their head and revising them . . . What will you do about those feelings: the love of the Homeland, the sense of duty? Is 'Homeland' just an empty sound to you? Just a word? Our consciences are clear . . .

What did we grab out there – what did we bring back? Those 'Load 200s' – the coffins with our comrades in them? What did we acquire? Sicknesses, from hepatitis to cholera? Wounds and damaged health? But I've got nothing to repent of. I was helping the fraternal people of Afghanistan. I was certain of it. The men who were out there with me were sincere, honest young guys too. They believed that we were there to bring good to that country, that they weren't on the front line by mistake. But some people want to see us as naive fools, cannon fodder. What for? What's the point of it? Are they looking for the truth? Don't forget what's in the Bible. Remember that when Pilate questioned him, Jesus said: 'To this end was I born, and for this cause came I into the world, that I should bear witness unto the truth.' And Pilate asked him: 'What is truth?'

That question remains unanswered.

I have my own truth. My own! Our faith might have been naive, but our belief in it was immaculately pure. What we thought was this: the new authorities are giving people land and everyone should be glad to take it. And then suddenly the peasants won't take the land! 'Who are you,' they said, 'to give away the land, when it belongs to Allah? Allah measures out and gives.' We thought that we'd build farm machinery depots and give them tractors and combine harvesters and mowing machines, and their lives would be completely changed. People would change. And then suddenly they destroy the farm machinery depots. They blow up our tractors as if they're tanks. We thought that in the age of space flight the idea of God was absurd. Absurd! We sent a young Afghan guy into space. 'Look,' we told him. 'Where is your Allah?' And then, suddenly, there's the unshakeable civilization of the Islamic religion . . . Is it possible to fight against eternity?

We used to think all sorts of things. But that's the way it was . . . It happened . . . And it's a special part of our lives. I cherish it in my heart; I don't want to destroy it. And I won't let anyone tar it all in the same black colour. We protected each other in action out here. You try standing in the way of someone else's bullet! You don't forget those things. And how about this? When I came back I wanted to make it a surprise, but I was afraid for my mother. So I called her: 'Mama, I'm alive. I'm at the airport.' I just heard the phone drop at the other end of the line.

Who told you that we lost the war out there? We lost it here, at home. In the Union. And we could have come back here so handsomely . . . All scorched and burned. After learning so much and going through so much. But they didn't let us. They didn't give us any rights here; they didn't give us anything to do here. Every morning someone puts up a poster on the obelisk marking the site of the monument to the internationalist soldiers who were killed. It says: 'Put it up at General HQ, not in the city centre . . .' My eighteen-year-old cousin doesn't want to go into the army: 'Carry out somebody's stupid or criminal orders? Turn myself into a killer?' He sneers at my military medals. But, at his age, my heart used to skip a beat when my granddad put on his red-letter-day jacket with his ribbons and medals. While we were fighting out there the world changed.

What is truth?

There's an old woman who lives in our five-storey block. A doctor. She's seventy-five. After all the articles, denunciations and speeches nowadays . . . after this avalanche of truth that has swept down on us she's gone mad. If she turns on the television and Gorbachev's speaking she opens her ground-floor window and shouts out: 'Long live Stalin! Long live communism, the bright future of mankind!' I see her every morning . . . They don't touch her; she's not bothering anyone. Sometimes I think that I'm a bit like her . . . Fuck it, I *am* like her!

But our consciences are clear before our Homeland.

A private, artilleryman

The doorbell rang. I went running outside, but there was no one there. I gasped, wondering if my son had come home.

Two days later some soldiers knocked at the door.

'Has my son gone?' I asked, guessing straightaway.

'Yes, he has.'

It went very, very quiet. I knelt down in front of the mirror in the hallway. 'Oh God! Oh God! My God!'

A letter I hadn't finished writing was lying on the table:

'Hello, son! I read your letter and it made me glad. There wasn't a single grammatical mistake in it. There were two syntactical errors, like the last time. "To my mind" should come at the beginning of a sentence and "just as" is two words. It should be "I'll do just as my father says." Don't be offended with your mother. It's hot in Afghanistan, son. Try not to catch a cold. You're always catching colds . . .'

At the cemetery no one said anything. There were a lot of people, but none of them said anything. I stood there with a screwdriver; they couldn't take it away from me. 'Let me open the coffin. Let me see my son . . .' I wanted to open the zinc coffin with my screwdriver.

My husband tried to kill himself: 'I won't go on living. Forgive me, mother, but I won't go on living.'

I tried to make him change his mind. 'We have to put up a headstone and tile the grave. Like other people do.'

He couldn't sleep. He said: 'When I lie down, our son comes. He kisses me and hugs me.'

I followed the old tradition and tried to keep a loaf of bread for the whole forty days after the funeral. It crumbled into little pieces after three weeks. That means the family will fall apart . . .

I put photographs of our son up all round the home. That made it easier for me, but it was hard for my husband. 'Take them down. He's looking at me.'

We put up a headstone. A good one, made of expensive marble. All the money we'd saved for our son's wedding went on his headstone. We covered the grave with red tiles and planted red flowers. Dahlias. My husband painted the little fence. 'I've done everything. Our son won't feel offended.'

In the morning he saw me off to work and said goodbye. When I got back from my shift he was hanging on a rope in the kitchen, right in front of my favourite photograph of our son. 'Oh God! Oh God! My God!'

You tell me if they were heroes or not? Why do I have to endure this grief? Sometimes I think: 'They *were* heroes!' He's not the only one lying there. There are dozens. There are rows of them lying in the municipal cemetery. Every public holiday there are military salutes there. And solemn speeches. People bring flowers. Children are accepted into the Young Pioneers . . . But I curse the government and the Party one more time . . . Our regime . . . Even though I'm a communist. I want to know what we did to deserve this. Why did they wrap my son up in zinc? I curse myself. I'm a teacher of Russian literature. I taught him: 'Duty is duty, son. It's what you have to do.' And in the morning I run to the grave and beg forgiveness: 'Forgive me for saying that, son. Forgive me . . .'

A mother

I got a letter: 'Don't worry if there aren't any letters. Write to the old address.' Then two months of silence. I had no idea that he was in Afghanistan. I'd packed a suitcase and I was going to join him at his new posting.

He wrote that he had got tanned and he was going fishing. He sent a photograph of himself sitting on a donkey that was kneeling in the sand. I didn't guess a thing until the first time he came back on leave. Then he confessed that he'd come from the war. His friend had been killed. Before that, he hadn't played with his daughter very much; he didn't have very strong paternal feelings, perhaps because she was still very little. But when he came back he would sit looking at her for hours, and the sadness in his eyes made me feel afraid. He got up in the morning and took her to kindergarten. He loved to sit her on his shoulders and carry her like that. We lived in Kostroma, a beautiful city. He collected her in the evening too. We went to the theatre and the cinema, but most of all he just wanted to be at home. To watch the television and talk.

He became greedy for love. If I went to work, or cooked something in the kitchen, he begrudged that time. 'Stay with me. We can do without rissoles today. Ask for some leave while I'm here.'

When the day came for him to go he deliberately missed the plane, so that we would be together for another two days.

The last night. It was so good I burst into tears. I cried and he just looked at me without saying anything. And then he said: 'Tamarka, if you have someone else later don't forget about this.'

'You've lost your mind,' I said. 'You'll never be killed! I love you so much that you'll never be killed!' He laughed.

He didn't want any more children. 'When I come back . . . you can have a child then. What would you do with them on your own?'

I learned to wait. But if I saw a funeral bus I felt ill. I wanted to scream and cry. I used to run home, and if we'd had an icon on the wall I would have gone down on my knees and prayed: 'Save him for me! Save him!'

That day I went to the cinema. I looked at the screen, but I couldn't see anything. I had this strange, anxious feeling: someone was waiting for me somewhere, there was somewhere I had to go. I barely managed to stay until the end of the film. That's obviously when the battle was taking place . . .

I didn't know anything for another week after that. I even got two letters from him. I was usually delighted with that – I used to kiss them – but this time I felt furious, wondering how much longer I would have to wait for him.

At five in the morning on the ninth day a telegram arrived; they simply stuck it under my door. The telegram was from his parents. 'Please come. Petya killed.' I screamed out loud and woke the child. What could I do? Where could I go? I didn't have any money. That was the day when his pay was due to arrive. I remember I wrapped our little daughter in a red blanket and went out into the road. The buses weren't running yet; I stopped a taxi. 'To the airport,' I told the driver.

'I'm going to the depot,' he said and closed the door.

'My husband's been killed in Afghanistan.'

He got out of the car without saying a word and helped me get in. We called at my friend's place and I sorted out the money. At the airport there weren't any tickets for Moscow and I was afraid to take out the telegram and show it to them. What if it wasn't true? If it was a mistake? What if . . . The most important thing was not to say it out loud . . . I cried and everyone looked at me. At last they put me on a rickety little plane to Moscow. I reached Minsk late at night. But I still had further to go, to Starye Dorogi. The taxi drivers didn't want to take me: it was too far, a hundred and fifty kilometres. I begged them. I implored them. One finally agreed: 'Give me fifty roubles and I'll take you.' I gave him everything I had left. I reached the apartment building at two o'clock. Everyone was crying.

'Perhaps it isn't true?'

'It is, Tamara. It is true.'

In the morning we went to the military commissariat. The officer told us: 'We'll inform you when they bring him.' We waited another two days. We called Minsk: 'Come and collect him yourselves.' We arrived at the regional military commissariat. They told us: 'They took him to Baranovichi by mistake.' That was another hundred kilometres, and our bus didn't have any petrol. None of the managers were there at Baranovichi airport; the working day was over. The watchman was sitting in his little booth.

'We've come . . .'

'Over there,' he said, pointing with his hand. 'Some kind of box. Take a look. If it's yours you can collect it.'

The dirty crate was standing out in the open, with 'Senior Lieutenant Dovnar' written on it in chalk. I tore a board off in the place where a coffin has a little window. His face wasn't damaged, but he was lying there unshaven. No one had washed him and the coffin was too small. And the smell. The unbearable smell. I couldn't lean down and kiss him . . . That was how they sent back my husband . . .

I went down on my knees beside what had once been the person dearest of all to me. The person I loved most of all.

That was the first coffin in the village of Yazyl in the Starye Dorogi district of the Minsk region. People's eyes were filled with horror. No one understood what was happening. I carried my daughter to him to say goodbye; she was four and a half years old. She started screaming: 'Papa's all black . . . I'm afraid . . . Papa's all black . . .' They lowered the coffin into the grave, and before they could even pull out the towels they'd used to lower it there was a terrible peal of thunder and a flurry of hail: I remember the hail, like white gravel on the lilac blossoms, and crunching under my feet. Nature herself was against it.

It was a long time before I could leave his home, because his soul was there . . . His father and his mother . . . His things: the desk, the school briefcase, the bicycle . . . I grabbed hold of everything that I could. I held his things in my hands . . . No one in the place said a word. I felt as if his mother hated me: I was alive, but he wasn't; I'd get married again, but her son wouldn't be there. She's a good woman, but at that time she was out of her mind. Her eyes were filled with a heavy darkness . . . Now she tells me: 'Tamara, get married.' But then I was afraid to meet her eye. His father almost went insane: 'Such a fine boy, and they destroyed him! They killed him!' Petya's mother and I tried to tell him that his son had been awarded a medal . . . That we needed Afghanistan . . . The defence of our southern borders . . . He wouldn't listen: 'The bastards! The bastards!'

The most terrible time came afterwards. It was awful getting used to the idea that I had nothing to live for, no one to wait for. But I waited for a long time . . . I moved to a different flat. In the morning I used to wake up soaking wet from fear: 'Petya will come back, and Oleska and I are living at a different address.' I simply couldn't understand that I was alone now, and I would carry on being alone. I looked in our postbox three times a day . . . I only got back my own letters, the ones he never received, with a stamp on them: 'No longer at this address'. I didn't like the public holidays any longer. I stopped going to visit people. I had nothing left but memories. I remembered the very best things. The things that came at the beginning . . .

On the first day we danced. On the second day we took a walk in the park. On the third day, two days after we met, he proposed to me. I already had a fiancé. The application was already in the registry office. I told him about that. He went away and wrote to me, with big letters covering the whole page: 'A-a-a-a-ah! A-oo-oo-oo-oo!'

In January I wrote back: 'I'll come and we'll get married. But I don't want to get married in January. I want a spring wedding! In a Palace of Weddings. With music and flowers.'

It was a winter wedding, in my village. A funny, hasty kind of occasion. At Epiphany, when people tell fortunes, I had a dream and I told my mother about it in the morning.

'Mama, I saw a handsome young man standing on a bridge and calling to me. He was in uniform. But when I got close to him he started moving away from me, further and further away, until he completely disappeared.'

'Don't marry a soldier, you'll be left alone,' my mother predicted.

He came for two days. 'Let's go to the registry office!' he said before he even set foot inside. At the village soviet building they looked at us and said: 'Why bother to wait two months? Go and get the cognac.' An hour later we were husband and wife.

There was a blizzard blowing outside. 'What taxi are you going to take your young wife home in?'

'Just a moment!' He raised his hand and stopped a tractor, a Belarus.

For years I've had a dream about us meeting and riding on a tractor. The driver honks his horn and we kiss. He's been gone for eight years now . . . Eight. I often dream about him. In my dream I always beg him: 'Marry me again.' But he pushes me away: 'No! No!' I feel so sorry for him, not just because he was my husband. What a man he was! What a handsome man! A big, strong body. In the street people turned round to look at him, not at me. It's a pity I never gave him a son. I could have done. I asked him, but he was afraid . . .

The second time he came home on leave he didn't send a telegram. He didn't warn me. The flat was locked: it was my friend's birthday and I was at her place. He opened the door and there was loud music and laughter . . . He sat down on a stool and cried. Every day he came to meet me: 'When I'm walking to collect you from work my knees tremble as if I'm going on a date.'

I remember we went to the river and sunbathed and swam. We sat on the bank and lit a fire. 'You know, I really hate the idea of dying for someone else's Homeland.'

And later, at night: 'Tamarka, don't get married again.'

'Why do you say that?'

'Because I love you very much. And I can't imagine you being with someone else.'

The days flew by fast. And a strange fear appeared . . . We were afraid. We even left our daughter with the neighbours so that we could be alone together more of the time. It wasn't exactly a premonition, but there was a shadow . . . This shadow appeared . . . He only had six months left to go. Here in the Union they were already planning a replacement for him.

Sometimes it seems to me that I've lived for a long, long time, but my memories are always the same ones. I've learned them off by heart.

My little daughter came home from kindergarten. 'Today we told the class about our fathers. I said my papa is a soldier.'

'Why?'

'They didn't ask if he was alive or not. They asked what he does.'

She grew up a bit, and when I was angry with her about something she said: 'You should get married, mama.'

'What kind of papa would you like to have?'

'I'd like to have my own papa.'

'And if it's not your own papa?'

'Someone like him.'

I was twenty-four when I became a widow. During the first few months, if any man had approached me I would have got married on the spot. I was going insane! I didn't know how to save myself. I was surrounded by the same old life: someone was building a dacha, someone was buying a car, someone had a new flat and they needed a carpet and a red cooker for the kitchen . . . beautiful wallpaper . . . Other people's normal life . . . But I was like a fish out of water. At night I choked on my tears . . . I've only just started buying furniture now. I didn't even have the heart to bake pies. Or put on a nice dress. How could there be any celebrations in my home?

From 1941 to 1945 everyone had their own grief. Everyone lost someone. They knew what they lost them for. The women all keened together. A hundred people are employed in the catering college where I work. I'm the only one whose husband was killed in that war; all the others have only read about it in the newspapers. The first time I heard on the television that Afghanistan was our disgrace I wanted to smash the screen. That day I buried my husband for the second time.

I loved him for five years when he was alive and I've loved him for eight years since he died. Perhaps I'm insane. But I love him.

A wife

They brought us to Samarkand . . . There were two tents standing there; in the first one we took off all our civilian clothes (the smarter guys had sold their jackets or sweaters on the way and bought some wine for the send-off) and in the other they handed out second-hand soldiers' gear – tunics from 1945, tarpaulin boots, footcloths. Show those boots to a black man used to real heat and he would faint. In underdeveloped African countries their soldiers have light low-cut boots, jackets, trousers and caps, but we sing as we build in forty degrees Celsius. For the first week we unloaded glass jars at a refrigerator factory. We lugged crates of lemonade about at a food depot. They sent us to the officers' houses and I clad one of them with bricks. I spent about two weeks roofing a piggery. If I nailed down three sheets of fibre cement, I swapped another two for a bottle of vodka. We sold off planks at one rouble a metre.

Before I took the oath they sent us to the shooting range twice; the first time they gave us nine cartridges and the second time we threw one grenade each. They lined us up on the parade ground and read out the order: 'You are being posted to the Democratic Republic of Afghanistan to perform international duty. Anyone who doesn't want to go – two paces forward.' Three men stepped out. The unit commander put them back in line with a knee up the backside: 'Right, that's your fighting spirit tested.' We got dry rations for two days and a leather belt – and off we went. That's the way it was . . . I wasn't upset about it. For me it was the only possible chance to see a foreign country. Well, and . . . Of course, it's true that I was dreaming of bringing back a cassette player and a leather briefcase. Before then nothing interesting had ever happened in my life. It was a boring life. Now I was flying in a huge Il-76. The first time . . . It was the first time I'd ever flown in a plane! I saw mountains through the little window. An empty desert. My people are from Pskov; we have meadows and woods there. We disembarked at Shindand. I remember the day and the month – 19 December 1980.

They took one look at me. 'One metre eighty centimetres . . . Put him in the reconnaissance company. They need men like him.'

From Shindand to Herat. And we built there too. We built a shooting range. Digging earth and carrying rocks for the foundation. I put on the fibre concrete roof and did carpentry work. Some of us never fired a gun until our first action. We felt hungry all the time. In the kitchen there were two fifty-litre vats. One for the first course: cabbage with water – no way could you get hold of any meat. The other was for the second course – dried potatoes or pearl barley without any oil. They gave us one tin of mackerel between four: the label had the year it was tinned, 1956, and its storage life, eighteen months. In a year and a half I only once stopped feeling hungry – when I was wounded. But apart from that I was constantly wondering where I could get hold of or steal something to eat. We used to climb into the Afghans' gardens and they shot at us. We could have stepped on a mine. But we wanted apples and pears, any kind of fruit, so badly. I asked my parents for citric acid, and they used to send it with their letters. We dissolved it in water and drank it. It was sour and we burned our stomachs.

Before our first action they played the Hymn of the Soviet Union. The political officer spoke. I remember he said that global imperialism remained constantly vigilant and they would welcome us home as heroes. I had no idea how I was going to kill anyone. Before the army I used to go bicycle racing and I developed big muscles. No one touched me; they were afraid to. I'd never even seen a fight with a knife and blood.

We rode on armoured personnel carriers. Before that they'd taken us from Shindand to Herat in a bus, and once I'd driven out of the garrison in a ZIL truck. We sat on the armour plate, holding our guns, with our sleeves rolled up to the elbows . . . It was a new sensation, something unfamiliar. A feeling of power, strength and being safe. The *kishlaks* immediately became small and low, the *aryks*, or irrigation ditches, became shallow and the trees were sparse. After half an hour I settled down and felt as calm as a tourist. I was viewing someone else's exotic country. Different trees, different birds, different flowers . . . I saw camelthorn for the first time. And I forgot about the war.

We drove over an *aryk*, across a clay bridge, which, to my surprise, could support tons of metal. Suddenly there was an explosion – someone had fired point-blank at the leading personnel carrier with a grenade launcher. And all of a sudden young guys that I knew were being carried by others. One of them with no head . . . a cardboard target . . . arms dangling loose . . . My mind couldn't immediately get to grips with this new and terrible life . . . The order was to deploy the mortars, 'cornflowers' we used to call them – a hundred and twenty shots a minute. All the rounds went into the *kishlak* that they had fired from, several rounds into every compound. After the battle we collected together the pieces of our boys, scraped them off the armour plate. There weren't any ID tags on the bodies; we simply spread out a tarpaulin and that was their communal grave. Just try finding where someone's leg is, or who a piece of skull belongs to. They didn't issue ID tags. What if they fell into enemy hands? First name, surname, address . . . Like in the song: 'Our address isn't a building or a street, our address is the Soviet Union . . .' That's the way it was.

We drove back without talking at all. We were simple guys, we weren't used to killing. In the garrison we calmed down. Got a bite to eat. Cleaned our guns. Then we started talking.

'Want to make a joint?' the 'granddads' offered.

'No thanks.'

I didn't want to smoke: I was afraid I wouldn't be able to give it up afterwards. You get hooked on drugs very quickly. It takes real willpower to give them up. Later on we all smoked, otherwise you'd just have croaked, your nerves would have snapped. If only we'd had the standard hundred grammes of vodka from the old war. It wasn't allowed. Total prohibition. But we had to handle the stress and zone out somehow. We sprinkled hash into the pilau rice, into the porridge . . . Our eyes were the size of fifty-kopeck coins . . . At night I could see like a cat. I was as light as a bat flying through the air.

Reconnaissance scouts don't kill in battle formation, but close up. Not with an automatic, but with a hunting knife or a bayonet. I learned to do it very quickly and I got used to it. The first man that I killed? That I killed close up? I remember . . . We approached a *kishlak* on foot and through the night-vision binoculars we saw a small torch glowing beside a tree, with a rifle leaning against it, and a man digging something up. I gave my comrade my automatic, moved in close enough and jumped the guy, knocking him off his feet. I shoved his turban in his mouth so he wouldn't shout. We hadn't taken hunting knives with us; they were too heavy to carry. I had a penknife that we used for opening tins of food. An ordinary penknife. He was already lying there. I pulled his head back with his beard and slit his throat. After you kill a man the first time . . . It's a shock, like after your first woman . . . But it passed off quickly. After all, I'm from the country: I'd killed chickens and goats! That's the way it was.

I was a senior scout. We usually went out at night. I used to sit behind a tree with my knife . . . Here they come. The one in front is the point man, the scout, he has to be taken out. We took turns to do that. This time it was my turn . . . When the scout drew level with me I let him move on a bit and then jumped him from behind. I had to make sure to grab his head with my left hand and jerk his throat up, so he couldn't shout. I stuck the knife in his back with my right hand, right under the liver. And I stabbed him right through . . . Back then I used to have a trophy, a Japanese knife thirty-one centimetres long. It slipped into a man real easy. He might squirm and fall, but he wouldn't call out. You get used to it. The technique of it was harder than the psychological side. Being able to hit the heart. I studied karate. How to take someone down . . . You have to find the painful points – the nose, the ears, just beside the eyebrow – and hit them precisely. Where exactly to jab in the knife.

We break into a *duval*: two of us by the door, two inside the yard and the rest search the house. Naturally, we take whatever we like . . . This one time my nerves gave out . . . We were combing a *kishlak*. We usually opened a door and tossed a grenade in first, before going in, to avoid running into a burst of gunfire. Why take the risk, when it's safer with the grenade? I tossed the grenade and walked in: the women were lying there with two boys and a little baby. In some sort of little box . . . instead of a baby buggy . . .

I remember it now . . . And it really bothers me.

I wanted to be a good man, but that doesn't happen in war. I came back home. I'm blind – a bullet took out the retinas of both eyes. It went into my left temple and came out of my right one. I can only distinguish light and darkness. I haven't managed to become a good man. I still often feel a desire to tear someone's throat out. I know them . . . The ones who deserve to have their throats ripped out. The ones who begrudge headstones for our boys' graves. Who don't want to give apartments to us invalids: 'I didn't send you out there . . .' The ones who don't give a rotten damn for us. When we were dying out there they watched the war on television. It was all entertainment for them! A spectacle! Something to give their nerves a thrill.

I've learned to live without eyes . . . I travel round the city alone; in the metro I make all the changes on my own. I cook – my wife's amazed that I cook better than she does. I've never seen my wife, but I know what she's like. The colour of her hair, what her nose is like, and her lips . . . I feel her with my hands and my body. My body sees. I know what my son's like . . . I changed his nappies when he was little and did his laundry. Now I carry him on my shoulders. Sometimes I think that you don't really need eyes. People close their eyes when they're happy, don't they, and that's the most important thing of all. An artist needs eyes, because that's his profession. But I sense the world. I hear it . . . That world means more to me than it does to all of you who have eyes. A word and a line of words. Sounds.

Many people think it's all over for me now – the boy's done all his fighting, so to speak. Like Yury Gagarin after his flight. No, all the important things are still ahead of me. I know that. You don't have to attach any more importance to a body than to a bicycle. I used to be a cyclist; I took part in races. The body is an instrument, like a power tool that we use to work with, that's all. I can be happy and free without eyes. I've realized that . . . There's so much that sighted people don't see. When I had eyes I was blinder than I am now. I want to purge myself of it all. All the filth that they dragged us into. My memories. You don't know how terrifying it is at night. It all comes tumbling down on me again . . . I'm jumping at a man, holding a knife again, sizing up where to stick it . . . A man's soft; I remember that a man's body is soft . . . That's the way of it!

The nights are frightening because then I can see. I'm not blind in my dreams.

A private, scout

Take no notice of how small and frail I am. I was out there too. I'm from out there . . .

Every year it gets harder for me to answer the question: 'If you're not a soldier, what did you go there for?' I was twenty-seven. All my friends were married, but I wasn't. I was friends with a boy for a year and then he married someone else. 'Jettison it! Wipe it from your memory, so that no one will ever know or guess that we were out there' – that's what one of my friends writes to me. No, I'm not going to wipe it from my memory. I want to figure it out . . .

We already started realizing out there that we'd been tricked. The question is: why is it so easy to trick us? Because that's what we want ourselves . . . If that's the right way to put it. I live alone a lot of the time; I'll forget how to talk soon. Stop speaking altogether. I can admit this . . . I'd hide it from a man, but I can tell a woman. My eyes popped out of my head when I saw how many women were going to that war. Beautiful ones and plain ones, young ones and not so young. Cheerful ones and spiteful ones. Bakers, cooks, serving women, cleaners . . . Of course, everyone had a practical motive of their own: they wanted to earn money and maybe sort out their personal lives. All of them were unmarried or divorced. Searching for happiness. For their destiny.

There was happiness out there. People did fall in love for real. And they had weddings. Tamara Solovei, a nurse . . . They brought in this helicopter pilot, black all over, scorched. And two months later they got married and she invited me to the wedding. I asked the girls I shared a room with what I should do, because I was mourning. My friend had been killed; I'd had to write to his mother. I'd been crying for two days. How could I go to a wedding? 'Her fiancé could be killed the day after tomorrow, but at least there'll be someone to cry for him,' the girls told me. 'Don't even bother thinking whether to go or not,' they said, 'find a present.' Everyone gave the same gift – an envelope with hard currency checks in it. The groom's crew arrived with a canister of pure spirits. And they sang and danced, and made toasts. They shouted out: 'Time for a kiss!' Happiness is the same everywhere. Especially for a woman . . .

All sorts of things happened, but I remembered the beautiful things . . . The battalion commander came into my room one evening: 'Don't be afraid! I don't want anything from you. You sit there and I'll just look at you for a while.'

But people had belief! Really strong belief! Believing in something is so beautiful. It's wonderful! Then that feeling of being tricked . . . Still, the belief. Somehow that was a part of us. Maybe I couldn't imagine a different kind of war, one that wasn't like the Great Patriotic War. I loved watching war films ever since I was little. The way I thought . . . The way I pictured things in my mind. The scenes I saw . . . How can a military hospital get by without women? Without women's hands? Men lying there, scorched all over. Mutilated. Just simply putting your hand on their wounds and passing on some kind of energy. That's mercy too! It's work for a woman's heart! But do you believe me? Do you believe us? You know, not all the women there were prostitutes or check grubbers. There were more good girls. I can trust you as a woman. Because you're a woman. It's best not to mention the subject with men. They'd laugh in my face . . .

At my new job (when I came back I left my old one) no one knows that I was at the war. That I'd come back from Kabul. I started arguing about Afghanistan – what kind of war it was, and why there was a war – and our head engineer interrupted me:

'What does a young woman like you understand about military matters . . . ? That's men's business . . .' (*She laughs.*)

At the war I met a lot of boys who were keen to go on dangerous operations. They died without a second thought. I watched men a lot out there. I spied on them. It was interesting . . . You know . . . What's going on their heads? What kind of microbes are in there? They're always fighting wars. I saw them risk their lives and I saw them kill. And to this day they still think that they're special somehow, because they've killed. They've been touched by something that the others don't know. Maybe it is a sickness? There's some microbe. Or a virus. And they get infected by it.

Everything had turned upside down at home . . . Among all the people I knew . . . We left a state that wanted this war and came back to a state that didn't want it. When your own socialism's crumbling, you lose interest in building socialism somewhere at the far end of the world. No one quotes Marx and Lenin any longer. They don't remember about world revolution any longer. The heroes are different now: farmers and businessmen. The ideals are different: 'My home is my castle . . .' But we were brought up on heroes like Pavel Korchagin and Alexei Meresiev. We used to sing songs round the campfire: 'First think of the Homeland, and then about yourself.' They'll start laughing at us soon. Frightening their children with us. What hurts isn't that we were denied something we should have had, that they didn't give out enough medals. We've just been crossed out, as if we never even existed. Crushed between the millstones . . .

Back here, for the first six months I couldn't get to sleep at night. And when I did fall asleep I dreamed of dead bodies and shelling. I used to jump up in horror. And when I closed my eyes the same pictures came back. I got an appointment with a neurologist. He listened to what I said and he was amazed: 'You mean you really saw that many dead bodies?' Oh, how I wanted to smack him across his young face! I barely managed to stop myself. I had to persuade myself not to. And I could swear a blue streak too! I learned that at the war.

I didn't go to any more doctors. And I started getting depressed.

In the morning I don't want to get out of bed, get washed and brush my hair. I have to force myself to do it all. I go to work and I talk to someone. Ask me in the evening and I don't remember a thing about it. I feel less and less desire to live. I can't listen to music. Or read poetry. But I used to love all that; it was what I lived for. I don't invite anybody to visit me. And I don't visit anyone else. I've got nowhere to hide, thanks to the damned housing problem. I live in a communal apartment . . . What did I earn from the war? I got a few clothes. I bought some Italian furniture . . . But I'm still alone. I didn't find anything in that life and I've lost my way in this one. I don't fit into this life either. I still want to believe in something. They've taken that away . . . I've been robbed . . . It's not just the money in the bank that's disappeared, with inflation, it's worse than that – they've confiscated the past. I don't have any past. Or any belief . . . How can I live?

Do you think we're cruel? Do you have any idea how cruel you all are? Nobody asks us anything and they don't listen to us. But they write about us . . .

Don't mention my name. I'm as good as dead already.

A civilian employee

I rush to the cemetery as if I was going on a date . . .

At the beginning I used to spend the night there. I wasn't afraid. Now I understand the way the birds fly and the way the grass ripples. In spring I wait for a little flower to break up through the ground to me. I planted snowdrops . . . So I would get a greeting from my son as early as possible. They grow up to me from down there . . . from him . . .

I sit at his grave until the evening. Until night. Sometimes I cry out, but I don't hear anything until the birds go flying up. A swirling crowd of crows. They circle round, flapping their wings above my head, and I come to my senses and stop calling. I've come here every day for four whole years. In the morning or the evening. I didn't come for eleven days when I was in hospital with a mild heart attack and they wouldn't let me get up. But I did get up and walked quietly as far as the toilet . . . That meant I could walk as far as my son; and if I fell it would be on his grave. I ran off in my hospital dressing gown.

Before that I had a dream about Valera. '*Mamochka*, don't come to the cemetery tomorrow. Don't come.'

I got there and it was very quiet; as quiet as if he wasn't even there. I could feel in my heart that he wasn't there. The crows were sitting on the headstone and the fence; they didn't fly away, they didn't hide from me, as usual. I got up off the little bench to go, and they flew ahead of me, trying to calm me down. They wouldn't let me leave. What was going on? What were they trying to tell me? Suddenly the birds calmed down and flew up into the trees. And I felt drawn to the grave. My heart was so peaceful; the feeling of alarm had passed off. His spirit had come back. 'Thank you, my birds, for telling me, for not letting me go. I waited and my darling son has come back.'

I feel uncomfortable among people. I'm like a wandering soul. They try to tell me things and keep bothering me . . . They get in my way. But at the cemetery I feel all right. I only feel all right with my son. You can always find me either at work or there, at the grave . . . That way it's as if my son is alive. I worked out exactly where his head is and I sit beside him and tell him about everything. What kind of morning I've had, what kind of day. We remember things together. I look at his photo. I look hard, for a long time. He either smiles a bit or frowns because he's annoyed about something. And that's how we live together. If I buy a new dress it's only to come and visit my son, so that he can see me in it. He used to kneel down in front of me: 'My mother! You're my beautiful mother!' Now I kneel beside him. I open the little gate and go down on my knees. 'Good morning, son . . . Good evening, son . . .'

I'm always with him. I was going to adopt a boy from the orphanage . . . Find a little blue-eyed boy like him. But I've got a bad heart. My heart wouldn't stand it. I force myself to work; it's like driving myself into a black tunnel. If I had time to sit in the kitchen and look out of the window I'd go mad. Only the suffering can save me. I haven't been to the cinema once in these four years. I sold my colour television and the money went on the headstone.

I haven't switched the radio on even once. As soon as my son was killed everything about me changed: my face, my eyes, even my hands.

I married for such wonderful love. I just rushed straight into it. He was a flyer, tall and handsome. In a leather jacket and flying boots. A real bear. Was he really going to be my husband? All the girls gasped at that! When I went into a shop I wondered why our Soviet manufacturers didn't make household slippers with high heels – I was so little beside him. I waited for him to get ill and start coughing, to get a head cold. Then he could stay at home for the whole day and I could look after him. I desperately wanted a son. And I wanted my son to be like him. The same eyes, the same ears, the same nose. It was as if someone up in heaven was eavesdropping: my son was exactly like him, alike as two peas. I couldn't believe that these two wonderful men were mine. I couldn't believe it. I loved my home. I loved washing and ironing. I loved it all so much, I wouldn't even step on a spider; I used to catch flies and ladybirds indoors and let them out though the window. Let all the creatures live and love each other – I was so happy! When I came home I used to ring the doorbell and switch on the light in the corridor, so my son could see how full of joy I was: 'Lerunka!' That's what I called him when he was little. 'It's me! I missed you!' I used to run home from the shops or from work.

I loved my son madly and I still love him now. When they brought the photos from the funeral I didn't take them . . . I still didn't believe it. I'm a faithful hound, the kind of dog that dies on its master's grave. And I was always faithful in friendship too. When my breasts were overflowing with milk I agreed to meet a friend: I had to give her back a book. So I stood out in the freezing cold for an hour and a half, waiting for her, but she didn't come. I thought no one could simply not bother to come if they'd promised, so something must have happened. I ran to her place and she was sleeping. She couldn't understand why I was crying. I loved her too, and I gave her my very favourite dress, a light-blue one. That's what I'm like. I was slow to get started with life, timid. Some people are bolder. I didn't believe that anyone could love me. When they told me I was beautiful I didn't believe it. I was a late developer in everything. But once I learned something and fixed it in my memory then it was there for the rest of my life. Forever. And I did everything joyfully. When Yury Gagarin flew into space I went dashing out into the street with Lerunka. At that moment I wanted to love everybody and hug everybody. We shouted out with joy . . .

I loved my son madly. Madly. And he loved me madly too. His grave draws me to it. It calls to me. As if he's calling my name.

When they asked him if he had a girl, he used to tell them, 'Yes, I do', and he showed them my student card, with a photo of me wearing my hair in long, long plaits. He liked to waltz. He invited me to have the first waltz at their school graduation party. I didn't know he could dance, but he'd learned. We swirled round and round together.

In the evening I used to knit at the window, waiting for him. Footsteps. No, that's not him. More footsteps . . . My son's footsteps! I was never wrong. We sat down facing each other and talked until four o'clock in the morning. What about? Well, what do people talk about when they're feeling good? About everything. About serious things and all sorts of nonsense. We laughed. He sang and played the piano for me.

I used to look at the clock and say: 'Bedtime, Valera.'

'Let's sit up a bit longer, my little mother.' He used to call me 'my little mother' and 'my precious little mother'.

'Well, my precious little mother, your son has joined the Smolensk Higher Military Academy. Are you glad?' He sat down at the piano and sang:

> Officers and gentlemen are princes of blue blood!
> Probably I'm not the first,
> And I won't be the last . . .

My father was a career officer who was killed defending Leningrad. My grandfather was an officer too. And nature herself made my son to be a soldier, with his height and strength, and his manners. He should have been a hussar! White gloves . . . Games of cards . . . 'Every inch a military man,' I used to laugh. If only the heavens above had wept at least one raindrop to give us an inkling . . . If there'd been a sign . . .

Everyone imitated him. Even I imitated him. I sat at the piano the same way as he did, half turned. Sometimes I caught myself walking like him. Especially after he died. I want him always to be here inside me . . . To go on living.

'Well, my precious little mother, your son's going away.'

'Where to?'

He didn't answer and I sat there crying. 'Where are you going, my dearest son?'

'How do you mean, "where"? That's obvious, isn't it? Now, to work, my little mother. We'll start with the kitchen. My friends will be arriving soon.'

I guessed immediately. 'To Afghanistan?'

'That's the place . . .' And he put on such a forbidding face, as if he'd lowered an iron curtain.

His friend Kolka Romanov came bursting in, as bright as a bell, and told me everything: when they were still in their third year at the academy they'd put in applications to be sent to Afghanistan, but for a long time they were refused.

The first toast: 'He who takes no risks, drinks no champagne.' Valera sang my favourite Russian romances all evening:

> Officers and gentlemen are princes of blue blood!
> Probably I'm not the first,
> And I won't be the last . . .

When there were four weeks left I went into his room early in the morning and sat there, listening to him sleeping. He slept beautifully too.

Destiny knocked so clearly on our door and gave us such a clear hint. I had a dream: I was lying on a black cross, wearing a long, black dress. And an angel was carrying me on the cross. I could just barely cling on, and I decided to look down to see where I would fall, into the sea or on to the land. And I saw a big pit, flooded with bright sunlight . . .

I was expecting him back on leave. He didn't write for a long time, and then I got a call at work. 'My precious little mother, I'm back. Don't be late. The soup's ready.'

I shouted out: 'My son! My dearest! You're not calling from Tashkent? You're home! There's a pan of your favourite borsch in the fridge!'

'Oh Lord! I saw the pan, but I didn't bother to look in it.'

'What sort of soup have you made?'

'It's called "the idiot's dream". Come home. I'm going to meet the bus.'

He came back with his hair all grey. He didn't admit that he wasn't on leave, that he'd got them to let him out of the hospital: 'To see my little mother for a day or two.' He rolled about on the carpet, growling in pain. Hepatitis, malaria – he'd caught everything. But he warned his sister: 'Mama mustn't know what's just happened. Go and read a book.'

I looked into his room again before work to watch him sleeping. He opened his eyes. 'What is it, my little mother?'

'Why aren't you sleeping? It's still early.'

'I had a bad dream.'

'Son, if you have a bad dream, you have to turn over. Then you'll have a good one. And you shouldn't tell anyone your bad dreams – then they won't come true.'

We went with him to Moscow to see him off. It was a sunny day in May. The marsh marigolds were in flower.

'How are things out there, son?'

'My little mother, Afghanistan is something we shouldn't be doing.'

He only looked at me, not anyone else. He held out his arms and pressed his forehead against mine. 'I don't want to go back into that pit! I don't want to!' He started walking, then looked back. 'And that's all, mama.'

On 7 July I woke up crying. I just stared up at the ceiling without seeing anything. He'd woken me up. As if he'd come to say goodbye . . . Eight o'clock. I had to get ready for work. I darted out of the bathroom holding my light-coloured dress, and then dashed from one room to another. But I just couldn't put that dress on. My head was spinning. I couldn't see anything. Everything was hazy . . . But I calmed down by the middle of the day, by lunch.

7 July . . . Seven cigarettes in my pocket with seven matches. Seven photos in my camera. Seven letters to me. And seven letters to his fiancée. My book open at the seventh page . . . Kobo Abe, *Containers of Death* . . .

He had three or four seconds to save himself. Their personnel carrier was heading straight over a cliff. 'Save yourself, boys! I won't make it!' He couldn't jump first and leave his friends . . . He couldn't do that . . .

This is a letter from the deputy regimental commander for political affairs, Major S. R. Sinelnikov. 'In fulfilment of my duty as a soldier I am obliged to inform you that Senior Lieutenant Valery Gennadievich Valovich was killed today at ten forty-five hours . . .'

The whole town already knew about it. The officers' club there was hung with his photographs and black crepe. The plane with his coffin was about to land. But no one had told me anything. No one had dared. At work everyone had red eyes from crying. 'What's happened?' I asked. They distracted me with all sorts of excuses. A friend of mine looked in. Then our doctor in his white coat. It was like I suddenly woke up.

'What is this? Have you all gone mad? Men like that don't get killed! No!' I started hammering on the desk. I ran to the window and banged on the glass. They gave me an injection.

'Have you all gone mad? Have you all lost your minds?' Another injection. But the injections had no effect on me. They tell me I was screaming 'I want to see him. Take me to my son.'

'Tell them to do it, or she won't survive this.'

A long coffin, rough wood . . . with 'Valovich' painted on it in big yellow letters. I hoisted up the coffin. I wanted to take it with me. My bladder gave out . . .

'I need a place in the cemetery. A dry spot. Nice and dry! You want fifty roubles? I'll give you it, I will. But I need a good spot. Nice and dry . . .' I understand inside that this is horrible, but I can't say that . . . 'A nice dry place. I'll give you everything I have, if you want!'

At first I stayed there at night. I didn't leave. They took me home, and I went back again . . . They were making hay. The town and the cemetery smelled of hay.

One morning I met a young soldier. 'Hello, mother. Your son was my commander. I'm willing to tell you everything.'

'Oh, son, just a moment.' We came back home. He sat down in my son's chair and began, then he changed his mind. 'I can't, mother.'

I bow when I get to him and I bow when I leave him. I'm only ever at home when I have visitors. I feel good with my son. I don't feel the cold even when it's freezing. I write letters to him there – I have a heap of letters that have never been posted. How can I send them to him? I come back home at night, the streetlamps are on, the cars drive along with their headlights on. I walk back. I've got so much strength inside that I'm not afraid of anything, neither man nor beast.

I still hear my son's words ringing in my ears: 'I don't want to go back into that pit!' Who's going to answer for that? Someone has to. I want to live a long life – I'm trying really hard to live – in order to be with my son. The most defenceless thing a man has is his grave. His name. I'll always defend my son.

His comrades came to visit him . . . One friend crawled on his knees in front of him: 'Valera, I'm soaked in blood. I killed people with these hands. I was never out of the fighting. I'm soaked in blood . . . Valera, I don't know any longer if it was better to be killed or to stay alive. I don't know any longer . . .' I'd like to know who's going to answer for all this. Why don't they tell us their names?

How he used to sing:

> Officers and gentlemen are princes of blue blood!
> Probably I'm not the first,
> And I won't be the last . . .

I went to the church and had a talk with the priest. 'My son has been killed. A remarkable son, my darling. How should I be close to him now? What are our Russian customs? We've forgotten them. I want to know them.'

'Is he baptized?'

'Father, I'd really like to say that he's baptized, but I can't. I was married to a young military officer. We lived in Kamchatka; it's covered in snow there all the time. We lived in dugout shelters made of snow . . . The snow here is white, but there it's blue and green, and it doesn't hurt your eyes. The air's clean there. Sound travels a long way . . . Do you understand me, father?'

'Mother Victoria, it's bad that he's not baptized. Our prayers won't reach him.'

Then I blurted out: 'I'll baptize him myself, then. With my love and my suffering. I'll baptize him through suffering . . .'

The priest took hold of my hand. It was trembling. 'Don't get so worked up, Mother Victoria. How often do you go to see your son?'

'I go every day. Of course I do! If he was alive we'd see each other every day.'

'Mother, you mustn't disturb him after five in the evening. They go to their rest.'

'I'm at work until five, and then I earn a bit on the side after that. I put up a new headstone for him. Two and a half thousand roubles. I have to pay back my debts.'

'Listen to me, Mother Victoria. Visit him every day when you're not working, and you must be there in time for the mass at twelve. He can hear you then.'

Let me have suffering and terrible, unbearable sorrow – just as long as my prayers reach him. And my love . . .

A mother

Here everything happens by some kind of miracle. Everything's based on belief . . . in a miracle!

They loaded us into the plane: 'At the double! At the double!' And right there, just a few dozen metres away, they lead up the drunken pilot, totally out of his head, and stuff him into the cabin. Honest to God! Well, it was okay . . . The plane took off and it flew. Down below there were mountains with sharp peaks. The idea of crashing into them was terrifying. Like crashing on to nails. Honest to God! I came out in a sweat . . . We got there fine, right on time. And the command came: 'Disembark! Fall in!' The pilot went swaggering past, splaying his legs out – sober. Well, so that was okay . . . What do you call that, if not a miracle? That's the way feats of heroism are performed here. But once we start repenting there are no limits. We rip the shirt open right across our chest and weep bitter tears. We really go all the way! Right down to the bottom. Like when we get drunk.

I came back and I told myself: 'To hell with it! To hell with it! They turn us into mental cases, into rapists and drug addicts.' I came back . . . And I have a normal life, like a normal man . . . Honest to God! Everything's okay . . . I used to drink wine, love women and give them flowers. Then I got married. And I had a son. Here I am sitting in front of you. Do I look like a madman? Or some kind of crocodile? I served in the special forces. All our men were fine boys. Lots of them from the country. From Siberia. They're healthier, they've got more stamina. We had one weirdo who liked to pierce the 'spirits'' eardrums with a cleaning rod. Honest to God! Just one. Only one . . . (*He pauses.*)

But strangely enough, life goes on. As Boris Slutsky says: 'When we came back from the war, I realized we weren't needed.' I've got Mendeleev's complete table of the elements inside me. The malaria still gives me the shakes, and all for what? No one here was waiting to welcome us. But out there they were shouting out 'You'll get perestroika moving. Stir up the stagnant brains . . .' A dead end. We came back and they didn't let us in anywhere. From the very first day they told us over and over: 'Study, boys. Start families.' Honest to God! So, fine, okay . . . Nothing but profiteering, mafia and indifference all around, and they won't let us get involved in anything serious. One practical person said to me: 'What can you do? Just shoot . . . ? And what do you know about? Do you think the Homeland can only be defended with a pistol? That justice is only restored with an automatic rifle?' Honest to God! So, okay, we're not heroes . . . Maybe in thirty years I'll tell my own boy: 'Son, it wasn't all as heroic as it says in the books; there was plenty of dirt too.' I'll tell him myself. But in thirty years . . . Right now it's an open wound. It's only just started healing over, growing a skin . . . (*He starts walking round the room.*)

I had one moment out there . . . (*He stops.*) Are you interested? When I thought about my last wish. It turned out to be very simple: a mug of water and a cigarette. Honest to God! I didn't want to die. I wasn't intending to die . . . My mind started wandering from loss of blood. My mind was wavering on the edge. Someone shouted at me and brought me round . . . Valerka Lobach, our combat medic, was slapping me across the face and shouting hysterically: 'You're going to live! You're going to live!' (*He sits down abruptly.*)

It's interesting to remember. Honest to God! So, it's okay . . . At night I still lug all the gear up into the mountains: an automatic rifle and two loads of ammunition – that's nine hundred cartridges – and then add to that four grenades, smoke rounds, flares, a flare pistol, a bulletproof vest, an entrenching tool, padded trousers, a waterproof cape, dry rations for three days (that's nine really heavy tins and three large packs of rusks). About fifty kilogrammes. On my feet I've got tarpaulin boots with footcloths, the ones they made us change into before we left the Union. I baked my feet right through before I took some Canadian trainers off a dead 'spirit' . . . To hell with it all! To hell with it! In a war everyone changes, even the dogs change. They're hungry . . . They're not yours; they look at you as food. A man never feels like he's food, but out there I did. I was lying there wounded. It's a good thing the boys found me quickly . . . (*He pauses.*)

Why did you come here? Why did I agree? We've meddled with this . . . What's the point? Who's it for? My granddad fought in the Great Patriotic War . . . I tell him about how we lost ten boys in a single battle. Ten coffins . . . Ten plastic bags. And my granddad says: 'Why, you've never seen a real war. In a battle we'd have a hundred or two hundred men who never came back. We put them in a mass grave in their tunics, or in nothing but their underwear, and threw sand over them.' To hell with it! I'm not saying any more. Honest to God! So, okay then . . . We drank vodka out there, Moskovskaya – the one they call 'crankshaft'. Three roubles, sixty-two kopecks.

Four years have gone by now. And one thing hasn't changed – death; the fact that my friends were killed. Everything else has changed.

Not long ago I went to the dentist. We all came back here with scurvy and periodontal disease. All that chlorine we swallowed! First they pulled out one tooth, then another. And the shock from the pain (I didn't take any anaesthetic) suddenly started me talking. I couldn't stop . . . And the way the dentist looked at me. She was almost disgusted. All her feelings showed in her face: 'His mouth's full of blood and he's still talking.' I realized that's what everyone thinks. Their mouths are full of blood and they're still talking.

A sergeant, special forces

Post Mortem

TATARCHENKO
IGOR LEONIDOVICH
(1961–1981)

In carrying out a combat mission, faithful
to his military oath and demonstrating fortitude
and courage, he lost his life in Afghanistan.
Beloved Igoryok,
You left this life before you knew it.

Mama and Papa

LADUTKO
ALEXANDER VICTOROVICH
(1964–1984)

Killed in the performance
of his international duty.
You carried out your duty as a soldier
with honour. You could not save yourself,
my son. You lost your life as a hero
in the land of Afghanistan, so that the
country would have peaceful skies.

To my dear son from Mama

BARTASHEVICH
YURY FRANTSEVICH
(1967–1986)

Died heroically in the performance
of his international duty.
We recall, love and mourn.

Your family remembers

BOBKOV
LEONID IVANOVICH
(1964–1984)

Killed in the performance
of his international duty.
The moon has set, the sun has gone out
without you, dear son.

Mama and Papa

ZILFIGAROV
OLEG NIKOLAEVICH
(1964–1982)

Killed in Afghanistan.
To my only son.

Mama

BOGUSH
VICTOR KONSTANTINOVICH
(1960–1980)

Killed while defending the Homeland.
The earth is empty without you.

Mama

Zinky Boys *on Trial*

A History in Documents

The trial transcripts refer to the book using its British title, *Boys in Zinc*.

Recently a group of mothers of internationalist soldiers who were killed in Afghanistan brought legal proceedings against the writer Svetlana Alexievich, the author of the book *Boys in Zinc*. Their complaint will be considered in the people's court of the Central District of Minsk.

The occasion for this application to the court was the play *Boys in Zinc*, presented on the stage of the Yanka Kupala Belarusian Theatre, and the publication of extracts from the book in the newspaper *Komsomolskaya Pravda*. The performance was recorded by the republican television channel and broadcast to the viewers in Belarus. The mothers, who have borne their boundless sorrow for all these years, were offended by the fact that their boys were portrayed exclusively as soulless killer-robots, pillagers, drug addicts and rapists . . .

L. Grigoriev, Vecherny Minsk, *12 June 1992*

'Put the Author of *Boys in Zinc* on Trial' – that was the title of the article printed on 22 June in the newspaper *Na strazhe Oktyabrya* and in several other publications. 'Following the publication of her book,' the article stated, 'a virtual war has been declared against the writer Svetlana Alexievich': the author is accused of distorting and falsifying the testimony of 'Afghanis' and their mothers. And now we have yet another attack, following the performance of a similarly titled stage play at the Yanka Kupala Belarusian Theatre and its airing on television screens. The judges of the Central District will consider the complaint brought by a group of mothers of internationalist soldiers who were killed. The date of the court hearing has not yet been set. The stage play has been taken out of performance . . .

We called the court of the Central District of the capital with a request to comment on this report, but our request merely provoked surprise. Secretary S. Kulgan said that the court had not received any such complaint . . .

The author of the article in *Na strazhe Oktyabrya*, V. Strelsky, explained to us that he had taken the information from the Moscow newspaper *Krasnaya zvezda*.

Chirvonaya zmena, *14 July 1992*

On 20 January the newspaper *Sovietskaya Belorussia* reported: 'In the people's court of the Central District of Minsk proceedings have begun in the case of the writer Svetlana Alexievich . . .'

One day previously, on 19 January, the newspaper *Vecherny Minsk* published an article on the same subject with the title 'Literature on Trial'. I have deliberately noted the dates of these publications. The point is as follows:

When I visited the people's court of the Central District of the capital of Belarus I learned that the case was being heard by Judge Gorodnicheva.

She would not allow me to switch on my dictaphone and categorically refused to provide any clarification, on the grounds that 'feelings should not be inflamed'. But Gorodnicheva did show me the file on the Alexievich case, and that file was opened on 20 January. In other words, it is obvious that press materials stating that the case was ongoing(!) had been prepared before the judge herself had opened the case . . .

Leonid Sviridov
Sobesednik, *no. 6, 1993*

Two complaints have been received by the people's court of the Central District of Minsk. A former 'Afghani', now an invalid, asserts that what S. Alexievich wrote about that war and about him personally is false and libellous, and therefore she should apologize publicly and make a payment of fifty thousand roubles in compensation for the insult to his honour as a soldier. In addition, the mother of an officer who was killed takes exception to the author's assessment of Soviet patriotism and its role in the upbringing of the younger generation.

Svetlana Alexievich met with both plaintiffs several years ago in the course of her work on the well-known book *Boys in Zinc*. Both of them now claim that they did not say what she wrote, and if they did say what is recorded in the book they have now thought better of it.

There are certain interesting nuances. In accusing the writer of distorting the facts the soldier who has lodged a complaint cites a newspaper publication of 1989. However, the name that appears in it is not his, but that of a different soldier. The mother who has lodged a complaint entangles the court in such a complex maze of politics and psychology that an entire brigade of scholarly experts would be powerless to liberate it. Notwithstanding this, the judge of the people's court has initiated proceedings concerning both complaints. The court hearings have not yet begun, but the pretrial questioning of the writer is going full speed ahead . . .

Anatoly Kozlovich
Literaturnaya gazeta, 10 February 1993

The well-known Belarusian writer Svetlana Alexievich, who once reminded us that 'war has an unwomanly face', is on trial. Apparently the ashes of Afghanistan have left a bitter residue in the hearts of certain enraged readers and they have not forgiven Alexievich for her *Boys in Zinc*, a documentary account of the Afghan War as we do not know it. The writer is accused of misrepresentation and selective use of the information provided to her by veterans of the war and the widows and mothers of soldiers who were killed; and, in addition, of libel, anti-patriotism and vilification. It is not yet clear if the case will be pursued further or the plaintiffs, who have demanded certain compensatory damages, will settle the case before it comes to (open) trial. But the signal is clear. Rising up before us we see the shade of Major

Chervonopisny, who lectured Academician Andrei Sakharov on the correct understanding of the Afghan War at a session of the Congress of People's Deputies . . .

Fyodor Mikhailov
Kuranty, *3 February 1993*

*From the Legal Claim of Oleg Sergeevich Lyashenko,
a Former Army Private and Grenadier*

The article 'We're Coming Back from Out There . . .', published in the newspaper *Litaratura i mastatstva* on 6 October 1989, included excerpts from Svetlana Alexievich's documentary book *Boys in Zinc*. One of the monologues is signed with my name (the surname given is incorrect).

The monologue represents what I told the author about the Afghan War and the time I spent in Afghanistan, the relations between people during the war, after the war, and so on.

Alexievich has completely distorted what I told her, adding things that I did not say or which, if I did say them, I understood differently, and she has drawn her own, independent conclusions, which I did not draw.

The statements that S. Alexievich attributes to me are demeaning and insulting to my honour and dignity.

The phrases concerned are these:

1. 'At the Vitebsk training camp it was no secret that we were being trained for Afghanistan . . . One guy confessed he was afraid that we would all get shot out there. I started despising him. Just before we left, another one refused to go . . . I thought he was a headcase. We were going to make a revolution!'

2. 'After two or three weeks there'll be nothing of the old you left, just your name. You aren't you any longer, but someone else. I think that's how it is . . . Clearly that's it. And that someone else . . . That person isn't frightened any longer by the sight of someone who's been killed. He thinks calmly or with a feeling of annoyance about how he'll have to drag him down a cliff or lug him for kilometres through the heat . . . You get this acute thrill

of excitement at the sight of a dead man: they didn't get me! That kind of transformation . . . It happens to everyone.'

3. 'I was taught to shoot at whatever I was told to shoot at. I shot without feeling any pity for anyone. I could have killed a child. Everyone wanted to get back home. Everyone tried to survive. There was no time to think . . . I got used to other people's deaths, but I was afraid of my own.'

4. 'Only don't write about our "Afghani" brotherhood. It doesn't exist. I don't believe in it. At the war we were all united by fear: we were deceived in exactly the same way . . . Here we're united by the fact that we've got nothing . . . We all have the same problems: pensions, apartments, good medicine, artificial limbs, furniture . . . If we solve those our clubs will fall apart. Let me just get myself an apartment, force it through, grab it with my teeth if I have to – with furniture and a fridge and a washing machine and a Japanese video – and that's it! . . .

'The young people haven't reached out their hands to us. They can't understand us. Supposedly we're equated with the men who fought in the Great Patriotic War. Only they were defending their Homeland; but what were we doing? We played the part of the Germans – that's what one young guy told me . . . And we resent them. Anyone who wasn't there with me, who didn't see it, experience it, suffer it – to me he's no one.'

All of these statements are profoundly insulting to my human dignity, since I did not say and do not think any such thing and I regard these comments as a defamation of my honour as a man, a human being and a soldier . . .

Unsigned, 20 January 1993

From the Transcript of the Pretrial Hearing

Judge: T. Gorodnicheva. *Solicitors*: T. Vlasova, V. Lushkinov. *Plaintiff*: O. Lyashenko. *Respondent*: S. Alexievich.

Judge T. Gorodnicheva: 'Plaintiff, do you claim that the writer distorted the facts as you told them to her?'

O. Lyashenko: 'Yes.'

Judge T Gorodnicheva: 'Respondent, please provide clarification concerning this matter.'

S. Alexievich: 'Oleg, I would like to remind you of how you told me your story and cried when we met, and that you didn't believe that your truth could ever appear in print. You asked me to make that happen. I wrote it. And now what? You are being deceived and used again, for the second time. But didn't you say that you would never let yourself be tricked again?'

O. Lyashenko: 'If you'd just been in my place: a beggarly pension, no job and two little children . . . my wife had just been made redundant too. How could I live? What could I live on? You get paid fees. You're published abroad. But it turns out that we're murderers and rapists.'

Solicitor T. Vlasova: 'I protest. Psychological pressure is being brought to bear on my client. My father was an air force general, and he too was killed in Afghanistan. Everything there was sacred. They discharged their oath of loyalty. They were defending the Homeland . . .'

Judge T. Gorodnicheva: 'What are the plaintiff's demands?'

O. Lyashenko: 'I demand a public apology from the writer and compensation for moral damages.'

Judge T. Gorodnicheva: 'Do you insist only on a refutation of the facts as published?'

O. Lyashenko: 'I insist that Svetlana Alexievich pay me fifty thousand roubles for the insult to my honour as a soldier.'

S. Alexievich: 'Oleg, I can't believe that this is you saying this. The words you are speaking are someone else's . . . I remember you differently . . . And you have placed too low a value on your burned face and lost eye. Only I am not the one who should be brought to trial. You have confused me with the Ministry of Defence and the Politburo of the CPSU.'

Solicitor T. Vlasova: 'I protest! This is psychological pressure.'

S. Alexievich: 'Oleg, when we met you were honest, and I was afraid for you. I was afraid that you might have problems with the KGB; after all, you had been forced to sign an undertaking not to disclose military secrets. And I did change your surname. I changed it to protect you, and now I must use that to protect myself against you. Since the surname is not yours, this is a composite character. And your claims are groundless.'

O. Lyashenko: 'No, those are my words. I said that . . . And it says how I was wounded, and . . . everything there is mine . . .'

From the Legal Claim of Yekaterina Nikitichna Platitsyna,
Mother of the Killed Major Alexander Platitsyn

The article 'We're Coming Back from Out There . . .', published in the newspaper *Litaratura i mastatstva* on 6 October 1989, included excerpts from Svetlana Alexievich's documentary book *Boys in Zinc*. One of the monologues, that of the mother of Major A. Platitsyn, who was killed in Afghanistan, is signed with my name.

This monologue is included in full in S. Alexievich's book *Boys in Zinc*.

The monologue as printed in the newspaper and the book is a distortion of what I said about my son. Although the book is documentary in nature S. Alexievich has added certain facts on her own initiative, omitted a lot of what I told her, drawn her own, independent conclusions and signed the monologue with my name.

The articles are humiliating and insulting to my honour and dignity . . .

Unsigned and undated

From the Transcript of the Pretrial Hearing

Judge: T. Gorodnicheva. *Solicitors*: T. Vlasova, V. Lushkinov. *Plaintiff*: Ye. Platitsyna. *Respondent*: S. Alexievich.

Judge T. Gorodnicheva: 'You may speak, Yekaterina Nikitichna.'

Ye. Platitsyna: 'The image of my son that I hold in my mind has nothing at all in common with the image presented in the book.'

Judge T. Gorodnicheva: 'Could you clarify what you mean: where, at what point and how are the facts distorted?'

Ye. Platitsyna (*picking up a book*): 'Nothing there is the way I said it. My son was not like that. He loved his Homeland.' (*She cries.*)

Judge T. Gorodnicheva: 'Please calm yourself and tell us the facts.'

Ye. Platitsyna (*reading from the book*): ' "After Afghanistan" (this was when he came home on leave) "he was even more loving. He loved everything about home. But there were moments when he sat there without saying anything, not seeing anybody. He used to jump up in the night and walk round the room. Once he woke me up by shouting: 'Flashes! Flashes! Mama, they're firing . . .' Another time I heard someone crying at night. Who could be crying in our home? We didn't have any little children. I opened the door of his room and he was holding his head in his hands and crying." '

'He was an officer. An officer on active service. But this shows him as a cry-baby. Why on earth did this have to be written?'

Judge T. Gorodnicheva: 'I am ready to cry myself. I cried more than once when I read this book and your story. But what here is insulting to your honour and dignity?'

Ye. Platitsyna: 'You see, he was an officer on active service. He couldn't have cried. Or take this: "Two days later it was the New Year. He hid presents for us under the New Year tree. A big shawl for me. A black one. 'Why did you choose black, son?' 'Mama, there were all kinds there. But by the time my turn came round, there were only black ones left. Look, it suits you.' " '

'So it turns out that my son stood in queues, but he couldn't stand shops and queues. And this shows him standing in a queue during a war. To get a shawl for me. Why did that have to be written about? He was an officer on active service. He was killed . . .

'Svetlana Alexandrovna, why did you write all that?'

S. Alexievich: 'When I was writing your story I cried too. And I hated the people who sent your son to be killed senselessly in a foreign country. You and I were in agreement, at one.'

Ye. Platitsyna: 'You say that I should hate the state and the Party . . . But I'm proud of my son! He was killed as an officer in action. All his comrades loved him. I love the state that we lived in, the USSR, because my son gave his life for it. But I hate you! I don't need your terrible truth. We don't need it! Do you hear me?'

S. Alexievich: 'I could listen to what you have to say. We could talk about it. But why do we have to talk about it in court? I can't understand that.'

* * *

Following an old moth-eaten Soviet scenario, Svetlana Alexievich is being systematically anathematized as a CIA agent and lackey of global imperialism who libels her great Homeland and its heroic sons, supposedly for two Mercedes and hand-outs in dollars.

The first trial was never concluded since the plaintiffs – former army private O. Lyashenko and Ye. N. Platitsyna, the mother of an officer who was killed – failed to appear for the trial. But six months later two new complaints were filed: by I. S. Galovneva, mother of the killed senior lieutenant Yu. Galovnev and chairwoman of the Belarusian Club of Mothers of Killed Internationalist Soldiers; and by Taras Ketsmur, a former army private who is currently the chairman of the Minsk Club of Internationalist Soldiers.

Prava cheloveka, *no. 3, 1993*

On 14 September a trial was held in Minsk, with the writer Svetlana Alexievich as the respondent. And then the most interesting part began.

'The complaint from I. S. Galovneva, the mother of an officer killed in Afghanistan, was submitted to the court without any date,' said Alexievich's solicitor, Vasily Lushkinov. 'We were provided with a copy without any signature and, naturally, with no date. However, this did not prevent the judge, Tatyana Gorodnicheva, from deciding to institute proceedings under Article 7 of the Civil Code. The surprising thing is that the case was not actually formalized in any procedural sense until the actual trial – that is, its number had already been entered in the court register, even though no determination of good cause for instituting civil proceedings had been made.'

However, the trial did take place, and it was presided over by a man who actually saw the case for the first time at the trial. Svetlana Alexievich and her lawyer only learned that T. Gorodnicheva had been replaced by Judge I. Zhdanovich ten minutes before the hearing began.

'This is perhaps more of a moral question than a legal one', was Vasily Lushkinov's reaction.

Perhaps that is true. In any case, yet another of Svetlana Alexievich's interviewees – Taras Ketsmur – made a sudden appearance as the plaintiff, and Judge I. Zhdanovich had before him a complaint that was unsigned and, naturally, unaccompanied by any procedural record relating to the case.

The respondent's solicitor drew the court's attention to this absurdity and protested. The court hearing was postponed.

Oleg Blotsky
Literaturnaya gazeta, *6 October 1993*

From the Transcript of the Court Hearing of 29 November 1993

Judge: I. N. Zhdanovich. *Lay judges*: T. V. Borisevich, T. S. Soroko. *Plaintiffs*: I. S. Galovneva, T. M. Ketsmur. *Respondent*: S. A. Alexievich.

From the Complaint of Inna Sergeevna Galovneva, Mother of Killed Senior Lieutenant Yu. Galovnev

Extracts from S. Alexievich's documentary book *Boys in Zinc* were published in the newspaper *Komsomolskaya Pravda* for 15 February 1990 under the title 'Monologues of Those Who Went through Afghanistan'.

The monologue published in my name contains inaccuracies and distortions of the facts about which I informed S. Alexievich, in addition to obvious lies and inventions, that is, the presentation, supposedly in my words, of things that I did not tell her about and could not have told her about. The liberal interpretation of my statements and also the obvious conjectures presented as my words denigrate my honour and dignity, and all the more so since the book is documentary in nature. I consider that a documentary author should present the information he or she has received accurately, keep recordings of conversations and obtain approval for texts from interviewees.

For instance, in her article Alexievich writes: 'It's not a good thing for a mother to admit, but I loved him more than anyone else in the world. More than my husband, more than my second son . . .' (This is about my son Yura, who was killed.) This quotation is invented (it does not correspond to what was said). The statement that I loved my sons to different degrees caused conflicts in my family and I consider that it denigrates my dignity.

Further on: 'In the first year at school he didn't know any fairy-tales or children's poems off by heart, but he knew whole pages out of *How the Steel Was Tempered* by Nikolai Ostrovsky.' These words suggest that my son was raised in a family of fanatics. What I told Alexievich was that at the age of seven or eight Yura used to read serious books, including *How the Steel Was Tempered*.

Alexievich has also distorted what I supposedly told her about the circumstances of my son being sent to Afghanistan. She cites what he supposedly said: 'I'll go to Afghanistan to prove to you that there is something exalted in life, that a fridge crammed with meat . . . [isn't] enough to make everyone happy.' Nothing of the kind was said. Alexievich's assertions denigrate me and my son. As a normal human being, a patriot and romantic, he volunteered to go to Afghanistan.

Nor did I say the following to Alexievich about when I suspected that my son intended to ask to go to Afghanistan: 'You won't die for your Homeland there, you'll just get killed for no reason at all. Nobody knows why. How can the Homeland just send its finest sons to their deaths without any great idea?' I sent him there myself. Myself!

This section denigrates my honour and dignity by presenting me as a two-faced individual with double moral standards.

The quarrel between my sons is described inaccurately. What

Alexievich wrote is: 'You don't read enough, Gena. I've never seen you with a book in your hands. It's always a guitar.' The quarrel between my sons was only about one thing: my younger son's choice of a profession. A guitar had nothing to do with it.

These words of Alexievich's insult me because they emphasize my lack of love for my younger son. I didn't say any such words to her.

I consider that Alexievich, having decided to present events related to the war in Afghanistan not only as a political error but as the guilt of our entire people, did so in a biased fashion and frequently simply invented things that supposedly happened in the interview. Her intention was to present our people – the soldiers who were in Afghanistan and their relatives – as unprincipled and cruel individuals who are indifferent to the sufferings of others.

To make Alexievich's work easier I let her have my son's diary, but that did not help her to present the facts in a genuinely documentary manner.

I ask Alexievich to apologize for distorting my authentic statements and for denigrating my honour and dignity in the newspaper *Komsomolskaya Pravda*.

Unsigned and undated

From the Complaint of Taras Ketsmur, a Former Army Private

The text of my first legal claim for the protection of my honour and dignity did not state any specific complaints against S. Alexievich for her publication in *Komsomolskaya Pravda* on 15 February 1990. I herewith augment and confirm that claim: everything stated by S. Alexievich in the newspaper article and in the book *Boys in Zinc* is invented and did not take place in reality, since I did not meet her and did not tell her anything.

When the article appeared in *Komsomolskaya Pravda* on 15 February 1990 I read the following:

'I went to Afghanistan with my dog Chara. If I called out "Die!" she dropped to the ground. If I was feeling out of sorts or seriously upset she used to sit beside me and cry. For the first few days I was absolutely thrilled that I was there . . .

'Please, don't you ever touch this. There are lots of wise guys here now, but why didn't anyone hand in their Party card or put a bullet through their head when we were out there? . . .

'Out there I saw them dig up metal and human bones in the rice fields. I saw the frozen, orange crust on the stiff face of man who'd been killed; yes, it was orange for some reason.

'The same books, photographs, cassette player and guitar are still there in my room, but I'm different. I can't just walk through a park, I keep looking round. In a café the waiter stands behind me and says, 'What will you order?' and I'm ready to jump up and run away. I can't bear anyone standing behind me. If I see a creep the only thought I have is that he should be shot.

'In the war we had to do the exact opposite of what we were taught in civilian life, and in civilian life we had to forget all the skills we learned in the war.

'I'm an excellent shot, I can throw grenades and hit the target – what good is that to me? I went to the military commissariat and asked to go back. They didn't take me. The war will soon be over, and men just like me will come back. There'll be more of us.'

I read almost precisely the same text in the book *Boys in Zinc*, with minor literary corrections, featuring the same dog and the same thoughts spoken out loud.

I confirm once again that this is pure invention, attributed to my name . . .

In view of the above, I request the court to defend my insulted honour as a soldier and a citizen.

Unsigned and undated

From I. S. Galovneva's Statement in Court

We lived abroad for a long time; my husband served there. We came back to the Homeland in the autumn of 1986. I was happy that we were home at last. But the joy in our home was mingled with sorrow – our son was killed.

I lay flat on my back for a month. I didn't want to hear anyone. Everything in our home was switched off. I didn't open the door to anyone. Alexievich was the first person to enter my home. She said she wanted to write the truth about the war in Afghanistan. I believed her. She came the day before they were going to put me in hospital and I didn't know if I would come back from there or not. I didn't want to live. I didn't want to live without my son. When Alexievich came she said she was writing a documentary book. What is a documentary book? It should be diaries and letters of the people who were there. That's how I understand it. And I gave her my son's diary, the one that he kept out there. 'If you want to write the truth,' I said, 'then here it is, in my son's diary.'

And then we talked. I told her about my life because I was feeling miserable. I was just stuck inside four walls, down on my knees. I didn't want to live. She had a dictaphone with her and she recorded everything. But she didn't say she was going to print it. I just told her because she was there, but she was supposed to print my son's diary. It's a documentary book. I gave her the diary; my husband typed it out especially.

She also told me that she was going to Afghanistan. She went on a business trip, but my son was killed there. What does she know about war?

But I believed her, and I waited for the book. I waited for the truth: what was my son killed for? I wrote a letter to Gorbachev, asking him what my son was killed for in a foreign country. No one was saying anything . . .

This is what Yura wrote in his diary:

'1 January 1986. Half the journey has already been covered, and there is so little left ahead. And once again flames, and once again oblivion and a new, long road – and so on and on endlessly until the will of the foreordained comes to pass. And memory, lashing with the whip of what has been suffered, breaking through into life in nightmarish dreams, and the phantoms of another world, other times and centuries, phantoms eye-catching in their similarity, but different, not knowing these days that have elapsed. And you can't stop, can't pause for breath, can't change what has once been foreordained – a dark void will gape open before those who defect, for, once having sat down to rest, you cannot rise up from the earth again. And weary, in despair and in pain, you will cry out to the empty heavens. What is there, when the circle is closed and the road is ended, and the new world has begun shining in its glory? Why are we accountable for them? It is not given to them to ascend to brilliant heights; and no matter how long the road, even so their days are numbered. But we shatter our lives, knowing no peace or happiness, wander weary and crushed, all-powerful and without rights, the demons and angels of this world . . .'

Alexievich didn't print this, my son's truth. There can't be any other truth. The truth belongs to those who were there. For some reason she described my life. In simple, childish language. What kind of literature is that? Disgusting little book . . .

Comrades, I raised my children honestly and justly. She writes that my son loved Nikolai Ostrovsky's book *How the Steel Was Tempered*. They studied that book in school then, along with Fadeev's *Young Guard*. Everyone read those books: they were in the school programmes. But she emphasizes that he read them, that he knew sections by heart. What did she have to write about that for? She tries to show him as abnormal. Fanatical. Or she writes that he regretted becoming a soldier. My son grew up on shooting ranges; he followed in his father's footsteps. His grandfathers, all his father's brothers and cousins – they're all in the army. A military family. And he went to Afghanistan because he was an honest man. He swore an oath of allegiance. It was necessary, so he went. I raised fine sons. He was ordered to go and he went: he was an officer. But Alexievich tries to prove that I'm the mother of a killer. And that my son killed people there. What does that mean? Did I send him there? Did I put the gun in his hands? Are we mothers to blame because there was a war there? Because they killed people out there, plundered and smoked drugs?

And this book has been published abroad. In Germany, in France . . . What right does Alexievich have to trade in our sons who were killed? Is it fame and dollars she's after? Who is she?

This is mine, I told her about it, I lived through it. And what has Alexievich got to do with it . . . ? She talked a bit and wrote down our stories. We wept out our grief to her . . .

She wrote my name wrongly. I'm Inna, but she has Nina Galovneva. My son's rank was senior lieutenant, but she wrote 'junior'. We lost our children, but she has her fame . . .

From Replies to Questions

V. Lushkinov (*S. Alexievich's solicitor*): 'Tell me, Inna Sergeevna, did Alexievich record what you told her on a dictaphone?'

I. Galovneva: 'She asked permission to turn on the dictaphone. I gave her permission.'

V. Lushkinov: 'And did you ask her to show you afterwards what she was going to take from the tape and use in the book?'

I. Galovneva: 'I thought she was going to print my son's diary. I've already said what I think documentary literature is – it's diaries and letters. And if it's my story, then word for word, the way I said it.'

V. Lushkinov: 'Why didn't you take Alexievich to court immediately, when *Komsomolskaya Pravda* published an excerpt from the book? Why did you only decide to do it three and a half years later?'

I. Galovneva: 'I didn't know she was going to publish this book abroad. To spread libels . . . I raised my children honestly for the Homeland. We lived all our lives in tents and barracks. I had two sons and two suitcases. That was how we lived . . . And she writes that our children are murderers. I went to the Ministry of Defence and returned my son's decoration myself . . . I didn't want to be the mother of a murderer. I returned his decoration to the state . . . But I'm proud of my son!'

Ye. Novikov (*S. Alexievich's public defender, chairman of the Belarus League for Human Rights*): 'I wish to protest. I request that it be entered in the record of proceedings that Svetlana Alexievich is being subjected to constant abuse in the courtroom. They are threatening to kill her . . . Even promising to cut her into pieces . . .' (*He turns towards the mothers sitting in the courtroom with large photographs of their sons, with their decorations and medals pinned to them.*) 'Believe me, I respect your grief . . .'

Judge I. Zhdanovich: 'I didn't hear anything. No insults.'

Ye. Novikov: 'Everyone heard them, apart from the judge . . .'

From Conversations in the Courtroom

'We're mothers. We want to say . . . They sent our sons to their deaths. And then they make money out of it. We've come to defend them, so that they can lie easy in the ground . . .'

'How could you! How dare you sling mud at our boys' graves? They carried out their duty to the Homeland to the end. You want them to be forgotten . . . All over the country hundreds of school museums and memorial displays have been set up. I took my son's greatcoat to the school too, and his school exercise books. They're heroes! Beautiful books should be written about Soviet heroes – they shouldn't be turned into cannon fodder. We're depriving young people of our heroic history . . .'

'The USSR was a great power, and a thorn in the side for many. And it's not for me at this moment to say where the collapse of our country was planned and by whom, including Judases well paid by the West . . .'

'They killed people there . . . Bombed people . . .'

'Have you ever served in the army? You haven't. You sat it out in college while our children were being killed.'

'Don't ask mothers if their son killed anyone or not. A mother only remembers one thing – *her* son was killed . . .'

'Every morning I see my son; I still believe that he's at home. When he was out there I told myself: "If they bring me a coffin I have two choices: go out into the street, to a meeting, or go to church." I call my generation "the generation of order-takers". The Afghan War was the peak of our tragedy. Why can they do anything they like with us?'

'Now the rabble will blame these eighteen-year-old boys for everything . . . That's what you've done! This war has to be separated from them . . . The war was criminal – it has already been condemned – but the boys should be defended . . .'

'I'm a teacher of Russian literature. For many years I used to repeat Karl Marx's words to my pupils: "The death of heroes is like the setting of the sun, not like the death of a frog that has burst from straining too hard." What does your book teach us?'

'Stop playing the hero, you "Afghanis"!'

'Curse you! Curse all of you!'

Judge I. Zhdanovich: 'Stop this uproar! Stop this racket! This is a courtroom, not a street market . . .' (*The courtroom is in pandemonium.*) 'I declare a fifteen-minute recess.' (*After the recess, police stand on guard in the courtroom.*)

From T. M. Ketsmur's Statement in Court

I haven't prepared a statement. I won't read from a piece of paper, just speak in plain, ordinary language. How did I get to know this extremely well-known – perhaps world-class – writer? We were introduced by Valentina Chudaeva, a front-line veteran of the Great Patriotic War. She told me that this writer had written the book *The Unwomanly Face of War*, which people were reading right round the world. Then, at one of the meetings with front-line veterans, I talked to other women, and they told me that Alexievich had used their lives to earn a fortune and become famous, and now she'd taken on the 'Afghanis'. I'm nervous . . . I beg your pardon . . .

She came to us in the Remembrance Club with her dictaphone. She wanted to record things about a lot of the guys, not just about me. Why did she write this book after the war? Why didn't this writer with the big world-famous name say anything at all during the war? Why didn't she shout out even once?

Nobody sent me there. I asked to go to Afghanistan; I wrote applications. I made up a story about a close relative of mine who had been killed there. Let me explain the situation a bit . . . I could write a book myself . . . When we met I refused to talk to her. I told her that we'd write our own book, the men who were out there. And we'd write a better book than she would, because she wasn't there. What can she write? She can only cause us pain.

Alexievich has deprived our entire 'Afghani' generation of moral justification. It turns out that I was a robot. A computer. A hired killer. And the place for me is Novinki, near Minsk, in the lunatic asylum.

My friends call me and promise to smash my face in for being such a great hero . . . I beg your pardon . . . She wrote that I served in Afghanistan with my dog . . . But the dog died on the way . . .

I asked to go to Afghanistan . . . Do you understand? I asked – myself! I'm not a robot . . . not a computer . . . I'm nervous. I beg your pardon . . .

From Replies to Questions

S. Alexievich: 'In your complaint, Taras, you wrote that you had never met me. But now you say that you did meet me, but you refused to talk to me. Does that mean you didn't write your legal complaint yourself?'

T. Ketsmur: 'I wrote it myself . . . We did meet. But I didn't tell you anything . . .'

S. Alexievich: 'If you didn't tell me anything, how could I know that you were born in Ukraine and were ill during your childhood . . . That you went to Afghanistan with a dog (although, as you say now, it died on the way there), and that the dog was called Chara . . .'

(*The reply is silence.*)

Ye. Novikov: 'You said that you asked to go to Afghanistan yourself, as a volunteer. I don't understand how you feel about that now. Do you hate that war or are you proud that you were there?'

T. Ketsmur: 'I won't let you confuse me . . . Why should I hate that war? I carried out my duty . . .'

From Conversations in the Courtroom

'We are defending the honour of our sons who were killed. Give them back their honour! Give them back their Homeland! You demolished the country. The strongest in the world!'

'You're the one who turned our children into murderers. You

wrote this terrible book . . . Look at their photographs . . . How young and handsome they are! How could murderers have faces like that? We taught our children to love their Homeland . . . Why did you write that they killed people out there? You wrote that for dollars . . . But we're poor. We don't have the money for medicine. Or anything to buy flowers for our sons' graves . . .'

'Leave us in peace! Why do you dash from one extreme to the other: first you showed us as heroes, and now suddenly we're all murderers? We didn't have anything except Afghanistan. That was the only place we felt like real men. None of us regret that we were there . . .'

'You want to convince us that a sick generation came back from out there, but I tell you a generation that found itself came back. At least we got to see what our boys are like – in real life! Yes, boys were killed. But how many of them are killed in drunken brawls, in knife fights? Every year more people are killed in road accidents than we lost in ten years of that war. Our army hadn't fought for a long time. And we tested ourselves, and our modern weapons. It's thanks to scribblers and hacks like you that we're losing ground all around the world . . . We've lost Poland . . . Germany . . . Czechoslovakia . . . We'll live to see the day when Gorbachev will be put on trial for that. And you too. You're traitors. Where are our ideals? Where is our great power? I went all the way to Berlin for that power in 1945 . . .'

'At the seaside in the south I saw some young guys crawl across the sand to the sea on their hands . . . They didn't even have one leg each . . . And I didn't go to the beach any more; I couldn't sunbathe there. I could only cry . . . They still laughed, and they wanted to flirt with the girls, but everyone ran away from them, like me. I want everything to be all right for those guys. I want them to know that we need them the way they are. They have to live! I love them for being alive.'

'Even now it's painful for me to remember. We were travelling in a train . . . And one of the women in the compartment said she was the mother of an officer who was killed in Afghanistan. I understand. She was a mother and she was weeping. But I said:

"Your son was killed in an unjust war. The *dushmans* were defending their own Homeland . . ." '

'It's such a terrible truth that it sounds like a lie. It's stupefying. You don't want to know it. You want to defend yourself against it.'

'They talk about orders. They say: "I was ordered to do it, and I obeyed." The international tribunals' answer to that was: "Carrying out a criminal order is a crime." And there's no statute of limitations.'

'In 1991 a trial like this couldn't have happened. The Communist Party was collapsing . . . But now the communists have started feeling strong again. They've started talking about "great ideals" again, about "socialist values". And if anyone's against them they take them to court! Next thing, they'll start putting them up against the wall. Or they'll collect us all together in a sports stadium some night, behind barbed wire . . .'

'I swore an oath. I was a soldier.'

'No one comes back from a war as a boy.'

'We raised them to love their Homeland.'

'Little boys. They put guns in their hands . . . And they told them: "There's your enemy" – a gang of *dushmans*, the *dushman* brotherhood, the *dushman* scum, gangs of bandits . . . But they didn't teach them to think.'

'Do you remember what Arthur Koestler said: "Why, when we tell the truth, does it always sound like a lie? Why, when we proclaim a new life, do we litter the ground with corpses? Why do we always intersperse the talk of a bright future with threats?" '

'When we shot up silent *kishlaks* and bombed the roads into the mountains we were shooting and bombing our own ideals. This is the harsh truth that we have to accept. And survive. Even our children have learned to play at "spirits" and the "limited contingent". Now, at last, let's summon up the courage to learn the truth about ourselves. It's unbearable! It's unendurable! I know. I've tried it for myself.'

'We have two choices: to learn the truth or to run away from the truth. We have to open our eyes.'

From Letters to the Court

Having learned the details of the court case that has been instigated against Svetlana Alexievich in Minsk, we regard it as persecution of the writer for her democratic convictions and an attack on creative freedom. With her genuinely humanistic work, her talent and her courage Svetlana Alexievich has won wide popularity and respect in Russia and other countries of the world.

We do not want to see a stain on the good name of the Belarus we love.

Let justice prevail!

The Association of Unions of Writers, the Union of Russian Writers, the Moscow Union of Writers

Is it possible to encroach on an author's right to tell the truth, no matter how tragic and cruel the truth might be? Is it possible to blame her for undeniable evidence of the crimes of the past, and particularly the crimes connected with the disgraceful escapade in Afghanistan, which claimed so many victims and mutilated so many lives?

One might think that in our time, when the printed word has finally become free, when there is no ideological press any more, no official guidelines and rigid policy of 'the only possible depiction of life in the spirit of communist ideals', there would be no further need to ask such questions.

Unfortunately there is. And eloquent demonstration of this is the trial, currently in preparation, of the writer Svetlana Alexievich, the same person who wrote the remarkable book *The Unwomanly Face of War* (about the fate of women who took part in the Great Patriotic War), and *Last Witnesses* (about the children of that same war) – and who, despite the efforts of official propaganda and the opposition of writers such as the infamous Alexander Prokhanov (during the Afghan War, he earned the title of 'the General HQ's tireless nightingale'), has also dared to tell the terrible, soul-searing truth about the war in Afghanistan in her book *Boys in Zinc*.

The writer, while respecting the personal courage of the soldiers and officers who were sent abroad by the Brezhnevite leadership of the CPSU to fight in a country that had formerly been friendly, and sincerely sharing the grief of mothers whose sons were killed in the mountains of Afghanistan, in this book also uncompromisingly debunks all attempts to present the shameful Afghan War as heroic and all attempts to romanticize it. She exposes all the false pomp and strident pathos.

This was evidently not to the liking of those who, even today, are convinced that the Afghanistan escapade, and other reckless ventures of a regime that is now a thing of the past – escapades paid for in the blood of our soldiers – were the fulfilment of a 'sacred international duty'; who would like to whitewash the dark dealings of politicians and vainglorious military commanders; and who wish to equate participation in the Great Patriotic War with participation in the unjust, essentially colonial, Afghan War.

These people do not engage in polemics with the writer. They do not dispute the appalling facts that she adduces. And in general they do not show their faces at all. They use others, who are still deluded or have been misled; years after the publications in newspapers and the appearance of the book *Boys in Zinc*, they initiate legal proceedings over 'the insult to the honour and dignity' of the soldiers who fought in Afghanistan, those boys about whom Svetlana Alexievich has written with such understanding, compassion and sympathy, with such heartfelt pain.

True, she did not depict them as romantic heroes. But only because she adhered firmly to Tolstoy's maxim: 'The hero . . . whom I love with all the strength of my soul . . . was, is and always will be – the truth.'

Well, then, is it possible to take offence at the truth? Can it be put on trial?

> *Writer-veterans of the Great Patriotic War: Mikola Avramchik,*
> *Yanka Bril, Vasil Bykov, Alexander Drakokhrust,*
> *Naum Kislik, Valentin Taras*

As Belarusian writers in Poland, we resolutely protest against the judicial persecution of the writer Svetlana Alexievich in Belarus.

The legal proceedings against the writer are a disgrace for the whole of civilized Europe!

> *Jan Cikvin, Sokrat Janovic, Victor Sved,*
> *Nadezda Artimovic*

I cannot remain silent any longer . . . And perhaps I have only just realized what kind of war it was. The poor boys, we owe them such a great debt of guilt! What did we know about this war? I would embrace every one of them and beg their forgiveness . . .

I recall what it was like at the time.

I had read in Larisa Reisner that Afghanistan was half-wild tribes jigging about and singing 'Glory to the Russian Bolsheviks, who helped us defeat the English'.

The April Revolution . . . The satisfaction of another country in which socialism is victorious. But the man next to me in the train whispers: 'More spongers for us to support.'

The death of Nur-Muhammad Taraki. At a seminar in the municipal Party committee on why Hafizullah Amin was allowed to kill Taraki, the lecturer from Moscow snapped: 'The weak must make way for the strong.' This left an unpleasant impression.

Our assault on Kabul. The explanation: 'The Americans were about to launch their own assault; we were only one hour ahead of them.' At the same time, rumours: things are bad out there – there's nothing to eat, there aren't enough medical supplies or warm clothing. I immediately remembered the events at Damansky Island in 1969 and the pitiful complaints of our soldiers: 'We haven't got any cartridges!'

Then the Afghan sheepskin coats appeared. They looked very classy on our streets. Women envied other women whose husbands were in Afghanistan. In the newspapers they wrote: 'Our soldiers are planting trees there, repairing bridges and roads.'

I was in a train from Moscow. In my compartment a young woman and her husband started talking about Afghanistan. I said something from the newspapers, and they laughed. They had been serving as doctors in Kabul for two years. They immediately started justifying the soldiers who brought back goods to sell, they weren't paid much. I helped them get out of the train at Smolensk. Lots of large cardboard boxes with foreign brand labels . . .

At home my wife told me that in the next block of flats the only son of a single woman was due to be sent to this war. She went somewhere, crawled on her knees and kissed boots. And she came back pleased: 'I got him off!' And at the same time she spoke calmly about 'the bosses buying out their own'.

My son came back from school: 'The paratroopers came and spoke to us.' And then, ecstatically: 'What great Japanese watches they all have!' One 'Afghani' was asked how much watches like that cost, and how much they were paid. After a pause he confessed: 'We stole a truckload of vegetables and sold them . . .' He admitted that everybody envied the soldiers on the fuel tankers: 'Millionaires!'

Out of recent events I recall the persecution of Academician Sakharov, with whom I agree about one thing: for us, dead heroes are always better than live people who dissent in some way. And again: not long ago I heard that 'Afghanis' – some privates and two officers – are studying at the seminary in Zagorsk. What motivated them to do that: repentance, the desire to hide from this cruel life or the desire to find a new path? After all, not everyone who gets his privileged college diplomas can feed his soul on meat at special prices, dress in imported trash and dig under the apple tree in his privileged vegetable plot, while avoiding seeing anything and keeping quiet.

N. Goncharov
Orsha

My husband was also in Afghanistan for two years (from 1985 to 1987), in Kunar Province – that's right beside the border with Pakistan. He's ashamed to call himself an 'internationalist soldier'. It's a sore point that he and I often discuss: should our Soviet forces have been there, in Afghanistan? And who were we there, invaders or friends, or 'internationalist soldiers'? The answers are always the same: no one invited us there and the Afghan people didn't need our 'help'. No matter how hard it is to admit it, we were invaders there. To my way of thinking we shouldn't be arguing now about monuments to our soldiers in Afghanistan (where we should put them and where we shouldn't), we should be thinking about repentance. We should all repent for the boys who were deceived and killed in this senseless war, repent for their mothers, who were also deceived by the authorities, repent for those who came back with mutilated souls and bodies. Repent before the people of Afghanistan, its children, mothers and old people – for bringing so much grief to their land . . .

A. Masyuta
Mother of two sons,
wife of a former internationalist soldier,
daughter of a veteran of the Great Patriotic War

The truth about the USSR's aggression in Afghanistan, confirmed by the documentary testimony of participants that is gathered in Alexievich's book, is not 'a mockery of honour and dignity', but a disgraceful fact of the recent history of Soviet communist totalitarianism, which has been unambiguously and vociferously condemned by the global community.

The practice of judicial persecution of a writer for her work is an equally well-known, shameful mode of functioning of the same regime.

What is happening today in Belarus – the massive, organized campaign against Svetlana Alexievich: the persecution of this writer and constant threats against her, the legal proceedings and attempts to ban her book – testifies to the fact that the vile eruptions of totalitarianism are not the past but the present of Belarus.

This reality makes it impossible to regard the Republic of Belarus as a free and independent post-communist state.

The persecution of Svetlana Alexievich, whose books are widely known in France, Great Britain, Germany and other countries, will bring the Republic of Belarus nothing but a reputation as a communist nature reserve in the post-communist world, and will define its role only as the unenviable one of a European Kampuchea.

We demand the immediate cessation of all persecution of Svetlana Alexievich and of the legal proceedings against her and her book.

Vladimir Bukovsky, Igor Gerashchenko,
Inna Rogachy, Mikhail Rogachy,
Irina Ratushinskaya

Attempts to discredit the writer Svetlana Alexievich, including by means of lawsuits, have been going on for a long time. In all her books Svetlana Alexievich has revolted against the insanity of violence and war, arguing that the highest value in life belongs to the human being, but that he is criminally transformed into a gearwheel of the political machine and criminally used as cannon fodder in wars unleashed by ambitious state leaders. Nothing can ever justify the death of our boys in the foreign land of Afghanistan.

Every page of *Boys in Zinc* is an appeal to people not to allow this bloody nightmare to happen again.

Council of the United Democratic Party of Belarus

Information is reaching us from Minsk about the judicial persecution of the Belarusian author and member of PEN International, Svetlana Alexievich, who is 'guilty' of no more than discharging the fundamental and immutable responsibility of any writer to share honestly with her reader the issues that concern her. The book *Boys in Zinc*, dealing with the Afghanistan tragedy, has travelled right round the world and earned universal recognition. The very name of Svetlana Alexievich, and her courageous and honest talent, command our respect. There is no doubt that, by manipulating so-called 'public opinion', revanchist forces are attempting to deprive writers of their most important right, as confirmed in the PEN International Charter: the right to free self-expression.

The Russian PEN Centre declares its unconditional solidarity with Svetlana Alexievich, the Belarus PEN Centre and all the democratic forces of that independent country, and appeals to the organs of the judicial system to abide by the international laws to which Belarus is also a signatory – first and foremost the Universal Declaration of Human Rights, which guarantees freedom of speech and freedom of the press.

The Russian PEN Centre

The Belarus League for Human Rights considers that the continuing attempts to punish the writer Svetlana Alexievich by means of legal proceedings are a political act on the part of the authorities, intended to suppress dissent, creative freedom and freedom of speech.

We are in possession of information that in 1991–2 various judicial bodies in the Republic of Belarus considered about ten political cases that had been artificially transferred to the sphere of civil law, but which were in essence directed against democratically inclined elected deputies, writers, journalists, publications and activists of public or political organizations.

We demand an end to the persecution of the writer Svetlana Alexievich and call for the reopening of similar cases in which the verdicts were motivated by political revenge.

The Belarus League for Human Rights

The war in Afghanistan began. My son finished school and went to a military academy. Throughout the ten years when other people's sons were in a foreign country with guns in their hands, my heart was in my mouth. My boy could have ended up there too. And it's not true that the people didn't know anything. The zinc coffins were brought into homes, maimed children came back to their stunned parents – everybody saw all this. Of course, they didn't say anything about it on the radio or the television, they didn't write about it in the newspapers (they only dared to just recently), but it all happened where everyone could see it. Everyone! So what was our 'humane' society doing then, including you and me? Our society was awarding our 'great' elders more Gold Stars, fulfilling and over-fulfilling the latest five-year plans (although our shops were still as empty as they had been before), building dachas and generally amusing itself. Meanwhile eighteen- and nineteen-year-old boys were facing hails of bullets, falling down in the foreign sand and dying.

Who are we? What right do we have to ask our children to account for what they did out there? Are we who stayed here really any purer than they are? Their suffering and torment has cleansed their sins, but there is no way that we can ever cleanse ourselves. The *kishlaks* that were shot to pieces and wiped off the face of the earth, the foreign land that was devastated, these are not on their consciences, but ours. We are the ones who killed, not our boys. We are the murderers of our own children and other people's.

But these boys are heroes! They didn't fight out there for a 'mistake'. They fought because they trusted us. We should all go down on our knees before them. The mere comparison of what we were doing here with what they went through is enough to drive anyone insane.

Golubichnaya
Civil engineer, Kiev

Of course, nowadays Afghanistan is a profitable, even fashionable, subject. And you, Alexievich, can be happy that people will read your book with avid interest. These days there are plenty of people in our country who are interested in everything that can be used to smear the walls of their own Fatherland with filth. You can even find some 'Afghanis' among them. For they (not all of them, not all!) will be handed the defensive weapon that they need so badly: 'Just look what they did to us!' Shoddy people are always in need of someone's protection. Decent people don't need that, because in any situation they always remain decent. And there are plenty of them among the 'Afghanis', but apparently they are not the ones you looked for.

I wasn't in Afghanistan, but I fought right through the Great Patriotic War. And I know perfectly well that there was filth there too. But I don't want to remember it and I won't allow anyone else to do so. The point isn't that that war was different. Nonsense!

Everyone knows that in order to live a man has to eat, and the consumption of food requires – begging your pardon – latrines. But we don't talk about that in public. Why have the people writing about Afghanistan and the Great Patriotic War started to forget that? If the 'Afghanis' themselves protest against these 'revelations', we should listen to them and study this phenomenon. It is clear to me, for instance, why they protest so furiously. There is a normal human feeling called shame. They are ashamed. And you noticed their shame. But for some reason you decided that wasn't enough. You decided to drag it out into the light for universal judgement. They shot camels there, civilians were killed by their bullets . . . You try to demonstrate that this war was unnecessary and damaging – without realizing that in so doing you insult the boys who fought in it, who are guilty of nothing.

N. Druzhinin
Tula

Our ideal, our hero, is a man with a gun . . . For decades we poured millions and billions of roubles into our defence forces, finding more and more new missions for them in the countries of Asia and Africa and, at the same time, more and more new leaders who wanted to build a 'bright future' in their own countries. A fellow student of mine at the Frunze Military Academy, Major – later Marshal – Vasya Petrov, personally drove Somalis into the attack, for which he was awarded the Gold Star . . . And there were so many like him!

But then the artificially shackled together Warsaw Pact and the so-called 'socialist camp', held together by the bayonets of Soviet military forces, started coming apart at the seams. To provide 'fraternal support in the struggle against counter-revolution' we started sending our sons to these countries – to Budapest, and then to Prague, and then . . .

In 1949 I travelled with our forces through countries liberated from fascism – Hungary and Czechoslovakia. Those were foreign lands, but it felt as if we were at home: the same greetings, the same joyful faces, the same hospitality, modest but from the heart . . .

A quarter of a century later our sons were greeted in that same land, not with hospitality, but with banners that read: 'The fathers were liberators, the sons are invaders!' The sons wore the same military uniform and bore the title of their fathers' successors, and we wore our shame in silence before the whole world.

There was more to come. In December 1979 the sons and the pupils of Great Patriotic War veterans – not least my pupil Borya Gromov, whom I taught tactics at the military academy – invaded Afghanistan. Over the years more than a hundred countries in the UN have condemned this crime, in committing which we set ourselves against the global community, like Saddam Hussein today. Now we know that in that dirty war our soldiers killed more than a million Afghans and lost over fifteen thousand of our own men . . .

In order to conceal the significance and true scale of this shameful aggression its instigators introduced into official circulation the term 'limited contingent' – a classic example of hypocritical cant. Equally hypocritical was the resounding title 'internationalist soldiers': a new kind of name for the military profession, intended to distort the meaning of what was happening in Afghanistan and mimic the name of the International Brigades who fought against the fascists in Spain.

The instigators of the invasion of Afghanistan, the big bosses in the Politburo not only demonstrated their own predatory nature but also made everyone who lacked the courage to oppose an order to kill accomplices in their crime. Killing cannot be justified by any kind of 'international duty'. What damned blasted duty?

I feel enormously sorry for their mothers and their orphaned children . . . And they weren't awarded medals for the blood of innocent Afghans, but zinc coffins.

In her book the author distinguishes them from those who sent them to kill; she feels pity for them, unlike myself. I don't understand what they want to put her on trial for. For the truth?

Grigory Brailovsky
Invalid, veteran of the Great Patriotic War,
St Petersburg

If only we'd seen the light sooner. But whom can we blame? Do they blame a blind man because he can't see? Our eyes have been washed clean with blood . . .

I ended up in Afghanistan in 1980 (Jalalabad, Bagram). Soldiers are supposed to carry out orders. It was back then, in 1983, that I first heard someone say: 'We should launch all our strategic bomber forces and wipe those mountains off the face of the earth. Look how many of our own men we've had to bury – and all for nothing!' It was one of my friends who said that. Like everyone else he had a mother, a wife and children. So, in our imaginations at least, we deprive those other mothers, children and husbands of the right to live in their own land, because they have the wrong 'views'.

But does the mother of one of our killed 'Afghanis' know what a thermobaric bomb is? The command centre of our army in Kabul had direct communications with Moscow at governmental level. The go-ahead to use this weapon was given from there. When the detonator is triggered an initial charge tears open a container filled with gas, which flows out, filling every cranny in the area. This 'cloud' explodes after a specific time period. Nothing is left alive in the area covered. A man's internal organs burst and his eyes pop out. Our air forces first used missiles packed with millions of tiny needles – the so-called 'needle missiles' – in 1980. There's nowhere to hide from needles like that – a man is transformed into a fine-mesh sieve . . .

I'd like to ask our mothers if even one of them has ever compared herself with an Afghan mother. Or do they regard that mother as a creature of a lower order?

What horrifies me is this: how many people we still have who fumble their way around, groping in the dark, trusting in their own feelings, without ever trying to think or compare one thing with another!

Are we people who are fully awake, are you and I even human at all, if we are still taught to spurn the reason that opens our eyes?

A. Sokolov
Major, military pilot

... And some of the high-ranking liars are still hoping to use their lies to bring back the old times that are so dear to their hearts. For instance, in the newspaper *Den*, General V. Filatov says the following in an appeal to the soldiers who fought in Afghanistan: '"Afghanis"! When the time for action comes we shall work as we did in Afghanistan ... There you fought for your Homeland on the southern front ... Now we need to fight for the Homeland as we did in 1941, on our own territory' (*Literaturnaya gazeta*, 23 February 1992).

This 'time for action' manifested itself in Moscow on 4 October 1993 outside the walls of the White House. But who knows if there will not be an attempt at political revanchism? Yes, justice does require a trial. A court of honour must try the initiators and inspirers of the Afghan crime – both the living and the dead. It is not required in order to fuel high passions, but as a lesson for the future to anyone who might think up new escapades in the name of the people – and for the moral condemnation of atrocities already committed. It is needed in order to dispel the false claim that guilt for the crimes in Afghanistan is shared only by the top five: Brezhnev, Gromyko, Ponomaryov, Ustinov and Andropov. Because there were sessions of the Politburo and secretariats, a plenum of the Central Committee of the CPSU and confidential letters to all the members of the CPSU. But out of all these active participants and audiences, not a single person objected...

A trial is required in order, at long last, to stir the consciences of those who were awarded decorations, commissions as officers or generals, honorariums and esteem for the blood of millions of innocent people, and for the lies in which, in one way or another, we were all implicated...

A. Solomonov
Professor of technical sciences,
Minsk

In the words of Solzhenitsyn, peace is not simply the absence of war, but above all the absence of violence against man. It is no accident that precisely now, when our post-totalitarian society is gripped by the insanity of political, religious and nationalist violence – including armed violence – an author has been presented with a bill for the truth about the war in Afghanistan. It seems that the scandal kindled around *Boys in Zinc* is an attempt to re-establish in people's minds the communists' 'myths about themselves'. Behind the backs of the plaintiffs other figures are visible: those who did not allow Academician Sakharov to speak about the inhumanity of this war at the First Congress of People's Deputies, those who are still counting on winning back the power that is slipping from their grasp and holding on to it by force . . .

This book raises the question of the right to sacrifice human lives while sheltering behind speeches about sovereignty and great power status. For what ideas are ordinary people now being killed in Azerbaijan, Armenia, Tajikistan and Ossetia?

Meanwhile, with the growth of pseudo-patriotic ideas based on violence, we are witnessing a new renaissance of the spirit of militarism, the arousal of aggressive instincts and a criminal arms trade, accompanied by sweet speeches about democratic reform in the army, military duty and national dignity. The bunkum rhetoric of various politicians in defence of revolutionary and military coercion, akin to the ideas of Italian fascism, German national socialism and Soviet communism, are generating ideological confusion in people's minds and preparing the ground for an increase of intolerance and hostility in society.

These politicians' spiritual fathers, who have already withdrawn from the arena of politics, knew how to manipulate human passions, and they drew their fellow citizens into fratricidal strife. Let us remember that in his own time Leo Tolstoy, who advocated a refusal to serve in the army, was not taken to court for his anti-military activity. Here again they wish to return us to a period when all that is most honest and decent was destroyed.

Behind the court case against Svetlana Alexievich lies a planned offensive by anti-democratic forces, which are fighting, under the guise of defending the honour of the army, to preserve a repugnant ideology and inveterate falsehood. The idea of a non-violent alternative, which is defended in Svetlana Alexievich's book, is alive in people's awareness, although officially this idea is not acknowledged and the concept of 'non-resistance to the evil of violence' is still ridiculed. But, let us repeat, the moral changes in the life of society result first and foremost from the formation of a self-awareness founded on the principle of 'a world without violence'. Those who wish to put Svetlana Alexievich on trial are pushing society towards hostility and the chaos of self-destruction.

Members of the Russian Peace Society:
R. Iliukhin
Doctor of historical science,
director of the group Ideas of Peace in History
at the Institute of World History of the Russian Academy of Sciences;
A. Mukhin
Chairman of the Initiative Group
for the Promotion of Alternative Service;
O. Postnikova
Writer, member of the April Movement;
N. Sheludyakova
Chairperson of the
Anti-Violence Movement

A writer cannot be judge and executioner – there have been plenty of those in Russia already . . . This expression of Chekhov's came to mind in connection with the pseudo-literary scandal concerning Svetlana Alexievich's book *Boys in Zinc* and the simultaneously launched campaign against the 'Afghanis' and their parents in our newspapers and even on foreign radio stations . . .

Yes, war is war. It is always cruel and unjust where human life is concerned. In Afghanistan the overwhelming majority of soldiers and commanders carried out their duty, faithful to their oath. Because the order was given by a legitimate government in the name of the people. Unfortunately, to our shame, there were certain commanders and soldiers who committed crimes, and there were some who killed and robbed Afghans and some (very few, but they did exist) who killed their own comrades, went over to the side of the *dushmans* and fought in their ranks.

I could adduce quite a number of other crimes committed by our men, but when certain writers and journalists compare our soldiers in Afghanistan with fascists that throws up a whole series of questions. Perhaps these gentlemen can show the world our government's decrees concerning our army's construction of concentration camps in Afghanistan, concerning the extermination of an entire people and the incineration of millions of people in gas chambers, as the Germans did? Or do you have documents, gentlemen, which demonstrate that for one Russian soldier who was killed hundreds of civilians were wiped out, as the Hitlerites did in Belorussia? Or can you prove that our doctors took blood from Afghan children for our wounded, as the German invaders did?

As it happens, I have a list of Soviet soldiers and officers who have been convicted of crimes committed against citizens of Afghanistan. Perhaps, gentlemen, you can present similar lists of Germans, or name at least one or two of them who were convicted during their occupation of our country for committing a crime against the civilian population?

Undoubtedly the decision of the Soviet government of the time to send forces into Afghanistan was criminal, and primarily so in relation to its own people. But in speaking of our military personnel, who were sent into hellfire to carry out their duty as soldiers with the tacit consent of the people – including yours, gentlemen – one must choose one's terms correctly. Those who took the decisions are the ones who should be shamed, and those with influential positions in society who remained silent . . .

Alexievich's humiliation of the mothers of soldiers who were killed is a nod in the direction of America – the country of great democracy! There, supposedly, forces emerged to oppose the war in Vietnam. However, anyone who reads the newspapers knows how America acted. Neither the American Congress nor the American Senate passed a resolution condemning the war in Vietnam. No one in America allowed, or will allow, anyone to say a single derogatory word about presidents Kennedy, Johnson, Ford and Reagan, who sent American soldiers to the bloodbath. About three

million Americans went through Vietnam ... Vietnam veterans
are among the highest circles of the political and military elite of
the country ... Any American schoolboy can buy the insignia of
the military units that fought in Vietnam ...

I wonder what would have happened to Radio Liberty, which
defends Alexievich, if its non-Belarusian staff called their own presidents who were involved in Vietnam 'criminals' and 'murderers'?
Of course, it's all right for them to call foreigners that, especially
when there are those willing to sell their own fathers for dollars
and German marks ...

N. Cherginets
Chairman of the Belarusian Union of Veterans of the Afghan War,
former military pilot in Afghanistan,
major-general of police,
Sovietskaya Belorussia, *16 May 1993*

... No one knows what we who were there know – except, perhaps, for our superiors, whose orders we carried out. Now they
remain silent. They say nothing about how they taught us to kill
and to 'frisk' the men we killed. They say nothing about the way a
caravan that had been intercepted was divided up between the helicopter crews and the top brass. Or how the body of every *dushman*
(as we used to call them then) was mined, so that whoever came to
bury it (an old man, a woman, a child) would also meet their death
beside their dear one, on their own native soil. And they say nothing about many other things.

I happened to serve in an airborne special forces battalion. We
were narrowly specialized, focusing on caravans, caravans and
more caravans. In most cases the caravans were not carrying weapons, but goods and drugs, most often at night. We had a group of
twenty-four men, and sometimes the other side could number
more than a hundred. How could we tell who was a peaceful caravan trader, a merchant who had bought goods in Pakistan and was
dreaming of selling them at a profit, and who was a *dushman* in
disguise? I remember every battle, every man I killed – old man,
mature man or young boy – writhing in his death agony. Like the

one in a white turban, with his frenzied howl of 'Allah Akbar' as he jumped off a five-metre-high rock after fatally wounding my friend . . . His guts were left on my singlet, and his brains on the metal butt of my assault rifle . . . We left half of our comrades behind on the rocks . . . We didn't get a chance to drag them all out of the crevices . . . Only the wild animals found them . . . And for their parents we invented 'heroic feats' that they had supposedly performed. That was in 1984 . . .

Yes, we should be put on trial for what we did. But together with the ones who sent us there, coercing us in the name of our Homeland and under the terms of our oath to do work for which the world at large passed judgement on fascism in 1945 . . .

Unsigned

The years pass by . . . And suddenly it turns out that people want more than what history leaves to them. The history that we are used to, where there are names and dates, events and evaluations of events, but there is no place for the human being. For the concrete human being who was not merely a faceless participant in these events, a statistical unit, but who was a distinctive individual, filled with emotions and experiences which, as a rule, are not recorded by history . . .

I don't remember when Svetlana Alexievich's book *The Unwomanly Face of War* appeared – about fifteen years must have gone by, I suppose – but even now I can visualize quite clearly one episode that shook me. A woman's battalion on the march, and here and there in the dust there are spots of blood. Even at war there are no breaks for the female organism.

What historian would leave us that fact? And how many people's stories must a writer listen to in order to extract it from the countless number of facts and experiences? That fact tells me more about the psychology of women at war than an entire volume of military history.

. . . And no matter how close to us events might be – the Afghan War, the Chernobyl tragedy, Moscow putsches, Tajikistani massacres – it suddenly turns out that they have become the property of history; new cataclysms arrive to take their place, and the attention of society is focused on these new events. People's testimonies are lost, because, in protecting us, human memory tries to black out the emotions and recollections that prevent a person from living and deprive him of sleep and peace. And then the witnesses themselves are lost to us . . .

Ah, how reluctant are the many wielders of power, who have disappeared from sight together with the regime, to admit that they also face judgement – the judgement of people and the judgement of history! Ah, how reluctant they are to believe that times have now arrived in which any 'pen-pushing hack' can presume to reach out to the 'sacred past' in order to 'sully and deride' it, to subject 'great ideals' to doubt! Ah, how acutely they are bothered by books filled with the testimony of the last witnesses!

It is possible to repudiate the criticisms made by KGB General Oleg Kalugin: people don't become KGB generals by accident. But it is impossible to repudiate the testimony of hundreds of simple mortals – 'Afghanis', Chernobyl victims, the victims of inter-ethnic conflicts, refugees from hotspots . . . However, it is possible to 'pressurize', 'put in her place' and 'stop the mouth' of a journalist, writer or psychologist who has collected these testimonies . . .

Of course, this is nothing new to us. We have already put Sinyavsky and Daniel on trial, anathematized Boris Pasternak, trampled Solzhenitsyn and Dudintsev into the mud.

And what if Svetlana Alexievich does fall silent? If the testimonies of the victims of our criminal age no longer appear? Then what will be left for posterity? The sickly sweet coo-cooing of the lovers of victorious communiqués? Rousing marches punctuated by stirring drum rolls? But we've seen all that before. We've already been through all that . . .

Ya. Basin
Medical doctor,
Dobry vecher, *1 December 1993*

I would like to address the court in these words . . . I counted myself as one of those who did not accept Svetlana Alexievich's book *Boys in Zinc*. I was due to appear at the trial in support of Taras Ketsmur . . . But now this could be called the confession of a former enemy . . .

After listening closely to everything that has been said in the courtroom and behind the scenes for the last two days I have realized that we are committing sacrilege. What are we tormenting each other for? Is this in the name of God? No! We are breaking His heart. In the name of the country? It didn't fight out there . . .

Svetlana Alexievich has described the obscenity of Afghanistan in concentrated form, and it is impossible for any mother to believe that her son could be capable of anything like that. But I will say more: what is described in the book is nothing compared with what happens in war, and everyone who really fought in Afghanistan can confirm that with his hand on his heart. We are now face to face with a harsh reality: after all, the dead know no shame, and if the shame is real the living must take it upon themselves. But *we* are the living! So it turns out that we were to blame for the war – the ones who carried out orders, that is – and we're to blame now, when responsibility has to be taken for the consequences of the war! But it would be more just if a book of such power and talent had appeared, not about the boys, but about the marshals and stay-at-home leaders who sent the young men to war.

I ask myself if Svetlana Alexievich should have written about the horrors of war. Yes! And should a mother stand up for her son? Yes! And should the 'Afghanis' stand up for their comrades? Yes again! Of course, a soldier is always culpable in any war. But at the Last Judgement the Lord will forgive a soldier first . . .

The court will find a legal way out of this conflict. But there has to be a human way out of it too, which consists in the fact that mothers are always right to love their sons, that writers are right when they tell the truth, and that soldiers are right when the living defend the dead. These are the elements that have really clashed in this civil lawsuit.

The directors and producers – the politicians and marshals – who organized this war, are not here in the courtroom. There are only injured parties here: love, which will not accept the bitter truth about the war; truth, which must be told, regardless of any love; honour, which accepts neither love nor truth because – remember the Russian officer's code of honour: 'I can give up my life for my Homeland, but I cannot give up my honour to anyone.'

God's heart embraces everything: love and truth and honour. But we are not gods. The one good thing about this civil lawsuit is that it that can bring people back to the fullness of life.

The only thing for which I can rebuke Svetlana Alexievich is not that she distorted the truth, but that the book contains almost no love for the youth that was led to the slaughter by the fools who organized the Afghan War. There has to be at least one 'Afghani' who will say that it is now a long time since we have been a grey, homogeneous mass; and that Taras Ketsmur's words, when he says that he does not condemn the war, are not our words – he does not say that for all of us . . .

I don't condemn Svetlana for the fact that her book let the man in the street know about the obscenity of Afghanistan. I don't even condemn her because, after reading it, people dislike us much more. We have to get through this reassessment of our role as a weapon of murder in the war. And if there is something to repent of then every individual must share in that repentance.

The trial will probably drag on painfully for a long time. But in my soul it is already over . . .

Pavel Shetko
Former 'Afghani'

From the Transcript of the Concluding Court Session, 8 December 1993

Judge: I. N. Zhdanov. *Lay judges*: T. V. Borisevich, T. S. Soroko. *Plaintiffs*: I. S. Galovneva, T. M. Ketsmur. *Respondent*: S. A. Alexievich.

From the Statement by Svetlana Alexievich, Author of Boys in Zinc

(FROM WHAT WAS SAID AND WHAT WAS NOT ALLOWED
TO BE SAID)

Until the very end I did not believe that this trial would take place, just as I did not believe until the last moment that they would start firing at the White House . . . That we could fire at each other . . .

I physically cannot bear the sight of frenzied, furious faces any longer. I would not have come to this trial if the mothers were not sitting here; although I know they are not the ones who are suing me, it is the former regime. Consciousness is not a Party ticket. You can't hand it in to the archive. Our streets, the signs on our shops and the names of the newspapers have changed, but we are still the same. Members of the socialist camp. With the same old camp mentality . . .

But I came to talk to the mothers. To ask their forgiveness for the fact that it is not possible to get at the truth without pain. I still have the same question that is there in my book: who are we? Why can they do anything they like with us? Send a mother a zinc coffin, and then persuade her to sue the writer who wrote about how she couldn't even kiss her son one last time and how she washed the zinc coffin with herbs and stroked it . . . Who are we?

Love for a man with a gun has been hammered into us, incorporated in our genes; it has been with us since we were children. It is as if we grew up during the Great Patriotic War, even those of us who were born decades after it. And our vision is regulated so that even after the crimes of the revolutionary Cheka units, the Stalinist blocking detachments that fired on their own men attempting to retreat and the prison camps, after the recent events in Vilnius, Baku and Tbilisi, after Kabul and Kandahar, we still imagine a man with a gun as a soldier in 1945, the soldier of the Victory. So many books have been written about war, so many weapons have been produced by human hands and minds, that the idea of killing has become normal. The finest minds ponder with childish stubbornness whether man has the right to kill animals, but we are able to justify war with barely a doubt, or by hastily trumping up a political ideal. Turn on the television in the evening and you will see the secret exultation with which we carry heroes to the graveyard. In Georgia, in Abkhazia, in Tajikistan . . . And once again we are making patriotic monuments of their graves, not religious memorials . . .

It is impossible to take away from men their most beloved . . . their most precious toy – war – with impunity. It is a myth . . . It is an ancient instinct . . . But I hate war and the very idea that one human being has a right to the life of another human being.

Recently a priest told me about a front-line veteran of the Great Patriotic War, already an old man, who brought his military decorations to the church. 'Yes,' he said, 'I killed fascists. I defended the Homeland. But even so, before I die, I want to repent for having killed.' And he left his medals in the church, not in a museum . . . But we are raised in war museums . . .

War is hard work and killing; but, as the years pass, the hard work is remembered and the thought of killing recedes. How could they possibly be invented, those details and feelings? And the terrible variety of them in my book?

More and more often, after Chernobyl and Afghanistan, after the events at the White House, I think that we are not equal to the events that happen to us. We don't work through our past properly; we always remain victims. Perhaps that's why everything is repeated?

Once, several years ago – four years ago, to be precise – we used to think in the same way: I myself, many mothers who are here at the moment in this courtroom and soldiers who had come back from the foreign land of Afghanistan. In my book *Boys in Zinc* the mothers' stories are the saddest pages. They are prayers. Mothers praying for their sons who have been killed . . . Why are we now sitting in court, facing each other? What has happened during this time?

During this time the country, the communist empire that sent them there to kill and to die, has disappeared from the map of the world. It does not exist. At first the war was timidly called a 'political error', and then a 'crime'. Everybody wants to forget Afghanistan. To forget these mothers, forget the cripples . . . Forgetting is also a form of lying. The mothers have been left alone with their sons' graves. They do not even have the consolation of knowing that their sons' deaths were not meaningless. No matter what insults and abuse I might hear, I have said, and I repeat it now, that I venerate the mothers. I also venerate the fact that, when the Homeland condemned their sons' names to ignominy, they became their sons' defenders. Today only the mothers defend the boys who were killed . . . What they are defending them from is a different question.

Their grief surpasses any truth. They say a mother's prayers can reach a child even at the bottom of the sea. In my book it brings them back from oblivion. They have been sacrificed on the altar of our painful enlightenment. They are not heroes, they are martyrs. No one dares to cast a stone at them. We are all guilty, we are all implicated in that lie – that is what my book is about. What is the danger of any totalitarianism? It turns everyone into accomplices of its own crimes. The good and the evil, the naive and the pragmatic . . . We should pray for these boys and not for the idea whose victims they became. I want to tell the mothers: you are not defending your boys here. You are defending a terrible idea. A murderous idea. I also wish to say that to the former soldiers from Afghanistan who have come to court today.

Behind the mothers I see generals' shoulder straps. The generals came back from Afghanistan with their Gold Stars, as Heroes of the Soviet Union, and with big suitcases full of junk. One of the mothers – she is also sitting in the courtroom today – told me how they sent back to her a zinc coffin and a little black suitcase containing a toothbrush and her son's swimming trunks. That was all that was left to her. All that he brought back from the war.

So from whom did you have to defend your sons? From the truth? The truth lies in the fact that your boys died from their wounds because there was no medical alcohol and no drugs – they had been sold to the *dukans* – just as they fed the boys out of rusty tins from the 1950s, and buried them in old uniforms from the time of the Great Patriotic War. Even on that they economized. I wouldn't like to say this to you at the graveside . . . But I have to say it . . .

You hear the shooting everywhere, and once again blood is spilled. What justification are you seeking for blood? Or helping others to seek?

At that time, five years ago, when the Communist Party and the KGB were still in power, in order to protect the heroes of my book against reprisals I sometimes changed names. I was protecting them against the regime. But today I have to defend myself against those whom I recently defended.

What am I obliged to defend? My right as an author to see the world in the way that I see it. And the fact that I hate war. Or do I have to prove that there is truth and there is specious plausibility, that an artistic document is not an official note from the military commissariat or a tram ticket? The books that I write are documents and also simultaneously my representation of the time. I collect details and feelings, not only from an individual human life, but out of the air of the time, its space and its voices. I don't invent things or make conjectures, I gather the book together out of reality itself. This document is what people tell me, and a part of it is also me, as an artist, with my own view and awareness of the world.

When I write I write down contemporary, current history. Live voices, live destinies. Before they become history they are still someone's pain, someone's scream, someone's sacrifice or crime. I ask myself a countless number of times how it is possible to make it through the midst of evil without increasing the evil in the world, especially now, when it is assuming such cosmic proportions. I ask myself that before every new book. That is my burden. And my destiny.

Writing is a destiny and a profession. In our unfortunate country it is even more than a destiny or a profession. Why does a court twice reject a request for expert literary testimony? Because it would immediately be clear that there is no case to be tried. They are putting a book on trial, putting literature on trial; assuming that since it is documentary literature it can be rewritten anew every time to indulge the requirements of the moment. God forbid that documentary books should be controlled by our biased contemporaries. We should be left with nothing but the echoes of political struggles and prejudices, instead of living history. Beyond the laws of literature, beyond the laws of genre, a primitive political reprisal is being perpetrated, one that has already been reduced to a communal, I would even say mundane, level.

Listening to this courtroom I often found myself wondering who would dare to call the people out into the street nowadays, the people who no longer believe anyone – not priests, nor writers, nor politicians. All they want is reprisals and blood . . . And they can only be controlled by a man with a gun . . . A person with a pen instead of a Kalashnikov automatic annoys them. But they have tried to teach me here how to write books.

The people who have summoned me to court reject what they said several years ago. The coding in their minds has changed and they now read the former text differently, or even refuse to recognize it. Why? Because they do not want freedom . . . They don't know what to do with it.

I remember very well what Inna Sergeevna Galovneva was like when we met, and I loved her. For her pain, for her truth. For her tormented heart. But now she is a politician, an official, the chairwoman of a club of mothers of soldiers who were killed. She is a different person. All that remains of the previous one is her name and the name of her son who was killed, and whom she has sacrificed for a second time. A ritual sacrifice. We are slaves – we romanticize slavery.

We have our own ideas about heroes and martyrs. If the matter at issue here were honour and dignity, we would rise and stand in silence to the memory of two million Afghans who were killed . . . Who were killed out there, on their own land . . .

How long can we go on asking that eternal question of ours: 'Who is to blame?' We are all to blame – you, I, they. The problem lies elsewhere – in the choices that each of us have: to shoot or not to shoot, to remain silent or speak out, to go or not to go. We have to ask ourselves – let everyone ask himself or herself . . . But we have no experience of entering into ourselves, going right down inside ourselves . . . to find the answers for ourselves . . . We are more accustomed to running out into the street under the familiar red banners. We still haven't learned.

Taras Ketsmur, one of my book's heroes . . . Not the one you see here now in the courtroom, but the other one, who came back from the war and told me about it . . . May I read to you from the book?

'It's as if I'm asleep and I see a great ocean of people . . . All around our house . . . I look round, but for some reason I can't get up. Then I realize that I'm lying in a coffin. It's a wooden coffin without any zinc covering it. I remember that clearly . . . But I'm alive – I remember that I'm alive, but I'm lying in a coffin. The gates open, everyone goes out into the road and they carry me out into the road too. Crowds of people, all their faces filled with grief and some kind of mysterious exaltation. I can't understand it . . . What's happened? Why am I in a coffin? Suddenly the procession stops and I hear someone say: "Give me the hammer." Then I get the idea that I'm having a dream. Someone says it again: "Give me the hammer." It's like it's reality and a dream at the same time. And then someone says "Give me the hammer" for a third time. I hear the lid slam shut and the hammer starts tapping, one nail hits me in the finger. I start banging my head against the lid, and my feet. Bang – the lid goes flying off and falls on the ground. The people watch as I rise up and sit there, exposed to the waist. I try to shout out: "That hurts! Why are you nailing me in? I've got nothing to breathe in there." They cry, but they don't say anything to me. They all seem to be dumb . . . faces filled with exaltation. Mysterious exaltation . . . Invisible . . . And then I see it . . . I get an idea of what it is. And I don't know how I can speak to them so that they'll hear me. I think I'm shouting, but my lips are pressed tight together, I can't open them. I really am dead, and I have to keep quiet. Someone says it again: "Give me the hammer" . . .'

He has not repudiated this. This will defend his honour and dignity in the court of history. And also me.

From Conversations in the Courtroom

'You say it's the communists . . . the generals . . . directors behind the scenes . . . But what about *them* – the ones who are deceived and who want to deceive themselves? Someone's to blame, but it's not them. The psychology of the victim. And victims always need someone they can accuse. They're not shooting here yet, but everyone's nostrils are flaring as if they can smell blood.'

'She's a millionaire, she has two Mercedes . . . Drives around in foreign countries . . .'

'A writer spends two or three years writing a book and gets as much for it nowadays as a young boy driving a trolleybus gets in two months. So where did you get those Mercedes from?'

'She drives around in foreign countries . . .'

'What about your own sin? You could shoot or not shoot. Well? Why don't you say something?'

'The people are humiliated and poor. And not long ago we were a great power. Maybe we weren't really like that, but we thought of ourselves as a great power because we had so many rockets and tanks and atom bombs. And we believed that we lived in the best country, the most just country. But you tell us that we lived in a different country – a terrible country, drenched in blood. Who's going to forgive you for that? You've trampled on the most sensitive spot . . . On the very deepest feelings . . .'

'We were all involved in this deception. Everyone.'

'You did the same thing as the fascists did! But you want to be heroes . . . And jump the queue to get a fridge and a suite of furniture into the bargain . . .'

'They're ants; they don't know that bees and birds exist. And they want to turn everyone into ants. A different level of consciousness . . .'

'And what do you want after this?' 'After what?' 'After all the blood. I mean our history. After blood the only thing people appreciate is bread. Nothing else has any value for them. Their awareness has been impaired.'

'We have to pray. Pray for our executioners. For our tormentors.'

'They paid her dollars. And she slings mud at us. And at our children.'

'If we don't tackle the past it will come back at us again in the future. And there'll be more deception, and more blood. The past is still ahead of us.'

From the Verdict of the Court

Verdict

IN THE NAME OF THE REPUBLIC OF BELARUS

The people's court of the Central District of the city of Minsk, comprising Judge I. N. Zhdanov, presiding; lay judges T. V. Borisevich and T. S. Soroko; and court clerk I. B. Lobynich, has considered in open session on 8 December 1993 the case of the claims for the protection of honour and dignity brought by Taras Mikhailovich Ketsmur and Inna Sergeevna Galovneva against Svetlana Alexandrovna Alexievich and the editors of the newspaper *Komsomolskaya Pravda*.

Having heard the parties to the case and investigated the case material, the court considers that the claims of the plaintiffs should be satisfied in part.

Under the terms of Article 7 of the Civil Code of the Republic of Belarus an individual citizen or organization may demand the retraction of statements that denigrate their honour and dignity if the persons disseminating such statements fail to prove that they are true and accurate.

The court has determined that issue no. 39 of the newspaper *Komsomolskaya Pravda*, on 15 February 1990, published extracts from Svetlana Alexievich's book *Boys in Zinc* as 'Monologues of Those Who Went through Afghanistan'. This publication included a monologue signed with the surname of the plaintiff I. S. Galovneva.

Taking into account that the respondents in this case, S. A. Alexievich and the editors of the newspaper *Komsomolskaya Pravda*, have failed to present any proofs of the truth and accuracy of the statements made in the said publication, the court considers them not to be true and accurate.

However, the court considers that the statements made are not defamatory, since, from the viewpoint of respecting the laws and moral principles of society, they do not belittle the honour and dignity of I. S. Galovneva and of her son, who was killed, in the opinion of the public at large or of individual citizens, and they do not include any statements asserting socially reprehensible behaviour by her son . . .

Inasmuch as the respondents have failed to present any proofs of the truth and accuracy of the narrative attributed to T. M. Ketsmur, the court considers the statements made in the monologue signed with the name of T. M. Ketsmur not to be true and accurate.

For the above reasons the court considers the statements in the following phrases to be untrue and inaccurate and defamatory to the honour and dignity of the plaintiff:

'Out there I saw them dig up metal and human bones in the rice fields. I saw the frozen, orange crust on the stiff face of a man who'd been killed; yes, it was orange for some reason.'

And: 'The same books, photographs, cassette player and guitar are still there in my room, but I'm different. I can't just walk through a park, I keep looking round. In a café the waiter stands behind me and says, "What will you order?" and I'm ready to jump up and run away. I can't bear anyone standing behind me. If I see a creep the only thought I have is that he should be shot.'

The court considers these statements to be defamatory, since they give readers grounds for doubting his psychological health and the adequacy of his perception of his surroundings. They portray him as an embittered individual, cast doubt on his moral character and create the impression that he is an individual who could present truthful and accurate information as false and inaccurate.

The other claims in T. M. Ketsmur's complaint are dismissed . . .

The respondent S. A. Alexievich has not acknowledged the complaint. She has shown that in 1987 she met with I. S. Galovneva, the mother of an officer who was killed in Afghanistan, and recorded their conversation on tape. This was almost immediately after the funeral of I. S. Galovneva's son. The plaintiff told S. A. Alexievich everything that is stated in the monologue signed with her name in the newspaper *Komsomolskaya Pravda*. So that Galovneva would not suffer persecution by the KGB, S. A. Alexievich unilaterally altered her name to 'Nina' and changed her son's military rank from senior to junior lieutenant; however the text did in fact refer to I. S. Galovneva.

S. A. Alexievich met with T. M. Ketsmur exactly six years ago. She recorded their face-to-face conversation on tape. What is said in the published monologue is presented in conformity with this recording and therefore it is true and accurate . . .

On the basis of the foregoing, and guided by the terms of Article 194 of the Code of Civil Procedure, the court has determined as follows:

The editors of the newspaper *Komsomolskaya Pravda* shall publish a retraction of the statements indicated within two months.

The complaint of Inna Sergeevna Galovneva against Svetlana Alexandrovna Alexievich and the editors of the newspaper *Komsomolskaya Pravda* for the protection of her honour and dignity is dismissed.

Svetlana Alexandrovna Alexievich shall be charged state duty in the sum of 1,320 (one thousand, three hundred and twenty) roubles to the benefit of Taras Mikhailovich Ketsmur and state duty in the sum of 2,680 (two thousand, six hundred and eighty) roubles to the revenue of the state.

Inna Sergeevna Galovneva shall be charged 3,100 (three thousand, one hundred) roubles to the revenue of the state.

An appeal against the verdict of the court may be lodged with the Minsk municipal court via the people's court of the Central District of the city of Minsk within ten days of the verdict's promulgation.

* * *

To: V. A. Kovalenko
Director of the Yanka Kupala Institute of Literature of
the Academy of Sciences of the Republic of Belarus

Dear Victor Antonovich,

As you know, legal proceedings against the writer Svetlana Alexievich in connection with the publication of an extract from her documentary work *Boys in Zinc* in the newspaper *Komsomolskaya Pravda* of 15 February 1990 have been completed at the level of original jurisdiction. Alexievich has effectively been convicted of insulting the honour and dignity of one of the plaintiffs (one of the characters in her book) by not conveying his words literally. The court twice declined applications for the provision of expert literary testimony.

The Belarus PEN Centre requests you to conduct an independent expert literary assessment, which will provide answers to the following questions:

1. What is the scholarly definition of a documentary narrative, taking into account that 'documentary' is understood to mean 'based on facts' (evidence) and 'narrative' is understood to mean 'a creative work'?

2. In what way does a documentary narrative differ from a newspaper or magazine publication, in particular from an interview, the text of which is usually agreed by the author with the interviewee?

3. Is the author of a documentary narrative entitled to employ artistic methods and impose an artistic concept on the work? Can she select from her material and adapt the literary style of spoken testimony? Is she entitled to have her own view of the world and to generalize from facts in the name of artistic truth?

4. Who owns the copyright, the author, or the people involved

in the events that she describes, whose statements and accounts she recorded while collecting material?

5. How can we determine the limits of an author's freedom from literalness, that is, from the mechanical transmission of the texts she has recorded?

6. Does Svetlana Alexievich's book *Boys in Zinc* correspond to the genre of documentary narrative (in connection with the first question)?

7. Does the author of a documentary narrative have the right to change the names of her characters?

8. And, arising from these other questions, the most important of them: is it permissible to put a writer on trial for an extract from an artistic work, even if those who provided oral material for the book dislike the extract? To be precise, Svetlana Alexievich did not publish interviews with the plaintiffs, but an extract from a book in the genre of documentary narrative.

The independent expert literary assessment is required by the Belarus PEN Centre for the defence of the writer Svetlana Alexievich.

Carlos Sherman
Vice-President of the Belarus PEN Centre,
28 December 1993

To: V. Bykov
President of the Belarus PEN Centre

We herewith comply with your request to provide an independent expert assessment of Svetlana Alexievich's documentary narrative work *Boys in Zinc* and reply to your questions in order:

1. From the definition of 'documentary literature' that is given in *The Encyclopaedic Literary Dictionary* (Moscow: Sovietskaya Entsiklopedia, 1987, pp. 98–9) and which is regarded by specialist scholars as the most adequate and accurate, it follows that documentary literature, including documentary narrative, belongs, in terms of its content, its methods and means of investigation and its form of exposition, to the genre of narrative literature, and

accordingly makes active use of the artistic selection and aesthetic evaluation of documentary material. 'Documentary literature,' says the author of this article, 'is narrative literature that investigates historical events and the phenomena of social life by analysing documentary materials, which are then transformed, either completely or in part, or in their manner of exposition.'

2. The same encyclopaedia article asserts that 'the quality of selection and aesthetic assessment of the facts that are presented, taken in historical perspective, broaden the informational character of documentary literature, taking it out of the category of newspaper and magazine documentary writing (general articles, listings, news items, reportage) and social or political journalism, and also of historical prose'. Thus, the excerpt from Svetlana Alexievich's *Boys in Zinc* that was published in *Komsomolskaya Pravda* on 15 February 1990 cannot be ascribed to the genre of interview, reportage, article or any other variety of journalism; it is *sui generis* publicity for a book that is soon to appear in print.

3. As for the right of the author of a documentary work to employ artistic methods as a specific means for generalizing from facts, to express her own concept of a historical event, to make a deliberate selection from the material, to adapt the literary style of the spoken testimony of witnesses to that event and to draw her own conclusions from the compilation of facts – the aforementioned encyclopaedic dictionary says the following, word for word: 'Reducing artistic invention to a minimum, documentary literature makes distinctive use of artistic synthesis, selecting real facts which carry a certain social significance.' Documentary literature is undoubtedly strictly oriented towards accuracy and truthfulness. However, is complete realism or absolute truth possible at all? As the Nobel Prize-winner Albert Camus said, complete truth would only be possible if a cinema camera were set in front of an individual and it recorded his entire life from birth to death. But in that case would another individual be found, willing to sacrifice his own life to the endless watching of this remarkable cinefilm? And would he be capable of discerning behind external events the inner reasons for the 'main character's' behaviour? It is easy to imagine

the situation that would have arisen if the author *of Boys in Zinc* had deliberately abandoned a creative approach to the facts that she had gathered and accepted the role of a passive collector. In that case she would have had to put down on paper literally everything that the 'Afghani' heroes said in the course of their hours-long confessional narratives and the final outcome (if a publisher could be found) would have been a bloated volume of raw, unprocessed material, which had not been elevated to its present aesthetic level, and which would not have found any readers. Furthermore, if Svetlana Alexievich's predecessors in this documentary genre had taken this approach then the world would not now possess such masterpieces as *Brest Fortress* by Sergei Smirnov, *The Nuremberg Epilogue* by Arkady Poltorak, *In Cold Blood* by Truman Capote, *Out of the Fire* by Ales Adamovich, Ya. Bril and V. Kolesnik and *A Book of the Blockade* by Daniil Granin and Ales Adamovich.

4. Copyright is the sum of the legal provisions that regulate the relations involved in the creation and publishing of literary works: these relations commence from the moment a book is created and consist of specific rights (both property rights and non-property rights). The most prominent among these rights are author's rights, the right to publish, reprint and distribute a work, and the right to the integrity of the text (only the author has the right to make any changes in his/her text or to grant permission for others to do this). The process of gathering material for a work in the genre of documentary literature requires a positive effort on the part of the author, who determines the problems and subjects addressed by the work. A violation of copyright is punishable under law.

5. As we have shown in our answer to the third question, a literally precise reproduction of what characters say is impossible in a documentary work. But this, of course, brings up the question of the intent of the author, with whom the characters have shared their memories in the course of their revelations and, as it were, transferred to him or her some of their rights to that testimony, hoping that their words will be conveyed precisely in their original form, relying on the skill of the author to separate out what is important and omit minor details that do not add depth to

an idea, to juxtapose the facts and see them as a single whole. In the end everything is decided by the author's artistic talent and moral stance, and the author's ability to combine documentation with artistic representation. In this case the degree of veracity and depth of insight into an event can only be judged by the reader and by literary criticism, which possesses instruments for aesthetic analysis. The degree of veracity is judged in their own way by the characters in the work; they are its most partial and attentive readers. Encountering the phenomenon of the transformation of the spoken word into the written and, especially, the printed word, their response to their own story is sometimes inadequate, just as someone hearing his own voice recorded on tape for the first time fails to recognize himself and believes that a crude substitution has been made. This sudden effect also arises as a result of the fact that, in the book, the story of one witness is juxtaposed and married with other, similar narratives, and it resonates or contrasts with them, or even disagrees and conflicts with the stories of the other witnesses and characters; and then their attitude to their own words also changes noticeably.

6. Svetlana Alexievich's book *Boys in Zinc* corresponds fully to the genre of documentary literature mentioned above. Veracity and artistry are present in it in proportions which allow the work to be classified as narrative prose and not as journalism. And, as it happens, the same author's previous works (*The Unwomanly Face of War, Last Witnesses*) are also classified by scholars as documentary literature.

7. In literature of the author's own time certain ethical limits become apparent, if the faithful communication of an individual's story and his truthful testimony concerning events, which have not yet been assessed in an appropriate fashion by society, could result in undesirable consequences, not only for the author, but also for the individual. In such cases the author undoubtedly has the right to change the names of her characters. And even when there is no danger to an individual, and the political climate is favourable to a book, authors quite often use this device. The author Boris Polevoi only changed one letter in the name of the

central character Meresiev in his book *The Story of a Real Man*, but an artistic effect was immediately created: the reader realized straightaway that the book was not about a single, specific individual but a typical phenomenon in Soviet society. There are numerous similar examples in the history of literature of the names of characters being deliberately changed.

8. Lawsuits, such as the one currently being pursued against Svetlana Alexievich, unfortunately happen in the world. In post-war England George Orwell, the author of a 'dystopia' entitled *Nineteen Eighty-Four*, was prosecuted and accused of libelling the machinery of state. Today we know that the subject of that book was totalitarianism of the variety that arose in the twentieth century. In our own time a death sentence was announced in Iran against the writer Salman Rushdie for a book which supposedly speaks about Islam in derisive terms. Progressive people everywhere regarded this act as a violation of the right to creative freedom that demonstrated civilizational backwardness. Not long ago the writer Vasil Bykov was accused of libelling the Soviet Army: many of the letters from pseudo-patriotic veterans that were published in the press sounded like serious public condemnation of a writer who was the first to dare to tell the truth about the past. And unfortunately history repeats itself. Our society, which has proclaimed the establishment of a state governed by the rule of law, is still only mastering the basics of the most important human rights, often substituting the letter of the law for its spirit and forgetting about the moral aspect of any legal proceedings. The right to the protection of personal dignity which, in the opinion of the plaintiffs, Svetlana Alexievich violated by publishing an extract from her book in a newspaper, should not be understood as the right to tell the author of a book one thing today and then something entirely different tomorrow, because it suits a changed mood or political situation. A question arises. When was the 'character' who appears in the book being sincere: when he agreed to share his memories of the war in Afghanistan with Svetlana Alexievich, or when, under pressure from his comrades in arms, he decided to defend the corporate interests of a specific group of people? And, in

that case, does he have any moral right to prosecute the writer in whom he previously confided, knowing that his confessions would be published? The facts communicated to the author by the plaintiff and published in the newspaper do not appear to be isolated or incidental, they are confirmed by other, similar facts in the book, which became known to the author from the stories of other witnesses of the same events. Does this not give grounds for thinking that the 'character' was being sincere at the moment when his oral narrative was recorded, and not when he repudiated his own words? And there is another important aspect: if there are no witnesses to the author's conversation with her 'character', and there is no other evidence of the correctness of one or the other party to the legal proceedings, the necessity arises to recheck all facts of a similar kind that the author adduces in her book – which could have been done in a sort of 'Nuremberg Trial', with tens of thousands of witnesses of the Afghan War taking part. Otherwise the danger exists of drowning in endless legal proceedings, at which virtually every word spoken by characters in the book would have to be proven, and that is already absurd. And therefore the request from the Belarus PEN Centre for the Institute of Literature to provide an independent expert literary assessment of the extract from Svetlana Alexievich's book *Boys in Zinc* that was published in the newspaper *Komsomolskaya Pravda* is quite natural in the present situation and is, perhaps, the only possible way to resolve the conflict.

V. A. Kovalenko
Director of the Yanka Kupala Institute of Literature of
the Academy of Sciences of the Republic of Belarus,
corresponding member of the BAS;
M. A. Tychina
Senior associate of the Institute of Literature,
candidate of philological science;
27 January 1994

After the Trial

The verdict of the court has been pronounced . . .

It is painful for me to write about us – about the people who sat in the courtroom. In her latest book, *Enchanted by Death*, Svetlana Alexievich asks: 'But who are we? We are people of war. We have either fought or prepared for war. We have never lived in any other way.'

We have fought . . . The women who seemed to have deliberately taken seats behind the writer compete to insult her, in quiet voices so that the judge wouldn't hear, but audibly enough for Svetlana Alexievich. Mothers! Using terms that I cannot even repeat . . . During a recess I. Galovneva approaches Father Vasily Radomilsky, who has come to testify on behalf of the writer. 'Aren't you ashamed of yourself, father, selling out for money?' Voices in the crowd exclaim: 'Powers of darkness! The devil!' and indignant hands are already reaching out to tear the cross off his chest. 'You say that to me? To me, who performed the funeral rites for your sons at night, because you said that otherwise you wouldn't receive the three hundred roubles of assistance that had been promised?' the priest gasps in amazement. 'What have you come for? To defend the devil?' 'Pray for yourselves and for your children. Where there is no repentance, there is no consolation.' 'We're not to blame for anything . . . We didn't know anything . . .' 'You were blind, and when you opened your eyes you saw only the body of your own son. Repent . . .' 'What do we care about the Afghan mothers . . . ? We lost our own children . . .'

However, the other side gave as good as it got. 'Your sons killed innocent people in Afghanistan! They're criminals!' a man shouts at the mothers. 'You're betraying your children for the second time,' another man rants.

What about you? After all, didn't we all obey our orders? Our orders to say nothing? Didn't we raise our hands in approval at meetings? I ask you . . . We all need a trial . . . That other trial, which Ye. Novikov, the chairman of the Belarus League for

Human Rights, spoke about in the courtroom, when all of us – the mothers of our soldiers who were killed, the veterans of this war and the other side, the mothers of the Afghans who were killed – will sit down together in silence and simply look into each other's eyes.

A. *Alexandrovich*
Femida, 27 December 1993

The civil proceedings for the defence of honour and dignity brought by Galovneva and Ketsmur against the writer Svetlana Alexievich have concluded. The final day of the trial attracted many journalists, and fleeting reports of the court's verdict have already appeared in some publications: Galovneva's complaint has been rejected and Ketsmur's complaints have been satisfied in part. I shall not cite the decision word for word, but only say that in my view it is relatively conciliatory in nature. But has it really reconciled the two sides?

Inna Sergeevna Galovneva, the mother of Senior Lieutenant Galovnev, who was killed in Afghanistan, is still on the warpath – she intends to submit an appeal on a question of law and carry on and on with her legal pursuit of the writer. What motivates this woman? What motivates this mother? Inconsolable grief. Inconsolable in the sense that, the further the Afghan War retreats into history, the more clearly society realizes what a foolhardy undertaking it was, and the death of our boys on foreign soil appears even more pointless . . . This is why Inna Sergeevna Galovneva does not accept the book *Boys in Zinc*. This is why, for her, it is an insult: the naked truth about the Afghan War is too great a burden for a mother to bear.

Taras Ketsmur, a former driver in Afghanistan, is the second plaintiff in these civil proceedings. His claim has been satisfied in part by the court. At Ketsmur's request two profoundly psychological and profoundly dramatic episodes in the monologue that carried his name – episodes which, to my mind, testified only that war never lets anyone go alive, even if his arms and legs are all still in place – were declared insulting to his honour and dignity. I must say that I can understand Taras. Do you recall the saying: 'Beware of the soul's first impulses, for they might be sincere'? Such is his monologue in *Boys in Zinc*. To my mind it is a soul's first, sincere impulse after Afghanistan. Four years have gone by. Taras has changed. So has the world around him. And he would also probably like to change many things in his memory of the past, if he cannot erase this memory from his soul completely . . . But here is *Boys in Zinc*, and the pen, as we know, is mightier than the sword.

Svetlana Alexievich left the court session before the proceedings had concluded – after the court had once again rejected the writer's request for expert literary testimony. She quite reasonably asked how it is possible to pass judgement on a documentary work without knowing the basic principles of the genre, or coming to grips with the fundamental elements of literary work, while at the same time not wishing to know the opinion of the professionals. But the court was adamant. After the request for expert literary testimony was refused for the second time, Svetlana Alexievich left the courtroom. As she left, she said this:

'As a human being . . . I have asked forgiveness for causing pain, for this imperfect world, in which it is often impossible to walk along the street without hurting another human being . . . But as a writer . . . I cannot, I have no right to ask forgiveness for my book. For the truth!'

The civil proceedings against Svetlana Alexievich and her book *Boys in Zinc* are our second defeat in the Afghan War . . .

Elena Molochko
Narodnaya gazeta, *23 December 1993*

In December 1993 the judicial marathon of the actions brought against the writer Svetlana Alexievich finally came to an end. The verdict of the court was that the writer must apologize to the 'Afghani' Taras Ketsmur, whose honour and dignity the court considered to have been 'insulted in part'. Without any hesitation the court ruled that the newspaper *Komsomolskaya Pravda* must print a retraction and also a written apology from the writer and the paper's editors.

The complaint of the second plaintiff, Inna Sergeevna Galovneva, the mother of an officer who was killed in Afghanistan, was rejected, although the court did acknowledge that 'some of the statements ascribed to Galovneva are not accurate and true'. The court was obliged to reject Galovneva's claims, since a cassette with a recording of what Galovneva said at a public meeting several years ago was presented in the course of the proceedings, and on it Galovneva completely supports Alexievich's book.

In this court, in these proceedings and in this system, Svetlana Alexievich had no chance of defending her human and professional dignity . . .

Taking fright at the worldwide indignation provoked by the political trial of a work of art and its creator, the stage managers of this Belarusian farce declared vociferously: 'This is in no way the trial of a book, or legal proceedings against a writer and her work! It is merely a civil action for the defence of dignity and honour, directed against the newspaper *Komsomolskaya Pravda* in connection with material published in 1990.'

'But what about the presumption of innocence?' Judge Zhdanovich was asked, after the trial had concluded, by Yevgeny Novikov, chairman of the Belarus League for Human Rights, and Ales Nikolaichenko, head of the Belarus Association for Free Media.

According to Zhdanovich, 'the presumption of innocence only applies in criminal cases'. So if Galovneva and Ketsmur had accused Alexievich of libel, in that case the presumption of innocence would have applied, since the very word 'libel' is a term of the Criminal Code, and in that case the plaintiffs would have had to present the court with hard evidence . . . But in the case of a civil suit for the defence of honour and dignity the presumption of innocence does not exist in Belarus . . .

It is possible that the civil proceedings might merge smoothly into a criminal case – the plaintiff Galovneva has promised this and spoken about it as her goal.

The pro-communist Belarusian newspapers that are persecuting the writer have been joined by *Komsomolskaya Pravda* in a comment published on 30 December 1993 and signed by the editor,

Victor Ponomaryov. 'Svetlana Alexievich "thought she saw generals' shoulder straps behind her mothers", but what they certainly do have behind them are their sons' graves. It is they, not the prize-winning, decorated writer, who are in need of protection. If an act of "civil execution" is being perpetrated, then it is certainly not the writer who is its object,' the newspaper declares, prissily and demagogically, in its haste to distance itself from Svetlana Alexievich.

This is the prologue to an official apology, a test of a voice that has been revamped – from the new back to the old. And they toy with the title of the book: '*Boys in Zinc*. Writers are all ironclad.' But are the journalists and editors of *Komsomolskaya Pravda* all elastic?

The truth has always cost those who speak it dear. Rejecting the truth has always plunged the cowardly into disaster. But there does not appear to have been any catastrophe in modern history more hopeless and all-embracing than the voluntary self-destruction of human nature by the subjects of communism – when there is nothing left of people but 'smoking holes', as Mikhail Bulgakov expressed it.

Smoking holes on the site of the Soviet conflagration . . .

Inna Rogachy
Russkaya mysl, 20–26 January 1994

During the ten years of the Afghan escapade many millions of people were pushed through it, ultimately bound together not only by their feeling of love for their Soviet Homeland but also by something far more fundamental. Some of them were killed, and as Christians we mourn their untimely deaths and honour the physical pain and emotional wounds inflicted on their families and dear ones. But it is hardly possible today to avoid the realization that they are not heroes with an indisputable right to national adulation, but only victims who arouse our pity. Are the 'Afghanis' themselves aware of this? In all probability this is too much for the majority of them to grasp. The American 'heroes of Vietnam', who share a similar fate, realized the true nature of their heroism and flung back the medals that they had been awarded by their president, but

our heroes only seem capable of feeling pride in their Afghan decorations. How many of them have pondered on what they were
really awarded for? It would be good if today these decorations
served only as a pretext for receiving benefits and privileges, in the
pursuit of which our entire impoverished society is engaged. But
the claims put forward by their owners go further than that. At one
of the 'Afghani' meetings in Minsk recently a far-reaching claim to
power in Belarus was openly proclaimed. Well, today such a claim
is not entirely groundless. By taking advantage of the moral
gobbledygook dominant in society (Afghanistan was a dirty war, but
the men who fought in it are internationalist heroes) it is possible to
achieve anything at all. In these conditions the mothers of those
who were killed are promising material in the hands of present and
former communist Reds and fascist-leaning Browns, who are
acquiring a new lease of life everywhere. And they use the mothers, exploiting their righteous anger and sacred sorrow to the hilt,
as their children's communist ideals and patriotism were once
exploited. They are basically on to a sure thing here – who is
going to cast a stone at a grieving mother? But behind the grieving
mothers familiar broad-shouldered figures loom up menacingly,
although the writer in *Komsomolskaya Pravda* pretends in vain that
he cannot see anyone there, that 'it is not a matter of generals standing behind them' . . . The ominous breathing of the imperial politics
that was not fully implemented in Afghanistan can be heard ever
more clearly in Belarus. The trial of Svetlana Alexievich is only a
single episode, one link in a long chain of concealed and open mani-
festations of this kind. It is not only Vladimir Zhirinovsky's party,
which has quite a number of followers in Belarus, that exudes nos-
talgia for a great power and warm seas. 'Rousing' post-totalitarian
society and 'uniting' it with fresh blood – that is the way to achieve
the same old goal: the shattered ideal of yesteryear . . .

Vasil Bykov
Literaturnaya gazeta, *26 January 1994*

No, this grim tussle with judicial proceedings was not concerned
with the truth about the war. It was a struggle for a living human

soul, for its right to exist in our cold and comfortless world – that soul which is the only thing that can block the road to war. War will continue for as long as it rages in our confused minds. For, after all, it is only the inevitable consequence of the malice and spite that has accumulated in our souls . . .

In this context the words of an officer who was killed acquire symbolic and prophetic significance: 'Of course I shall come back, I have always come back . . .' (From the diary of Senior Lieutenant Yury Galovnev.)

Pyotr Tkachenko
Vo slavu Rodiny, *15–22 March 1994*